Steering a
Middle Course

The **ISEAS – Yusof Ishak Institute** (formerly Institute of Southeast Asian Studies) is an autonomous organization established in 1968. It is a regional centre dedicated to the study of socio-political, security, and economic trends and developments in Southeast Asia and its wider geostrategic and economic environment. The Institute's research programmes are grouped under Regional Economic Studies (RES), Regional Strategic and Political Studies (RSPS), and Regional Social and Cultural Studies (RSCS). The Institute is also home to the ASEAN Studies Centre (ASC), the Singapore APEC Study Centre, and the Temasek History Research Centre (THRC)

ISEAS Publishing, an established academic press, has issued more than two thousand books and journals. It is the largest scholarly publisher of research about Southeast Asia from within the region. ISEAS Publishing works with many other academic and trade publishers and distributors to disseminate important research and analyses from and about Southeast Asia to the rest of the world.

Steering a Middle Course

From Activist to Secretary General of Golkar

SARWONO KUSUMAATMADJA

ISEAS YUSOF ISHAK INSTITUTE

First published in Singapore in 2020 by
ISEAS Publishing
30 Heng Mui Keng Terrace
Singapore 119614
Email: publish@iseas.edu.sg
Website: bookshop.iseas.edu.sg

Originally published in Indonesian as
MEMOAR SARWONO KUSUMAATMADJA
"Menapak Koridor Tengah"
© 2018, Sarwono Kusumaatmadja
Licensed through PT Kompas Media Nusantara
All rights reserved.

Translated by Johannes Nugroho.

ISEAS Library Cataloguing-in-Publication Data

Name(s): Kusumaatmadja, Sarwono, author. | Nugroho, Johannes, translator.
Title: Steering a middle course / by Sarwono Kusumaatmadja.
Description: Singapore : ISEAS – Yusof Ishak Institute, 2020. | Includes
   bibliographical references and index. | English translation of
   Menapak Koridor Tengah.
Identifiers: ISBN 9789814881654 (soft cover) | ISBN 9789814881661 (PDF) |
   9789814881746 (epub)
Subjects: LCSH: Kusumaatmadja, Sarwono—Biography. | Cabinet officers—
   Indonesia—Biography. | Politicians—Indonesia—Biography. |
   Indonesia—Politics and government—1966-1998. | Indonesia—Politics
   and government—1998-
Classification: LCC DS644.62 K97A3

Typeset by International Typesetters Pte Ltd

Dedicated to the current and future generations.
May you succeed in your endeavours so that our nation can stand tall.

Contents

Foreword by Senior Minister and Coordinating Minister for National Security, Singapore, Teo Chee Hean

I have known Pak Sarwono Kusumaatmadja for more than twenty years, going back to the time when he was Indonesia's State Minister for the Environment when I served as Singapore's Minister for the Environment from 1995 to 1997. I readily agreed when I was invited to contribute a foreword for the English translation of his memoir.

Pak Sarwono has had a long and distinguished career in politics and government, spanning the New Order and *Reformasi* eras. He cut his teeth as a member of the House of Representatives (DPR) from 1971 to 1988, during which he served as Secretary of the Golkar faction from 1973 to 1987. He was an astute politician who became the first civilian to be appointed Secretary General of Golkar in 1983. His appointment, when he was just forty years old, injected youth, energy and fresh ideas into the party. Having established a strong track record, Pak Sarwono was appointed to then-President Soeharto's Cabinet in 1988.

Pak Sarwono is a social activist at heart. His spirit of service and dedication to the Indonesian people became his hallmark throughout his years in government. As State Minister for Administrative Reform from 1988 to 1993, he improved the public service and professionalized

the bureaucracy, including the education sector. As State Minister for the Environment from 1993 to 1998, Pak Sarwono recognized that environmental sustainability was key to long-term national development, and he introduced policies to incentivize Indonesian companies and people to preserve and protect the environment. He depended not only on his formal authority as the Minister, but also astutely drew on his instincts as a social activist and his links to NGOs and the media to achieve his aims. He was among the first to recognize the link between corporate practices and the environment. As Minister for the Environment, he proactively worked with the international community to manage environmental challenges such as transboundary haze. Pak Sarwono was subsequently appointed Indonesia's first Minister of Marine Affairs and Fisheries from 1999 to 2001, during which he laid the groundwork for the development and sustainable management of Indonesia's marine and fisheries resources.

Pak Sarwono made several working visits to Singapore, in both his capacities as Golkar Secretary General and Cabinet Minister. He engaged our leaders with candour about Indonesia and its views about Singapore and the world, and he worked hard to strengthen Singapore-Indonesia cooperation for mutual benefit.

Pak Sarwono's memoir traces his formative experiences as a young man coming of age in a newly independent Indonesia. No doubt these experiences shaped his orientation as an activist and a patriot, and his journey in becoming an important actor in Indonesia's remarkable development over the decades. His memoir provides insights on key events in Indonesia's post-independence history and the crucible of Indonesian politics. For friends and observers of Indonesia, there are many valuable lessons to be learnt from this vivid, engaging and important memoir.

Teo Chee Hean

A Testimonial *for Steering a Middle Course*

By Dr Siti Nurbaya Bakar, Minister of the Environment and Forestry of Indonesia (2014–)

The period between 1948 and 1988 was noteworthy in the post-independence history of Indonesia, a period rife in political, economic and social upheavals. Examining the available literature on the period, we are presented with an array of opinions and interpretations on the expositions of great ideas for the nation and on those who carried them out.

This book is one such undertaking; narrated in a communicative way that truly evokes the atmosphere of the period described by Sarwono Kusumaatmadja, replete with acute observations and first-rate wit. What impressed me most was how Sarwono's childhood and teenage years—coupled with the family values instilled in him and the multitude of life's challenges overcome through perseverance, creativity and resolve—made him the man he is.

The journey of the republic between 1948 and 1988 was crucial in laying the foundation for the young nation-state. For Sarwono, who was born in 1943, the period was unique as it corresponded with his own formative years and his growing maturity as an individual.

What is compelling about *Steering a Middle Course* is how the great events of national importance have been translated into how they affected the many, resulting in a very down-to-earth and tangible narrative. Another distinguishing factor is that not only was Sarwono a witness to the political events and the modern development of Indonesia but he was an active participant in them.

To date, even in retirement, Mas Sarwono continues to be in public service through, among other things, his role as chairman of the national Advisory Board on the Management of Climate Change. His role has shifted from being at the forefront to being in the background, encouraging and counselling the younger generations by interacting with them.

How Mas Sarwono has reached this milestone is also what this book is all about. It is my personal hope that, in time, *Steering a Middle Course* will be followed by another memoir covering the period between 1988 up to the present time. The great changes that have taken place in Indonesia since 1989 were no less interesting or less dramatic than the earlier period in our history. To Mas Sarwono, I convey my congratulations on the release of his memoir *Steering a Middle Course*.

Jakarta, September 2018
Siti Nurbaya Bakar

Preface

After a long process that culminated in the first half of 2018, this memoir was finally completed, just in time to be published for my seventy-fifth birthday. In many ways, efforts for this memoir began long before its actual writing, when I was Minister of State for Administrative Reform. It was during this period that I instructed a group of young people at the ministry to conduct interviews of their colleagues and seniors, with the view to collecting material for an autobiography. Unfortunately, for reasons unknown to me, those I charged with the task were half-hearted in their efforts, and the few interviews they made were never handed in to me.

Around the early part of 2000, my journalist friend Dwi (Donny) Iswandono—who was a sports reporter when I was President of the Indonesian Association of Lawn Tennis (PELTI)—and his colleague Iput Bambang Putranto came to talk me into reviving the idea of a memoir. We also discussed the issue of the forest fires that had ravaged Sumatra and Kalimantan in 1997, the horrors of which were still fresh in our minds.

In turn, I suggested to both Donny and Iput that they begin collecting information and data on the forest fires, which then became a book titled *Kemelut Politik di Balik Asap: Refleksi atas Bencana Nasional Kebakaran Hutan 1997–1998* (Political Crisis behind the Haze: A Reflection on the National Disaster of the Forest Fires of 1997–1998). Alas, this book is not discussed in depth in this memoir, which only covers the period between 1948 and 1988.

Early in 2000, my brother Mochtar Kusuma-Atmadja and I discussed whether we both needed to write our own respective autobiographies for posterity. At the time, Mochtar did not feel the urgency to do so. He felt he had been sufficiently productive in writing about foreign policy, legal reform, the environment and new initiatives in the cultural sphere. Mochtar believed his works should speak for themselves as part of his legacy. In fact, he tended to believe that any text on his life might end up becoming a string of self-justifications, not to mention being an egocentric exercise.

My own views on the matter were similar to Mochtar's, even though I could not claim to match his prolific writing or his track record of public service in general. But, over time, Mochtar gradually came to the conclusion that a memoir might not be such a bad idea after all, especially when its creation was supported by one's family members, colleagues and friends.

In the same light, this memoir was also the product of long deliberation, initiated long ago, pushed along with sporadic efforts, all of which culminated in the first half of 2018, when I became convinced that this memoir could be a meaningful endeavour. The project received support from my close friends, family members and even people who only knew me from afar. In the end, I decided to write this memoir, assisted by a team comprising Donny Iswandono, Iput Bambang Putranto and Apolonius Lase.

The memoir's title is *Steering a Middle Course*, and it is the first book in a series. The next book will undergo preparation—and let us hope that it will be completed—soon enough.

This memoir begins with snapshots of events that occurred in 1948, when I first became aware of my surroundings, and ends at the time I quit as Secretary General of the Golkar Party and was about to start my tenure as Minister of State for Administrative Reform.

This memoir was the product of my own penmanship—so to speak—a book of four chapters, with the help of the many people I have mentioned.

Chapter 1 covers events in my childhood up to the year 1963, when I came home from my overseas studies and continued my secondary school education. The initial text for Chapter 1 was finalized in 2006, and parts of it were used in the writing of my brother Prof. Mochtar Kusuma-Atmadja's biography, which was written by Nina Pane. Readers will discover parts in this memoir that are similar to, even identical to, the earlier sections of Mochtar's biography. Indeed, I gave Nina Pane my permission to use my account of what our family life was like when she was writing my brother's biography. In case any reader would like to make a further study of my family's history, Nina Pane's biography of Mochtar, titled *Rekam Jejak Kebangsaan* (A Record in Nationhood) provides a more comprehensive account.

Chapter 2 narrates my life as a young adult. It opens with me as a university student at ITB (Bandung Institute of Technology) at a time marked by political tension and economic meltdown, which came to a head with the end of the Guided Democracy era and the rise of the New Order. It was also during this period that my activist friends and I in Bandung were recruited by the military to become members of parliament for Golkar.

Chapter 3 is an account of what I experienced as a member of the House of Representatives (DPR) amid consolidation efforts within Golkar towards a system of membership based on individual active volition, and the repositioning of mass organizations under Golkar. The chapter also discusses initiatives to maximize the role of the DPR through the Golkar Fraction at a time when restrictions were widespread in the country.

Chapter 4 is a record of my time as Secretary General of Golkar, under the chairmanship of Sudharmono. The chapter contains accounts that many will find interesting on the New Order's preparations for the country's political maturation through the structural transformation of Golkar. It also features events and details hitherto unknown to the public about figures with whom I interacted frequently, particularly Sudharmono, Benny Moerdani and Moerdiono.

My account was naturally based on my recollection of events, which, as I discovered during the course of writing, had the capacity for greater scope and clarity as the text developed. Of course, exact recall within the right context requires crosschecking with the available literature and, beyond that, assistance from many people, to whom I am indebted. These include in particular my contemporaries during my days of student activism, as a DPR member, and my time in Golkar. They also include colleagues who worked in the press in the 1990s and many others who helped me in various ways during the writing of this memoir.

Indeed, help came to me in the most variegated ways. The most meaningful assistance given to me during this project came in the form of the personal interviews sat for me by several people, such as my senior Rahman Tolleng in the early 2000s. Interviews with both Jusuf

Wanandi and my cousin Hartini Sofiati proved indispensable, too. However, other forms of help were also invaluable. There were instances in which I was given a document, a photo or even had my memory jogged about a seemingly insignificant event that later proved to be significant. A telephone conversation or an ordinary chitchat was often very meaningful. I could not possibly rank those who contributed to the writing of this memoir, so I will instead name them in alphabetical order. I hope I did not leave anyone out:

Agung Nugroho
Agus Sukanda
Aidy Halimanjaya
Akbar Tandjung
Albert Hasibuan
Anak Agung Oka Mahendra
Arief Witjaksono
Bruno Kaka Wawo
Diandri Kusuma Agus
Djoko Sudyatmiko
Erna Witoelar
Fred Hehuwat
Hangga Yudha Widya Putra
Hartini Sofiati
Heri Ahmadi
Ipong Witono
Jakob Tobing
Jusuf Suroso
Jusuf Wanandi
Lannya Kandar
Marzuki Darusman
Muchtar Abbas
Nina Pane
Padmono S.K.
Rahman Tolleng
Rahmat Witoelar
Rhesa Noviar
Rum Aly
Sudarko Prawirojudo

Sugeng Setiadi
Toriq Hadad
Wahyu Mulyana
Wimar Witoelar
Yoyon Suharyono
Veronika Wiyarsi

Last but not least are my own children: Rezal Ashari, Krisnan Kusmara (Nino), Devyandra and Kendisan.

I would also like to express my deep appreciation for the members of my writing team, who had the unenviable task of being my constant companions in the journey. It is never easy, as I found out, to write about oneself, a process which necessitates a support team consisting of patient, thorough and conscientious people. I would also like to thank my publisher Kompas and Tempo's Centre for Data and Analysis.

Jakarta, July 2018
Sarwono Kusumaatmadja

A Testimonial

To Remain Unaffected by Power

"May you live in interesting times", a proverb says. Many would count their lucky stars to have lived through important moments in history.

Accordingly, we welcome the publication of Sarwono Kusumaatmadja's (SKA) autobiography, which will surely help us understand the moments he experienced through a more discerning eye: the early days of the newly independent republic, the Soekarno era and the New Order. For me personally, this book is not just something that jogs my memory. SKA is an important figure in my life, and the scope of this book covers the time during which both of us started to become acquainted with the world.

This book also reveals my good friend to the world in new dimensions. SKA relates his life experiences with great clarity and depth, but manages to avoid being tedious with his witty SKA-esque repertoires.

The book stands as proof that to be intellectual is not merely about education but also enlightenment born out of awareness. In this regard, the book has the potential to cultivate intellectuality and maturity in its readers.

This book covers the period in which SKA grew up and eventually became Secretary General of Golkar. It is a story of great interest since not many are familiar with SKA's background. Those who are somewhat familiar with his background will also benefit from the intimate details imparted by this book. One thing I know about SKA: he is an honest man, which makes this book credible.

The story of Sarwono's life from childhood till high school took place in the setting of the war for independence and with Soekarno at the pinnacle of his power. Yet, somehow, this is not a political book. What makes it interesting lies in the accounts of everyday life, in the socio-economic snapshots it gives of Jakarta at the time, something unfamiliar to most young people today. Perhaps not many will even consider things like this important. But they are important if we want to understand why and how Jakarta became the city we know it today. So, in a way, this book is a testimony on "Jakarta in the Making".

This book has no shortage of anecdotes that I found compelling because I was in many of them. But I am convinced that anyone whose life was touched by SKA would also have an equally compelling experience to remember. So, this book is a study of growing up during revolutionary times—the history of reaching adulthood during the Soekarno era.

After graduating from high school in 1963, Sarwono's life revolved around the ITB campus, particularly his activism within the Association of Bandung Students (PMB). There, SKA received his early political education and formed his network of self-confident young people. These fellow students continued to hold Sarwono in high regard throughout his milestones: a university student, an activist, an MP, a grandee of the most powerful political party in the country, and a minister.

This is a compelling book because of its strength in content and context. Contextually, SKA manages to recreate the mood of the period of history in his narrative, thoughtfully letting us glimpse his experiences and the people he came into contact with. In terms of content, every part of this memoir is of substance, making it an ideal historical reference. In the hands of a cinematographer, this book could be the basis of a film on Jakarta in the early days of Indonesian independence. The film could follow the life of a child growing up and going to school in the politically stringent era under President Soekarno and the revolutionary dynamics of his rule—encompassing domestic politics and with an anticolonial tinge—in the lead-up to the Gestapu rebellion.

This book is no doubt an even more useful tool for the serious political observer. In describing his rise within Golkar, Sarwono also tells us how the party went from its early days of Soeharto's rule as an Amalgamated Secretariat to a fully fledged political entity, and even an effective bureaucracy. To use his own language, SKA retreated voluntarily into the outer circle of the elite, even though he had been one of the principal architects of the development of Golkar into an idiosyncratic force in Indonesian politics. Along with Sudharmono, Sarwono moulded the character of Golkar at the heights of its influence, before it degenerated because of the excesses of Soeharto's power and those around him. Although Sarwono was part of the Golkar leadership, he remained unaffected by power. In many ways he never truly shed his being an activist, which allowed him to keep his conscience. But, since I may be subjective in this regard, I will allow the readers to form their own conclusions.

Those wishing to study how Indonesian politics came to accommodate, nurture and then in turn be nurtured by Golkar, this volume is an important source. The book has the authority to occupy a special place among Indonesia's classical works as one that captures Indonesia holistically. The book is indeed a kaleidoscope of being Indonesian: the expressed emotions, feelings and reactions of a citizen, to the political instincts honed through experience, and the carrying out of government business by Sarwono, with his characteristic curiosity, deference and a real love for Indonesia.

Jakarta, July 2018
Wimar Witoelar

1

A Clumsy Boy from Sentiong

The first three months of my tenure as Minister of State for Administrative Reform were nothing short of strange. Instead of seeing me during working hours at the presidential office Bina Graha as he did with other ministers, President Soeharto liked to summon me to his private residence in Jalan Cendana in the evening. Odder still, during those night-time meetings, never once did he bring up the matter of my portfolio or duties, preferring to dwell on colourful past events that he wanted to talk about.

I decided to ask Vice President Sudharmono and the Minister of Defence and Security L.B. "Benny" Moerdani why I was being treated differently. The two senior figures in government were in agreement— that the President was trying to size me up, with a view to making me part of his inner circle, commonly known as the Cendana Group.

Both of them also cautioned me that being in the inner circle was a great burden, going by their own experiences during the 1988 General Session of the People's Consultative Assembly (MPR). But they also told me that I alone had to decide whether or not I wanted this course.

I mulled over what they had said for some time before resolving to choose the "Middle Course". Consequently, I decided to send a clear signal to the President that I wished merely to serve as minister, and not to be inducted into the inner circle. My opportunity arrived when the President started telling me some very private matters about himself, which I thought was inappropriate between a President and his minister.

At that moment, I made up my mind to speak up. I pointed out to him that I had been minister for three months but never once had he informed me of what he expected me to do in that capacity. I also told him frankly that I was uncomfortable with discussing private affairs.

As he listened to my declaration, I noticed the President's face becoming tense. He then said rather curtly, "Please have a drink!" I knew this was an unmistakable signal that our conversation was over. It was therefore with relief that the next time he summoned me it was to Bina Graha at 10 a.m.

We had a thorough and productive discussion on my department's new supervisory programme for government departments known as "Pengawasan Melekat". At our first "proper" meeting, I formed a clear impression that the President was very well informed about government policy and was in full mastery of his brief as both head of state and government.

In my mind, had I chosen to become part of the inner circle, I might have found myself languishing in grey areas whereby I would have had to constantly guess what was on the President's mind. I wanted my position to be unambiguous, and being part of a small clique—however hallowed—would have placed me in a position that was neither here nor there. If I had forced myself to go through with it, the consequences would have been dire, both for myself personally and for my ability to carry out my tasks as a public official.

Yet, it was not a decision taken lightly. During my career in public service there were several occasions on which I had to make difficult decisions like this, all of which I will relate in this memoir. Looking back, I cannot help but reflect that my actions, and who I was, were the fruits of my formative years, beginning with my own birth.

A Brief Family History

I was born on 24 July 1943 in Jakarta, during the Japanese Occupation. I was the second child of my father Mohammad Taslim and my mother Sulmini Surawisastra. My eldest brother, Mochtar, was already fourteen years old when I was born. My father, an assistant apothecary by trade, grew up in Tasikmalaya. He was born into a family of village bureaucrats known during the Dutch era as *klein ambtenaar*.

His family background ensured that my father received Dutch schooling. He was first enrolled at an elementary school known as Hollandsch-Indlansche School (HIS), then Meer Uitgebreid Lager Onderwijs (MULO), the equivalent of junior high school, and eventually he completed his training at the apothecary assistants' school in Bandung.

Judged by today's standards, my father's education may not seem much. However, by the standards of his day, when the literacy rate in the Dutch East Indies was merely ten per cent, an assistant apothecary belonged to an elite class of well-to-do and respectable professionals.

My mother hailed from Cirebon and she trained as a teacher. Her lineage was strongly connected with the religious school (*pesantren*) Balerante in Palimanan, Cirebon. Her father, Badjoeri Surawisastra, was a *santri* (someone educated at a *pesantren*) who lived as a wealthy farmer and who died in Mecca while performing the hajj in 1947. I remember that he once held my hand as we walked down a road in Palimanan, carrying Ade, my sister, close to his chest.

My mother trained as a teacher at Bandung's Hollandsch Indische Kweekschool (HIK) and went on to Hoogere Kweekschool (HKS). I cannot recall any family tradition to explain how a daughter of a *santri* came to study at a Dutch school.

My parents met in Bandung while they were studying. My mother told me they became close after my father introduced himself in a most unusual way: by tapping my mother's head from behind a window. After they were married, they moved to Jakarta, where my father worked at De Gedeh Chemist's while my mother taught at Kartini School in Jalan Gunung Sahari. We lived in a house my parents built in Jalan Kramat Sentiong.

Late Birth

There are several versions of our family history to make sense of the long span between the births of Mochtar and myself, but suffice it to say the many years that elapsed between my mother's first and second pregnancies were said to be the reason my birth was a complicated affair.

My entry into the world was assisted by the able hands of the gynaecologist later widely known as Professor Sarwono Prawirohardjo. In the days to come, the good doctor was to become chairman of the Indonesian Institute of Science (LIPI). His daughter Sumarti and I were in the same class at Sekolah Rendah Perwari, and later we would both attend university at the Bandung Institute of Technology (ITB).

To honour Professor Sarwono's role in my birth, I was named after him. My last name, Kusumaatmadja, was taken from that of my paternal grandfather, Idris Kusumaatmadja.

The difficulties surrounding my birth were told in several versions of our family history, but all accounts were in agreement that I was in my mother's womb for more than nine months. My mother recalled that Dr Sarwono had advised her to take good care of me because I might have some motoric dysfunction. There was definitely some truth in this, as it turned out. I was to grow up to be a clumsy and accident-prone person. Countless cups, plates and other breakables became casualties in my accidents. A great deal of time and energy were also spent on rectifying my condition.

Another feature of my childhood was the fact that our family often had to move around, sometimes leaving Jakarta for another town. Towards the end of the Japanese Occupation we moved to Bandung, Cirebon, Tasikmalaya and finally to a village near Cirebon in Palimanan where my mother's family was from. In April 1945, in Cirebon, my sister, Sudaryati, known to us as Ade, was born.

Earliest Memories

One of my earliest childhood memories was of a house located opposite a building surrounded by a high wall. The building was the Cirebon prison, and the house opposite belonged to Dr Soedarsono—called by most people as *Oom* (Uncle) Son—who worked at the Health

Department. Later on, during the war for independence, he was to serve as the Minister of Social Affairs in Syahrir's first cabinet and Minister of Home Affairs in the second.

I remember another occupant of the house, a young boy with a booming voice, who was Juwono, Oom Son's youngest child. Juwono would also serve as a minister in several cabinets. In 1998 he replaced me as Minister of the Environment in the Development Cabinet VII, Soeharto's last cabinet. Both of us served in the National Unity Cabinet under President Abdurrahman "Gus Dur" Wahid. Juwono would go on to become Minister of Defence in the United Indonesia Cabinet under President Susilo Bambang Yudhoyono (SBY).

From this period I also remember different landscapes and different locations that served our family as temporary homes. The need to keep moving, living a kind of nomadic lifestyle as it were, was necessary on account of the raging conflict taking place around us between the invading Dutch forces and our republican guerrilla fighters.

My mother, Ade and I had to keep moving to stay ahead of the fighting, while my father and later Mochtar joined the guerrilla forces. They were part of the freedom fighters then known as the "republicans". My father served with the Indonesian Red Cross (PMI) while Mochtar enrolled with the Student Soldiers Battalion 400. Both operated within Tasikmalaya.

Oom Son, Harbinger of the Future

Oom Son had a notable presence in Cirebon. While working at the Kesambi Hospital, he was also part of an underground movement to prepare for the independence of the Republic of Indonesia. As a well-educated man, Oom Son quickly proved indispensable to the movement, and he was an up-and-coming man of politics, a path he took to with alacrity.

Upon learning that Emperor Hirohito had declared Japan's unconditional surrender to the Allies after Hiroshima and Nagasaki had been reduced to ashes by atomic bombs, Oom Son lost no time in declaring Indonesia's independence on 15 August 1945 in the Cirebon town square, witnessed by members of the public.

The document of the declaration never saw the light of day again, but it was said to contain no more than three hundred words. His declaration was later considered a prologue to the republic's Proclamation of Independence by Soekarno and Hatta on 17 August 1945.

The historical account of the "Cirebon Declaration" was recounted by witnesses to the event, including the version related to me by a contemporary of Oom Son's. Details about the declaration were also reported from time to time in the local press, such as *Radar Cirebon* and *Pikiran Rakyat*, with verification by historians at the University of Padjajaran.

Oom Son's place in the history of Cirebon was further cemented when a major artery road on which the Sunan Gunung Jati Public Hospital—formerly the Kesambi Hospital—is located, was named Jalan Dr Soedarsono. As a politician, Oom Son later joined the Indonesian Socialist Party (PSI) under Sutan Syahrir and served in the cabinet when Syahrir became Prime Minister. While serving as minister in the first and second Syahrir cabinets, Oom Son spent much of his time in Yogyakarta, where the nation's capital was relocated between 1945 and 1949 after the capture of Jakarta by the Dutch.

It was during this time that Oom Son accomplished the extraordinary task of sending Indonesia's famine relief contributions for India in the form of several rice shipments. The success of this act of solidarity was exceptional because of the Dutch naval blockade against republican forces and the ongoing war for independence. The feat earned him the sobriquet of "Rice Minister".

While organizing the shipments of rice for India, Oom Son also worked tirelessly to set up Indonesia's official embassy to India and Burma. Beginning in 1948, he started making multiple trips to India. In 1952 he was appointed Indonesia's first ambassador to India and Burma.

Mimi the Saviour

During our family's nomadic years, one noteworthy event took place at the estate of my mother's family, known as Jalan Kiori in Palimanan, near Cirebon. The estate comprised three houses with vast front- and backyards where, at the time, female members of the family and their children lived. No adult male members of the extended family were present, since all of them were away fighting the Dutch.

The event revolved around how Mimi—that was how my mother was known to her friends and relatives—saved the lives of her extended family and neighbours in the village. I learned about the details of the event later, as an adult, from different people who were present, but I remember Ade, Mimi and myself sitting together and a tall white man with a short iron stick standing next to us. Later on, I came to learn that the "short iron stick" was really a Sten gun.

I also remember seeing many pale-skinned men with blonde hair in green-striped clothes. They were carrying long iron sticks, which turned out to be rifles. One of them, sitting on a bench, carried a large box with a long wire sticking out from his back. Later on in life I was told the box was a field radio communicator.

This is the story of how Mimi saved us all. A Dutch soldier had been captured by local fighters, who then executed him in the field behind our Palimanan house. A few days later, a platoon of Dutch soldiers—all Caucasians—appeared at our doorstep to look for the missing soldier. All the inhabitants nearby were gathered together. Adult males were separated from the women and children. They were all ordered to squat down. Several of the soldiers stood guard over the inhabitants while the others spread out to search the houses and the surrounding fields.

We were all tense, not only because of the search for the missing soldier but also because Oom Son had entrusted republican government documents into our care by burying them underground. People had heard that after having their property searched, an interrogation would ensue. In some cases a few adult males would then be shot dead. Should the body of the missing soldier have been found or, worse, the concealed documents discovered, more innocents lives would have been lost, including women and children. The whole village might have been burned to the ground.

It was at that moment that Mimi, fluent in Dutch, engaged the commander of the platoon, a lieutenant, in conversation. I learned about the details of the conversation from Mimi later on and from the stories of my aunts and uncles. Their conversation ran as follows:

"Why have you come all the way here? Wasn't the war in Europe enough already? Why are you behaving like the Nazis?" chided Mimi in Dutch.

The lieutenant was visibly shocked to hear precisely correct Dutch being spoken by a villager. He replied that he was looking for his subordinate who had last been seen in the vicinity. He then asked Mimi, "Where is your husband? Where did you learn how to speak Dutch?"

Mimi replied that her husband had not been seen for three years and was likely "to have been killed by one of you". Mimi also told him, succinctly, about herself and how she had learned Dutch.

According to eyewitnesses, what subsequently happened was like a miracle. The lieutenant approached Mimi and told her that he himself hated war and that he thought it was not right for the Dutch to return to Indonesia. He showed her a photo of his family and pointed to several of his soldiers whom he identified as his own neighbours back in the Netherlands. He told her that as their commanding officer he was responsible for the lives of these young soldiers and that he had to answer to their parents as well. The commander further said that war was a cruel taskmaster. In truth, he only wanted peace so that he and his soldiers could go back home. He told Mimi back at home he was also a teacher.

Mimi then suggested that the soldiers stop searching the village and join her in a singalong. The lieutenant then blew his whistle to gather his soldiers. Mimi started singing a nursery rhyme and the soldiers joined in. The atmosphere of fear dissipated and the Dutch soldiers duly left.

Cases similar to this of the war-weary lieutenant were not unheard of among Dutch soldiers serving in Indonesia during the war for independence. We know of others such as Hj Princen, the ex-Dutch soldier who defected to the Indonesian side and became an Indonesian citizen and a human rights activist. There was also Rokus Bernardus Visser, a former elite forces Dutch commando who also chose to become an Indonesian citizen and assumed a new identity as Mohammad Idjon Djanbi. He became one of the founders of RPKAD, now Kopassus (Army Special Forces), along with Colonel Alex Kawilarang.

Mimi's encounter with Dutch soldiers. Dutch language text: Fred Hehuwat.

Shared Parental Values

So that was my Mimi, an extremely intelligent person and a skilled negotiator whose prowess would shine in more than one emergency situation. Her personality was a cheerful one. She was an extrovert and always dressed neatly. Mimi always wore a *kebaya* (a blouse worn with a full-length sarong; traditional womenswear in Indonesia), even at home. She was a happy-go-lucky person with an optimistic outlook on life best summarized by the Sundanese expression of *kumaha engke* (let tomorrow take care of its problems), always believing there was no such thing as an insurmountable problem.

Mimi was quite the social activist. Running orphanages, teaching at elementary school and being actively involved in the movement to eradicate illiteracy were all in a day's work for her. She also adored her children. At home we would speak to each other in the affectionate toddler talk we had invented, a habit we continued well into adulthood. Mimi was meticulous when it came to her children's education and health. Even in the most difficult circumstances, she always ensured that we ate nutritious food and went to the best schools possible.

In general, Mimi's health was excellent. She was rarely ill, except for the occasional complaints on account of her rheumatism. She liked her sweets and chocolate—always the Dutch Droste brand. But she never had any problems with her teeth, even if she never chewed betel leaves like so many women of her generation did.

Not long after the dramatic incident with the Dutch soldiers in Palimanan, I saw that people were cheering and looking happy. I later learned that this was because they were celebrating the fact that international diplomatic pressure had compelled the Dutch to recognize the sovereignty of the Republic of Indonesia and, as a preliminary step towards this momentous event, a ceasefire had been declared.

Suddenly, out of the blue, there appeared in our family home a bespectacled young man with wavy hair. He was wearing a white shirt with rolled-up sleeves and a pair of shorts. This is the first memory I have of Mochtar, my eldest brother. A few days later, my father came home as well. He had a roundish figure, wore glasses and was balding. The hair he had remaining had turned grey.

For the first time in four years, our family was together again. Much gratified by our reunion, we soon set out for Jakarta again. We were all pleased that the Dutch would soon be leaving our beloved country.

As time went by after our reunion, and coupled with stories told by my relatives about him, I was to find out that the character of my father was different to that of my mother. He was someone with a strong personality and he had the tendency to do as he pleased or what he thought was right, even if it meant neglect of himself and his own needs. This strain of altruism was also present in Mimi, but Father concentrated his efforts on providing healthcare for others personally, not through organizations. He was fundamentally a dedicated caregiver, and the funds that he used to treat sick neighbours or relatives came out of his own pocket.

Father never talked about himself: all the stories I heard about him were related by other people, all of whom remembered good things about him. Relatives and friends of the family told of how his health had been affected by his long service during the war. He carried out humanitarian missions on behalf of the Indonesian Red Cross, and he was tireless in his tasks, which included tending to the bodies of the slain and treating wounded freedom fighters, or people in general. The long hours took their toll on him and his health deteriorated. He was diagnosed with diabetes, an affliction that runs in the family, but he refused to treat himself, and over time his condition became worse as complications set in.

Father was also someone without racial, religious or social prejudice. He dealt with everyone in the same way. There is a family story in which he came to the rescue of a young woman distantly connected with our family. The young woman in question had married a man of a different religion. This created a family scandal as the match was opposed by both sides. Father and Mimi both acted as mediators, and in the end they managed to bring the two sides to accept the match, after a difficult yet touching process of negotiation.

In resolving family conflicts over religious differences, Father and Mimi relied on the counsel of two revered members of the family: Hajji Abdul Kadir, a cousin of Father's, and Hajji Hasan Djohari, Mimi's younger brother from Cirebon. Both had an inclusive view on relations between people of different faiths. While they still believed that ideally a couple should consist of two people of the same faith, they acknowledged that faith was a basic individual right that had to be respected.

I once bore witness to how my father dealt with a recently married young couple of different faiths who had come to him for protection and help with convincing their families to accept their marriage. Father said, "I will defend your right to get married, but don't take it as a sign of my approval of what you have done. To be clear, what I will defend is your right, even though I feel uncomfortable with what you have decided."

Father was not one to beat about the bush. He was often curt, but he had a gentle heart and never considered himself superior. When he encountered someone in distress, he would come forward to help, and Mimi would support him. But it did not stop Mimi from reminding him about his own state of health. What she wanted was for my father to spare the time for his own treatment before he went about treating others. My own conclusion was that their respective characteristics complemented each other. Father was an idealistic social justice warrior, so to speak, while Mimi was ever the diplomat, the compromise-seeker and the formidable problem-solver.

Father and Mimi had a lot in common when it came to basic principles. But in other aspects, such as lifestyle and social conduct, they were worlds apart. Consequently, they argued a lot—in Dutch, so that their children would not be involved.

Father never told us what had caused any of his arguments with Mimi. But Mimi was not one for bottling up, and she often got things off her chest when in the company of close relatives. One of her concerns was about Mochtar, who had completed high school and wanted to study at university. Mimi wanted to set aside funds to send him to university. Father, however, objected, saying that there were other children around who needed urgent help.

At the time this particular issue was brought up, our days of being war refugees were over. We were all back in Jakarta, but we could not return directly to our Sentiong house for reasons I will explain shortly. We were then living temporarily with one of our relatives—whom we called Aki Daud—in Rawamangun, near the Genjing Market.

While our parents were arguing about Mochtar's future, my brother was busy doing business with Djoni Abdurrahman, who was Mochtar's age but was technically our uncle, if the family tree was to be respected. *Mang* (how young men are addressed in the Sundanese culture) Djoni had served with Mochtar in the Student Soldiers' Force. He was then trying to get into the Armed Forces (TNI). Later in his life he was to reach the pinnacle of his career as Commander of the Regional Military Command (Kodam) I/Iskandar Muda in Aceh. Mang Djoni would come by from Cirebon once a week in a truck known to us as the "power wagon", loaded with foodstuffs such as fish-paste, crackers, soy sauce, rice and other commodities. His wares would be offloaded at Aki Daud's house. Ade and I were then recruited to help re-package them into smaller portions. Mochtar would then do the rounds of stalls and shops at the Genjing Market, delivering consignments to the businesses that sold his wares.

Back to Sentiong

There is another incident involving Mimi that I have never been able to forget; Ade and I were both witnesses to it. It also involved soldiers working for the Dutch. Whilst Aki Daud had been generous in putting us up in his house, we were eager to return to our own home in Jalan Kramat Sentiong. The problem was, the house had been commandeered by personnel of the KNIL (Koningklijk Nederlands Indisch Leger, or the Royal Netherlands East Indies Army) and their families. KNIL soldiers had been recruited from the indigenous Indonesian population, so they were not Caucasians like the ones who had come to Palimanan. Caucasian Dutch soldiers usually belonged to the KL (Koningklijk Leger).

There was a lot of frustration among KNIL units after the Dutch had lost Indonesia and were in the process of leaving the country, particularly as these soldiers were not ethnic Dutch. They may have felt their future was bleak and uncertain, and they might have been afraid of retribution from other Indonesians. When my parents tried to talk to them, they behaved roughly towards my father, pushing and shoving him. Father was already very ill by then and could not do much to fight back. In the end, Mimi took over, shouting at them in Dutch, her arms akimbo.

As it turned out, the KNIL soldiers were confused. Their own knowledge of the language was sketchy and they could not reply in

My father Mohammad Taslim. My mother Sulmini Surawisastra, known as Mimi.

proper Dutch. They tried to engage my mother in the street language commonly known as *bahasa pasar* (market talk; an amalgam of Malay and local languages), but Mimi persisted in speaking in Dutch. Impressed by her mastery of Dutch, the KNIL soldiers started behaving themselves. They may have wondered with whom they were talking. In the end, Mimi decided to lodge a complaint with the military over the continued occupation of our house.

Mimi, Ade and I subsequently made several trips to KMKBDR (the Military Command of Greater Jakarta), which later became Kodam V/Jaya. We found out that matters concerning KNIL personnel were handled by Captain Erwin Baharudin (who, after retirement, sat on the Indonesian National Sports Committee) and Lieutenant Tombokan. Mimi sat with the two officers and told them of her grievances, which were well received. Things looked promising. Lieutenant Tombokan was polite and friendly. And whilst the bespectacled Captain Erwin was rather quiet, he clearly had the air of an educated man.

As luck would have it, the KNIL soldiers were to be moved to Jalan Kernolong anyway, as they were about to set sail for the Netherlands. They had apparently been promised by the Dutch that they would be able to return home once the newly independent Indonesia lay in ruins.

As the negotiations proceeded for us to return to our home, Mimi would often go to the Sentiong house, and there she would treat the depressed soldiers like family, bringing them food and talking to them. After they were moved to Jalan Kernolong, Mimi continued to visit them. So in the end we were able to return to our Sentiong house, although it was in a state of disrepair.

Ade and I, being children, and having moved house so many times, were somewhat reluctant to leave Aki Daud's house. It had a vast backyard, and beyond this were paddy fields and fish ponds owned by the locals. The whole place had become our playground. We were very fond of playing in the open space, looking for fish, frogs and eels, and learning how to fly kites. Every day was full of play for us there. We also made our own toys from the materials available all around us; quite unlike what children are used to nowadays, with their mass-produced toys.

Sentiong, however, did not disappoint us. The River Sentiong, which ran alongside the rail tracks, had clear water and a healthy population of fauna. We were used to drinking the water from the well in our front yard without boiling it first. Between the rail tracks and the Kawi-Kawi cemetery there was also a stretch of swampland with an abundance of fish, where we would often take a net and go fishing.

Back in the family home, our parents were busy settling into their old lives. Father was once again working at the De Gedeh Chemist's. As a senior employee, a chauffeured car was available to collect him from home in the morning and to drive him back after work. But Father refused to be picked-up or dropped-off in front of our house, preferring instead the major road nearby, Jalana Kramat Raya, as his pick-up point. In the end he refused to use the car altogether, travelling instead to and from work on the electric tram.

My father (second from right) with his fellow employees at De Gedeh Chemist's

"The junior employees need the car more than I do because most of them live in the outer suburbs", Father said. "If the chauffeur only drove me, it would be a waste of time."

Mimi was kept busy running the household, as we had a steady stream of visitors from the provinces. Ade and I started school at SR Perguruan Rakyat near St Carolus Hospital. We walked to and from our school every day. Mochtar was studying law at the University of Indonesia while moonlighting as an English tutor. He was a keen sportsman. He also ran an open-air cinema in the neighbourhood with his friend Hamid Attamini, who would later become Cabinet Secretary. Mochtar was an all-round success story. He was the first person in Sentiong to ride a Mobylette motorbike. He would often ask me to start the engine before he set off on it.

Mochtar's time in university seemed very brief. He soon graduated and received a scholarship to do his post-graduate studies at Yale. Father was right; Mochtar could achieve anything if he set his mind to it. Everyone knew him to be a smart, fastidious young man who liked to stand on his own feet.

Father, Ade and I liked to visit the fish market, the Cikini Zoo and to see the dog races. We also liked to watch children's movies, including Indian films, the plots of which we sometimes found to be fantastical, especially when it came to the excessive singing, dancing and weeping they contained. In addition, we regularly paid visits to our various relatives, with Father always bearing gifts of cough mixture and skin ointment.

My father's main hobbies were fishing and hunting, which he pursued in the company of his friend *Pak* Katimin. Father had three hunting rifles: a 5.5 mm BSA air gun, a Diana double-barrel and a Mauser bolt rifle.

I thought that hunting was the most contradictory hobby my father could have had, given that he chose not to take up arms during the war and instead served as a medic because he did not wish to kill. If he was largely tight-lipped about himself and his past life, Father was unusually chatty when talking about his hunting trips. He always brought back large quantities of fish and grouse when he returned from his trips, which he liked to give away to the neighbours as cooked parcels.

Naturally, this did not please Mimi, who often protested at having to prepare dozens of grouse and a few basketfuls of fish in her kitchen. Nor was she impressed when she had to listen to Father boast to his fishing and hunting buddies.

Mimi insisted we should take what they said with a pinch of salt. "You can only believe half of what they are saying", she would opine, while gutting the fish Father had brought back.

She related to us how once Father returned home with a great quantity of fish he claimed to have caught. But Mimi later found a fishmonger's receipt in his pocket for exactly the same type and quantity of fish Father had given to her.

Political Education at Home

The guests that frequented our home were not just my father's colleagues and fishing and hunting buddies, but also our relatives from different parts of the country. Some came to Jakarta to study, some looking for employment, and others for a host of other reasons. Many of our relatives had taken part in the war for independence, and some of them thereafter joined various political parties. Some even claimed to have special access to party bosses, but not everyone was convinced by these assertions.

Now that our colonial masters had departed, new sources of tension surfaced in the new republic. It became common to criticize government policies. No cabinet lasted very long because of the frequent motions of no confidence in parliament, the members of which changed their allegiances rather too easily. Armed rebellions against the central government also took place in several provinces.

It was therefore inevitable that in our house, when the guests sat together with the hosts in the evening, whilst they were eating, drinking coffee and smoking, political issues would come up as topics of discussion. At times the discussion would become heated, and even raucous, since our guests came from different political affiliations. My impression of politics then was that it was a field for idealists who worked hard to apply their ideologies to statecraft. I never heard anything about corruption or abuses of power. Whether Indonesian politics in those early days was pure or, as it happened, the guests at our home were all idealists, to this day I still do not know.

I personally became very interested to listen to all the political discussions taking place in our home. In a bid to be acquainted with current affairs, I tried to read as much as possible of all the newspapers. I had three preferred sources—*Indonesia Raya, Pedoman* and *Merdeka*—with the respective figures behind them being Mochtar Lubis, Rosihan Anwar and B.M. Diah.

At that time I was full of admiration for these young press figures and I always enjoyed the debates between them. If there was something I did not understand, I would try to clarify it with the guests at home. Gradually, I began to have a picture of what was going on in the country. Freedom of the press was still robust. The exchange of ideas between different groups was as invigorating as it was during the discussions at our home.

Mochtar, however, behaved differently. Whenever our home was full of guests, he would go around offering his hand to them, engage in chitchat and then leave the house or ensconce himself in his room to read.

Father was not a political person. He was more like someone with a great commitment to uphold humanity, which was why his guests saw him as an impartial figure. He acted as a moderator for the discussions, which was also apt since he was the host. He facilitated the discussions patiently, sometimes resorting to his dry humour or sarcasm to ease tensions between the debaters.

Meanwhile, Mimi would be busy preparing food. We did not have to worry about stockpiling food since most of the guests would arrive at our doorstep with produce from the provinces: rice, eggs, vegetables and spices. Still, the sheer number of guests who came and went meant that Mimi was kept extraordinarily busy looking after them. Our guests would sometimes carry on their discussions into the early hours of the morning. Consequently, many of them were forced to stay overnight, sleeping on straw mats in our living room.

Father's Death

In time, Father's health took a turn for the worse, to the point that he was forced to quit work and to rest at home. The number of visitors we received dwindled accordingly as our former guests felt they would be intruding on his convalescence. Ade and I would keep him company, giving him massages and plucking out his grey hairs. His face and body had become swollen, he suffered sores that refused to heal, and his vision had become blurred. But in spite of this we never heard him complain. On a few occassions he would point at the door and say "Look, it's your grandparents coming to fetch me". We of course saw no one. We started to feel his days with us were numbered.

Towards the end he asked for all his favourite meals, even when they were strictly forbidden for someone in his condition. He gave away all his rifles to Pak Katimin. Father died on the morning of 11 April 1956 after dining on rich carp *pepes* (West Javanese method of preparing a dish by steaming or grilling spiced fish or meat wrapped in banana leaves).

Life Gets Tougher

Two years before Father died, Mimi went back to teaching. This time she taught at the Perwari Elementary School. She still had to run the household at Jalan Kramat Sentiong and to look after any guests who turned up at our doorstep.

Ade and I moved schools from Perguruan Rakyat Elementary to where Mimi taught. My brother, Mochtar, in the meantime had come home from his studies in the United States and married Siti Chadidjah (Ida). The newly-weds moved into the Sentiong house. By setting up their household there with us they were helping to pay for the upkeep. Our house then became a boarding house (*indekos*) in a further effort to generate more income. We saw it as a way of economizing as well because we also partook of the food we had to prepare for the boarders.

Our lifestyle remained simple. There was one difference, however: when Father was still around, we lived simply out of choice. We chose not to buy a car, a refrigerator, telephone or a kerosene stove. The excessively simple way we lived then was because Father had chosen to use the greater portion of his income to help others. Mimi, however, thought differently. Although she had no intention for us to wallow in luxury, she did want our lives to be comfortable and less troublesome than was necessary. We had previously maintained our wood-fired stove because Father wanted to live as "the ancestors" did, even though the soot coated the walls and ceiling of our kitchen. It was no surprise then that not long after Father died Mimi bought herself a kerosene stove.

Father's death though also meant we had to live simply because Mimi's income was derived only from her teacher's salary and the rent collected from our tenants. Mochtar and his wife eventually moved out of Sentiong. I do not know why Father was never paid any pension from De Gedeh Chemist's, and at the time we did not think to enquire why. Ade and I went to and from school with Mimi on a tricycle driven by Mang Ading or *Kang* (brother) Wardi. Most of our schoolmates, by contrast, were driven in cars, as anyone would expect of a student at Perwari Elementary. Perwari was then a school for children of the city's elite families—a far cry from our previous school, Perguruan Rakyat.

I felt more comfortable at Perwari, which had nothing to do with elitism. From birth I was predisposed to be left-handed. Left-handedness was not an issue at Perwari. At Perguruan Rakyat, my previous school, the teachers were harsh with left-handed students because of the social stigma that the left hand was "the ugly hand". I was forced by the teachers there to use my right hand. They often struck at my left hand with a ruler whenever they caught me using it. Although in the end I was able to write with my right hand, Father encouraged me to use my left at home. "Don't give it up! Your left-handedness is a gift from God", he said.

Father's view was vindicated by various researches on left-handedness, which have concluded that it is a sign of the dominance of the right side of the brain. Left-handed people tend to be creative and artistic and usually have good intuition.

The Soedarsonos to the Rescue

The family tradition of hosting out-of-town visitors that we inherited from Father continued. For both Father and Mimi, who actively took part in the independence movement, this tradition of hospitality, of sharing and solidarity, was important. Never did Mimi consider ditching it, even when our income had dwindled. Consequently, there were times when she indeed ran out of money to keep up our hospitality. Thus, the three of us—Mimi, Ade and I—became frequenters of the pawnshop at Jalan Kramat Raya where Mimi would trade family belongings for cash. At the beginning of the following month, after receiving her salary and the lodgers' rent, she would redeem her goods. This went on month after month.

Oom Son and his family were our frequent benefactors. After coming home from India, where he was ambassador, Oom Son worked at the Ministry of Foreign Affairs. Our families visited each other often, and I was quite close to Juwono.

In mid-1956, Oom Son received a new ambassadorial posting to Yugoslavia. He came to see Mimi to ask her permission to take me along with him to Europe to study. I never learned first-hand his reason for this overture, but according to family accounts he wanted to repay Mimi's kindness for having, in the past, paid for the schooling of Moespiah (Aunt Moes), Oom Son's wife—who was Mimi's younger sister.

I was overjoyed to hear about his offer because at the time very few Indonesians had the opportunity to study abroad, especially at such a young age. I felt nothing but full of joy because I knew and trusted the Soedarsonos and was convinced they would guide and help me. I also heard that during his teenage years Mochtar had stayed at Oom Son's house in Cirebon and had learned a lot there.

I must confess that I had minimal knowledge about what life was going to be like overseas. Nor did I dwell much on the unknown because I felt everything would be revealed in time. Most of my relatives took the news of my imminent departure in their stride, though some were surprised that a shy and awkward boy like me had been chosen to go abroad.

Most of the daily essentials I needed would be purchased in Europe when I got there, so I only took a small briefcase with me. Neither did I take any photo or memento with me. In fact, it was no different from preparing for a trip out of town. One special part though was when I accompanied Oom Son's children on their trip to Surabaya and Malang to bid their relatives farewell. When our ship set sail, there was no large contingent of well-wishers. Everything about our departure was quite ordinary.

I still remember the name of our ship, the SS *Willem Ruys*, which belonged to Royal Rotterdam Lloyd and had a gross tonnage of twenty thousand. Aboard the ship were mostly Dutch passengers on their way home. Our voyage took three weeks, with stopovers in Singapore, Colombo (Sri Lanka), Djibouti (Somalia), Port Said (Egypt) and with its final destination in Naples.

It was fun on the ship because of the multitude of recreational activities, including races and competitions. I learned how to play table tennis, though I was not very good at it. I spent much of the voyage with Budi Soedarsono who was teaching me English. If I had not been so introverted, I might have used the opportunity to meet new friends and learn more new things. But, such is my disposition that I would only participate in something when asked, so I ended up focusing on my English. I would also sketch, which was something I enjoyed doing.

Life in Europe

My first experience of being abroad was when I was in Italy. We spent several days between two cities: Naples and Rome. Italy was a wonderful place to be since it had so many historical sites such as Pompeii, Tivoli and the Coliseum. Even though I did not understand the language, Italian sounded very musical. The Italians I saw spoke in an expressive way, using their eyes, hands, shoulders and intonation, the nuances of which conveyed different things.

Italian society was in some ways similar to Indonesia. Discipline on the road was poor. The people were friendly and good-looking. There were counterfeit goods, scalping and pickpockets; a bit like 'Pasar Senen' in the old days. The food was good, and a week in Italy just flew by for us. To this day I still have a keen desire to learn the Italian language.

My first ever trip by plane took place when we flew from Rome to Yugoslavia's capital, Belgrade—in terrible weather conditions. Upon reaching Belgrade, we went to stay at Hotel Palas, a humble bed-and-breakfast by today's standards, though it was considered a luxury hotel at that time. Asians were a novelty in Belgrade, so many people would try to befriend us and ask us all sorts of things. We were often stopped in the street and invited into people's homes on the spot, where they would serve us food and drinks spontaneously.

A first social visit to a Serbian family would usually begin with fruit pickle being served from a bowl using a spoon, which was passed around from one person to the next. Afterwards, there would be a choice of two things to drink: *slivovic*, which was a liqueur, or Turkish coffee, which was so strong that after a few sips one could hear one's heart thumping. Conversation then followed; in our case in all sorts of languages, including sign language.

The Yugoslavs admired President Soekarno enormously for being a champion of freedom for colonized nations. After Soekarno's visit to Belgrade, he and President Josip Broz Tito became good friends on account of the good chemistry between them, not to mention their shared dream of realizing true freedom for developing nations. Tito was widely revered for his leadership against the Nazis during World War II, and he was a world-class leader.

Although Yugoslavia was ruled by a communist regime, I did not think the general atmosphere there was repressive. Citizens and the press were still able to criticize the government. Tito also often stood up to the hegemony of the Soviet Union, which felt entitled to lead the global Communist bloc. Tito's disaffection with Stalin was one of the things that inspired the creation of the Non-Aligned Movement.

As more and more Yugoslavs became acquainted with Indonesia, relations between the two nations and peoples became easier. "Payung Fantasi" (Imaginary Umbrella), a song by the Indonesian singer Bing Slamet, became a hit because it was often played on the Yugoslav radio, courtesy of the Indonesian Embassy.

Toni Pogacnik's Sorrow

Not long after Oom Son took up his post in Belgrade, our national soccer team came to play against its Yugoslav counterpart. The match saw a full stadium. The Indonesian team were beaten 4-1, but they managed to hold themselves against their Yugoslav counterparts better than anyone had expected. The coach of our national team then was a Yugoslav Croatian, Toni Pogacnik, who was to make his permanent home in Indonesia. I was present at the welcome reception at Hotel Palas but stood at a distance to watch my favourite soccer players. For some of them I had had the opportunity of carrying their bags and shoes to the Ikada Stadium in Jakarta, partly so that I could get in for free. They would arrive on tricycles, motorbikes and some even on bicycles. But Toni Pogacnick spotted me at the reception and came over. "Hey, young man, don't be shy! Come and meet your brothers!" he said with kindness in Indonesian. He then grabbed my arm and took me around the room. I shook hands with Djami'at Dhalhar, Ramang, Ade Dana, Maulwi Saelan, Ramli, Tan Liong Houw, Kwee Kiat Sek, Witarsa, Paidjo, Danu and the other members of the Indonesian national team. I felt very proud that day.

I got my nerve up to ask Toni Pogacnik about his strategy in training the Indonesian soccer team, which back then was among the top Asian teams, with it winning most of its matches.

"Indonesians are different from Europeans", he observed. "In my own country anyone with enough skill and common sense can become a coach. But Indonesians need to be treated like siblings, so I have to be brother and father to my team. By having that special bond, I can coax every bit of their potential out."

The team coached by Toni went on to become a sensation when it played a 0-0 draw against the Soviet Union at the 1956 Melbourne Olympics. Unfortunately, however, a number of the players from the same team were later banned from playing in the 1962 Asian Games as they were found to have taken bribes. Toni was understandably devastated, and he refused to coach again.

It is not hard to imagine how crushed he would have been, knowing that his own players had betrayed all his love and dedication for money. I wondered whether similar incidents, which often occurred involving our compatriots, led to Indonesians being known for their lack of principles. Even after this disappointment, Toni stayed on in his adopted country as a citizen. In the 1970s, when Ali Sadikin was President of the Indonesian Football Association (PSSI), Toni came out of retirement and briefly coached the national team again. Indonesian soccer had experienced a rebirth in the 1970s after the shambles of the 1960s. Not long after that, Toni Pogacnik passed away.

Seeds of Discord in Yugoslavia

In the days I spent in Belgrade, there were already signs of what
was to come. When Yugoslavia disintegrated, I thought the seeds of
discord had been there all along. I befriended many local children my
age when I was in Belgrade, especially those aged between ten and
fifteen. I quickly picked up the Serbian language from them. Even then,
there was obvious ethnic disharmony that was not present in Jakarta.
Serbian children liked to tell stories that denigrated the Croats and
Bosnians and vice versa. Every ethnic group tried to monopolize my
relations with them.

"Don't make friends with Croats, they were Nazi spies", a Serbian
child said.

"Your president [Tito] is a Croat and he is the leader of Partizan",
I reminded him.

"But his wife, Jovanka, is a Serb", the Serbian retorted passionately.

When I was with Croatian friends, they would badmouth the Serbs,
whom they thought were backward and Russian spies. When I was
with both Croatian and Serbian children at the same time, they would
talk disparagingly about the Bosnians. "The Bosnians are Slavs like us
but they became lackeys of the Turkish Ottoman Empire and converted
to Islam", was the standard line both Croats and Serbs would use to
find a common enemy in the Bosnians.

This polarized outlook was evidently passed down through the
generations, having its roots in history. When Yugoslavia broke apart
in the 1990s, the children I interacted with would have been in their
fifties and they would have come to occupy important places in their
country. Reliant only on Josip Broz Tito to unite all the ethnic groups
in Yugoslavia, and without any efforts to resolve the issues of the past,
the country eventually disintegrated along the ethnic divide.

Oom Son has a surprise

Our accommodation at Hotel Palas came to an end when we were
granted a house in the district of Diplomatska Kolonija. It was there
that, out of the blue, Oom Son told me the reason he had brought
me abroad was he had noticed I was a smart young man with a lot
of potential. "It would be a pity if you wasted this opportunity", he

added. He also said that in his view I was not a person who could be cajoled into things. It would save everyone time, he said, if I were just "plunged" into the unknown.

He then asked me where I wanted to go to school: Britain, France or Germany. I replied I would go wherever he thought best for me, but he insisted I choose because he trusted my judgment. "Your ability to make decisions is to be honed. If you don't use it, it will become dull."

His high opinion of me was something new to me, even a bit of a shock. I had almost accepted my lot in life as a shy, awkward person who walked on eggshells for fear of making mistakes. Moreover, I thought my position in Oom Son's household was owed to his gratitude towards Mimi, so I would not want to appear too forward.

My late father had told me to avoid dangerous activities. "Don't play in the field too often", Father said. "If a papaya fruit were to fall, it would most likely do so on your head."

There were three Sundanese words that had been instilled in me by Father to keep my path straight. *Montong* (don't, or you shall not), *kade* (take care) and *bisi* (if, used to indicate something bad might take place).

Even when I was in my teens back home, I could not swim or ride a bicycle. My clumsiness was so well-known that a neighbour in Sentiong used to tease me, "Do take care when you walk! Don't run yourself into a car!"

An Experiment in Self-Confidence

The extra dose of confidence that Oom Sun injected into me proved to be a catalyst for my endeavour to overcome my weaknesses. I started learning how to ride a bicycle. I did this in secret, with my riding sessions beginning at eleven at night. I always made sure that I returned the bicycle to the shed in good order. If a tyre went flat, I would mend it with whatever was available around me, using the tools in the kitchen. I made my own adhesive by dissolving sheets of rubber in petrol.

A child with normal motoric functions would take no more than two days to be able to cycle. I, on the other hand, needed ten, and I was thankful that no one had caught me during my nocturnal sessions.

Everyone was pleasantly surprised when I showed them I could ride a bicycle. They held their breaths as I tried to show off by letting go of the handlebars. They were bemusedly sympathetic when my little stunt had me crash into a nearby gutter.

Next, I learned how to swim in the pool at the residence of the military attaché Colonel Ibrahim Adjie. I did not have to do this in secret, since my bike ride had proved to everyone that I could engage in physical activities without doing myself irreparable harm.

I also took up tennis at the Avala Tennis Club, although not very

successfully. The senior coach there—Ristic was his name—became sufficiently exasperated with me to turn me over to the junior coach, Todorovic. In the end, Todorovic also threw in the towel and suggested I practise by hitting the ball against the wall.

As I was in the process of deciding which country to study in, I was temporarily enrolled at the American International School. I was able to follow the lessons there, although my English proficiency left much to be desired. A major complaint the teachers had of me was that I was too shy and withdrawn and that my physical coordination was below par. "Like Pinocchio the wooden puppet", a friend of mine at Perwari Elementary used to say.

In the end I told Oom Son I would very much want to study in Britain, reasoning that my English was improving, among other things. He agreed with me and asked Pak Moerdowo, the Indonesian Education Attaché in London, to look for a suitable school for me. After further inspection by Aunt Moes and Siti Sundari, Juwono's elder sister, it was decided I would go to King's School in Gloucestershire. Juwono had already been enrolled somewhere else, the Bedales School, where Budi his elder brother had also gone. At King's School I was enrolled as Sarwono Soedarsono because, as far as they were concerned, I was Dr Soedarsono's son.

As I was about to leave for my new school, I thought I would be accompanied throughout the journey, since I was a thirteen-year-old on the cusp of travel in a foreign land. But that was not what Oom Son had in mind. Instead, I was given a train ticket, a few traveller's cheques, a letter of introduction to the headmaster at King's School and road directions. I was saddened by this but chose not to say anything. Oom Son picked up on my mood and he said, "If I thought you were a stupid boy, I would take you there all the way. But I'm sure you can get there by yourself. Don't doubt yourself, just go for it." He was indeed right. I managed to arrive at my new school without undue difficulty.

Managing Oneself

King's School was an all-boys boarding school with only 150 students, and it was categorized as an independent school under the British accreditation system. The owner and headmaster of the school was James H. Mosey, who also taught general knowledge. His wife was also a teacher, though I have forgotten what she taught because I was never in her class. The majority of the students were Britons, with the school's foreign students made up mostly of ethnic Indians who grew up in Africa. The number of Asian students was very low, and I was the only Indonesian student there.

The façade of King's School in Gloucestershire, United Kingdom.

As part of the admission process, an interview with the student was conducted to place him in a suitable class or student group. The school's best subjects were in humanities, so the curricula in literature, languages, history and geography were excellent. The sciences were also taught, since interest in science subjects among the foreign students was high. In general, no subject would be taught in depth to any student who did not specialize in the subject.

My own interview was conducted by the headmaster himself, which was uncommon. Like Oom Son, Mr Mosey was also convinced I was a person of many talents. He asked me to think carefully about the subjects I would specialize in. In the meantime I was placed in the school's most junior class—which made me the oldest student there—because of my lack of proficiency in English.

In order to make my choices, I decided to observe the culture and atmosphere of the school. I found that the students there tended to socialize and to be ranked according to ethnicity and personal prowess. The British in general saw themselves as a superior ethnic group, but even among them there were social ranks.

At the top were the so-called "toffee-nosed" or "toffs" who spoke with a posh Southern accent. These students were good at humanities and sports. Generally speaking, they came from families of scientists, government officials and military officers.

At the other end were those seen as unsophisticated, who spoke in strong regional or Northern accents, and who came from families with business or non-gentry backgrounds. Although their families could afford to send their children to private schools, students from this group tended to be seen and treated as second class.

The two groups strictly did not mix with one another. Those perceived as belonging to the lower classes were often mocked as "working class", which was derogatory because at the time there was strong criticism of the British working class as having bad work ethics. Some students from the "unsophisticated" group would also try to prove themselves by picking on other students, especially Asians. They were bullies, a term that is now universally used in the Indonesian language.

My own position was a tricky one. As the only Indonesian, I belonged to no group, and my own communication skills were limited. This was not just because I was an introvert, but also because my English proficiency then was far from ideal. I concluded that my priority was to escape my social isolation and become "sophisticated". This meant I had to excel at subjects that they revered, such as languages, history, geography and literature.

Consequently, I joined one of the humanities study groups, which each had between five and eight students and a tutor of its own. This was supplementary to the normal class, which had a maximum of twenty students. By necessity I became a very diligent student, including doubling my efforts to catch up on my English.

Myself (second from right, standing) in the schoolyard.

Every night, between 10 p.m. and 1 a.m., I practised my English alone in my bedroom, under the blanket, aided by torchlight. I did not want to be caught by the on-duty teacher or get detention for breaking the rules on sleeping hours. I also started reading books, beginning with those easiest to digest such as Enid Blyton and Billy Bunter comics. I then switched gradually to more challenging books. My burning the midnight oil paid off, as my English was fast improving.

After the term break, three months after I first set foot at King's School, I was finally admitted into a class with students my age.

Things got easier from that point on. The Asian students approached me and told me that I was one of their own. "You are one of us. We have to stick together." The posh students also started talking to me.

I began to receive protection from the Asian group against the school bullies. The protector within this group turned out to be a Thai student. He was of small build but he was a tough fighter. His name was Suraphol. After a few moves attempted against him, an English bully would be writhing on the floor in pain. But I did not want to be protected. I decided to come up with a strategy of my own to ward off bullies using my own strengths.

I noticed how the posh students dealt with bullies. Characteristic of their kind, they would tear through any bully with their withering insults and sarcastic wit, delivered in an upper crust BBC accent. This was the strategy I adopted for my needs, and it worked wonderfully with bullies. They started to look at me in a different light. "Stay away from that cheeky chocolate-coloured Asian bastard!" I heard a bully say to his mates.

Coming Full Circle

My time of just surviving at King's School was firmly behind me now. But it occurred to me that I could not afford to be complacent, and that I must now aim for greater heights. I began to get involved in extracurricular activities, one of which was working on the school farm, which produced mushrooms, vegetables and chicken eggs. The project was considered important by the headmaster as he felt intellectual capacity alone was insufficient without real work experience. The money made by the farm went to the construction of a basketball court and a swimming pool.

Another bonus for me in working on the farm was that I struck up new friendships with English students who spoke with regional accents. A few bullies also became friends with me in the end. They spoke to me about how vexed they were with the arrogance of the English upper classes.

It was my view that Mr Mosey used the farm project to lend prestige to the English country folk who were often looked down upon. Those farm boys were accorded the sobriquet "stalwarts" and wore special pins of pride. I also worked at a carpentry workshop that saw a lot of participation by students of Indian heritage.

I tried all manner of sports, including the quintessentially English cricket. My gambit with cricket, sadly, ended with a minor incident in which I fractured one of my fingers catching the ball wrongly. I also played soccer, but only managed to make it into Team B, and I was placed in unenviable positions on the field. Initially I was told to be

1592

THE NEW SCIENTIST, 25 DECEMBER 1958

LETTERS

Mushrooms and mic
behaviour

Sir,—In your issue of 27 N
I was most interested to read a
by Dr. David Park on antagor
tolerance in microbial beh
particularly as it concerned the
of edible mushrooms. I discu
with my deputy, who is also m
science master, and he was as i
as I. In this school we try to
as many sides of true educ
possible and, of course, mar
together. Among other things
duce a considerable area of mu
spawned in boxes, and the l
practically the whole of the wo
first composting to final pickin
do this in their spare time. Y
see immediately how this kind
can help with biology in the la
and *vice versa*.

This is an independent school
no grant whatsoever from an
and we therefore try to use th
play of physical and mental ef
to add to our income, ev
a trifle.

I wonder if Dr. Park could
further guidance—and even
that we could use, if only expe
—to test out his findings.

JAMES H. Mo
Headn
King's School,
Sherborne Park,
Northleach, Glos.

Dr. David Park replies:

Most growers regard fresh hors
as the best basis of commercial m
production. Straw may be adde
crease the concentration of food
to the fungus. It is important
"fermentation" or "composting
material be properly done. A 5
heap is made and covered with a 3
of loam soil. This is left for
during which the internal tempera
to 60°-70° C. The heap is then "
so that the ends go to the centre,
outside material to the inside of
heap.

After a further four days thi
heap is turned and left for three da
when the temperature should have
to about 30° C, and the compost
for "spawning." In wet or cold
the whole process is best done and
The micro-organisms performing t
stages in decomposition are norm
sent in the material and in the soil
a cover, and inoculation would no
be useful.

Mushrooms and microbial behaviour

Sir,—In your issue of 27 November I was most interested to read an article by Dr. David Park on antagonism and tolerance in microbial behaviour— particularly as it concerned the growth of edible mushrooms. I discussed this with my deputy, who is also my senior science master, and he was as intrigued as I. In this school we try to develop as many sides of true education as possible and, of course, marry them together. Among other things we produce a considerable area of mushrooms, spawned in boxes, and the boys do practically the whole of the work from first composting to final picking. They do this in their spare time. You can see immediately how this kind of thing can help with biology in the laboratory and *vice versa*.

This is an independent school and has no grant whatsoever from any source and we therefore try to use this interplay of physical and mental effort also to add to our income, even if it is only a trifle.

I wonder if Dr. Park could give us further guidance—and even material that we could use, if only experimental —to test out his findings.

JAMES H. MOSEY,
Headmaster.

King's School,
Sherborne Park,
Northleach, Glos.

ature of the
ion can affect
ness of the
ork, for good

ect corollary
mply cannot
k, the work
re; but obvi-
to be driven

add to this
ral Secretary
commission
1948, I had
of visiting
ies here and
know direc-
ts have been
s health has
led that it is
first go for
nt lessons in
and research

. PRESTON.

pools

. J. G. Borth
hair lines on
ve frequently
nenon which

alm stagnant
h should be
iled for the
stir the water
nsuing com-
a wavering
may be seen
velocity onto
The circle
ible " plop "
nvergence a
pples travels
behaviour
e hair line is

phenomenon
ioned.
but it looks
of the water
as, repairing
e.
ALEXANDER.

Letter to the Editor by King's School Headmaster James H. Mosey, revealing his great interest in agriculture.

the goalkeeper. Then, after my glasses fell off and got trampled, I was moved to the left midfield with the task of harrying our opponents. I guess my clumsy Pinocchio-esque movements were useful in distracting the other side.

I also had a go at rugby, but I was only trusted with making short passes to my teammates. I was never able to become good at any sport as a result of my poor physical coordination. But the British appreciated my efforts. My physical education teacher, Mr Cummings, thought I was "hopelessly lost" when it came to sports, but he urged me not to stop trying. "If you live long enough, you'll be a champion because the others will have died first", the retired sergeant major once told me in his dry English humour. As it happened, he could be right. In my middle age I began winning at tennis tournaments, not because I had outlived my competitors but because I was a state minister.

Getting through the Hurdles

I started 1958 with renewed determination. I leapfrogged again and became the youngest student in my new class. Mr Mosey advised me to aim for General Certificate of Education (GCE) A levels, which would have meant I could start university in 1961 at the latest. I could have aimed lower, for the O Levels, and finished high school by 1959. A GCE was awarded for every subject the student passed.

To enter tertiary education, a student needed a combination of A-level certificates for the field of study he or she wanted to enrol in. If state scholarship was sought, there was another level beyond A's, which is S Level. Mr Mosey believed I had a chance of being accepted at Cambridge. Mr Dennis—the science teacher whom I had been avoiding because his subject was not on my priority list—tried to talk me into applying myself to mathematics and physics. "Science will continue to evolve", he said. "In the near future, the sciences and humanities will need each other and come together. There are signs it is already happening. You still have untapped talent. So, let's put it to use and join my study group."

His prediction proved accurate, since the fusion of mathematics and economics became econometry. Statistics is used in conducting polls before national or regional elections, pioneered by Gallup in the United States. There are other examples in which the sciences and humanities synergize at higher levels of complexity. But I was obsessed with perfecting my achievements in the humanities and did not heed his invitation.

At that stage in my life I was devouring literary books of various kinds. Many of these did not leave a lasting impression, as literature then was only a means to an end for me—a way to be recognized as part of the educated elite. Some did, however, impress me greatly on a personal level, such as the novels of Charles Dickens, the essays and plays of Bernard Shaw, the novels and essays of George Orwell, the Sherlock Holmes series by Sir Arthur Conan Doyle and the short stories of William Somerset Maugham.

I also enjoyed Voltaire's satirical works, which I tried to read in their original French, although this was a challenge on account of my basic mastery of the language. There were other literary works that might have proved invaluable and offered deeper insights, such as treatises on philosophy. However, becoming immersed in such things required a considerable investment in time and thought. They also demanded an emotional maturity that may have exceeded my abilities at that age.

My status as an upcoming student brought with it all kinds of recognition, including the honour of being invited to join the school debating club. Debates between club members were regulated by the rules and conventions prevalent at all schools in the United Kingdom, and debating events were very much sought after by students. My desire to better the posh students resurfaced, so I put in extra efforts to become an effective debater, and I think I succeeded.

Being part of the debating club meant I needed to master every branch of the humanities, the information of which was readily available in the library. I also had to keep abreast of current affairs through newspapers, the radio and television, which was still a new medium then. I also ramped up my focus on all my school subjects, doing additional research beyond the material my teachers gave me.

My monumental efforts led to my next adventure: being asked to take part in the school play, which that year was Shakespeare's *Twelfth Night*. At the time, my English proficiency was deemed sufficient to be given a role in the play. However, as I had expected, according to the literature teacher, I was too self-conscious to be a stage actor. Mr Thomas nicknamed me "sostenuto" for my understated stage performance.

In the end it was decided I would be the stage prompter, with the task of whispering lines forgotten by actors. As the prompter, I was required to be out of sight and out of the audience's hearing, below the stage, reciting lines in a proper British accent.

The cast of our school play, Shakespeare's *Twelfth Night*. I took part as a prompter, situated below the stage with the main task of whispering forgotten lines for the actors on stage.

Political Forecaster

The year 1958 saw France engulfed in a political crisis, brought about by economic slowdown and the demands by various French colonies for independence. The French Fourth Republic was in jeopardy, and the demands for constitutional reform were vociferous.

Amid the pandemonium, the controversial Charles de Gaulle came to the fore.

General de Gaulle was popular with the masses, being the wartime hero who had led the French Resistance against Nazi Germany during the occupation. Both Churchill and Roosevelt, however, did not like de Gaulle, who was often at loggerheads with the other leaders of the Allies. Perhaps because he was a French nationalist and was seen as anti-British, de Gaulle was widely disliked in the UK. Because he was popular with the masses, he was rejected by the French elite. To many people, therefore, de Gaulle was simply another "garrulous and overbearing" general.

Consequently, he was often not given a second thought, even when the future of France was a major talking point at our school. It was the main topic at the debate club, and it was discussed every time Mr Mosey gave a public lecture on current affairs.

At the debate following one lecture, I was the only student to predict that de Gaulle would become President and what he would do as France's leader. My prediction was disputed by others. I rebutted their arguments, using data and information from various sources, including newspapers and Radio France.

"Well, let's see what happens", Mr Mosey said. "But we must ponder on what Sarwono has said today because his arguments were weighty and his intuition is sharp."

After the debate, Mr Mosey came to see me and said, "I think you were spot on." He then left me after fixing me with a thoughtful look.

A few months later, the French Constitution was rewritten. The Fifth Republic was born and de Gaulle was elected President with an overwhelming majority of seventy per cent. King's School was rocked by the news. Soon after, Mr Mosey called for a general assembly. To my surprise, the purpose of the assembly was to congratulate me on being the only student to have predicted de Gaulle's rise to power. I was presented with a trophy, and Mr Mosey spoke of me highly in front of the whole school. "This young man will play an important role in his home country", he said, to the applause and hurrahs typical of school children in the UK.

Putting My Feet Up

In short, 1958 was a year of unqualified success. The school holiday, which I usually spent gallivanting with Juwono, was more enjoyable because I was no longer his useless sidekick, dawdling in his wake. I had apparently matured into a dependable travelling companion.

Our holiday would start with a trip to London, where we would stay at a guesthouse in Paddington owned by Mrs Travell. It was well frequented by Indonesian students, boasting guests such as Flight Lieutenant Sudibyo Rahardjo, a naval officer who would later become Chief of Staff of the Indonesian Armed Forces (Kasum ABRI). At the time, he was training how to fly the Gannet anti-submarine aircraft. Apart from the Paddington guesthouse, we, like other Indonesian youngsters in the UK, would also stay at the residence of Lieutenant Colonel Sutoyo Siswomihardjo, the assistant military attaché in London. We now remember him as one of the Revolutionary Heroes of 1965. One of his sons, Lieutenant General (Retired) Agus Widjojo, would also distinguish himself by making invaluable contributions to our military reforms of 1998.

Juwono and I never had much in the way of pocket money, so we could only afford to go to the cinema. At times we were able to watch plays when there were extra last-minute tickets sold at discounted rates. We would only eat cheap fare such as newspaper-wrapped fish and chips or hamburgers and milkshake. If we wanted to look for books or records, we would head for the street markets in Petticoat Lane.

There was one restaurant we often dined in where we always sat at the same table and ordered the same meal because it was the cheapest. The proprietor was used to our ritual and would serve our food without asking for our order. One day, to his amazement, we ordered something else. Raising his eyebrows he said, "Well, you must have come into some inheritance!"

From London we would also often travel to Continental Europe. My German and French were then sufficient for conducting everyday conversations, which I enjoyed doing. When the Indonesian Embassy purchased a car for the use of the ambassador, Juwono was tasked with picking it up from the Mercedes Benz factory in Stuttgart. I was

In London during a school holiday.

asked to accompany him and was told to keep talking to Juwono while he was driving so he would not nod off! In Austria we stayed at the (late) Rusdi Husain's house, the husband of Juwono's sister Sofiati.

With Oom Son's children: (from left) Hartini Sofiati, Juwono, Siti Sundari, the (late) Rusdi Husain (Hartini Sofiati's husband), Budi Santoso and myself in Vienna, July 1958.

Reunion with My Brother in Geneva

I was able to see Mochtar again that year, as he attended a UN Conference on the Law of the Seas in Geneva. He was part of the Indonesian delegation headed by our Ambassador to Switzerland, Achmad Soebardjo. When we met him at the train station, he at first did not recognize me. It took him sometime before he realized his own brother was there as well. He told me he had not expected to see me so grown up. I stayed in the same room as Mochtar, and I was proud to be able to observe the Indonesian delegation in action from the visitors' gallery.

During this period the Indonesian government had begun efforts to have the concept of the Archipelagic State—as enshrined in the Djuanda Declaration of 13 December 1957—recognized for Indonesia by the International Law of the Seas. Seeing that Mochtar was buried in his work, and that he was also ill with influenza, I spent much of my time in Geneva sightseeing. Sometimes I was accompanied by a member of staff from the UN Secretariat, a British national called Ada Barfoot. She treated me like her own brother. She even took me to places across the French border to buy food because it was cheaper there.

Homebound

At the end of 1958 we received news that Oom Son's posting would end soon and that we would all have to go back to Indonesia. I immediately informed Mr Mosey of my imminent departure, and he was saddened to hear it.

"You can be put on an accelerated programme to complete GCE O Level and A", he said. "I will write to your father."

But Oom Son asked me to decide for myself what was best, by saying, "You have proved to everyone, against all odds, that you can do well at school and in other things. After such a feat, it no longer matters where you go to school."

Mr Mosey might have guessed that the decision to go back to Indonesia had something to do with financial difficulty, which was why he offered me a full scholarship until I completed my A levels. His deduction might have been right, but what in the end made up my mind to go home was not what he thought it was. I had previously received a letter from Mimi that both surprised and touched me. It was in English—good English, too. She had always written to me in Sundanese before. She had apparently taken up learning English at the age of fifty-four through a language course at Schroevers, aside from teaching at elementary school and running the boarding house. Her classmates, some of whom I knew personally, were all much younger than she was. When I got home they told me Mimi was a conscientious learner, was highly disciplined, never missed a class, and was careful and quick to learn.

Mimi, in her letter, did not ask me to return home. But the letter turned out to be a decisive factor in my decision. I also felt I had become very British. Not because I had consciously wanted to change my identity, but because I wanted to prove to myself I could excel at my studies and to not be a disappointment to Oom Son. I had also "gone British" so that I would not be ostracized in an environment where social and racial prejudices were strong.

I also thought at the time that I had accomplished everything I had set out to do. I was therefore convinced I could succeed in learning anything. I duly told Mr Mosey that it was with the greatest regret that I had made up my mind to return home. He was upset and told me he assumed I would have limited opportunities for growth in Indonesia, because not too many Europeans—apart from the Dutch—knew much about the country. He also had the notion that life there would be very backward.

If I had accepted Mr Mosey's offer of the scholarship—and he was as objective as one could hope for in a headmaster, who often berated the posh students—I would still have found myself in a discriminatory and denigrating environment, and over time I might have been frustrated by it. I thought, try as I might, I would never have been accepted as one of them. So it was better for me to go home and live among my own people.

So, at the beginning of 1959, I said my farewell. In our last meeting before the long holiday, Mr Mosey, teary-eyed, looked at me and held my hand tight, "Any time you want to come back, let me know. My offer is still on. What would become of you if you went home now?"

Lessons from the UK

If I were asked what the benefits of studying in the UK were, I would say there was quite a lot of them. Chief among them was gaining proficiency in English, which opened doors of communication otherwise closed and gave me an advantage in the acquisition of knowledge.

Being fluent in another language is always useful because it accords a person respect from others. That was why Mimi was so successful at negotiating—her mastery of several languages that could be put to use at the right moment.

The British education system was also empowering because it did not seek to spoon-feed students with memorized texts, but rather it taught students ways of seeking knowledge and of the relationships between different disciplines. History, geography and literature are distinctive branches, but they are ultimately interconnected. Under the British system, people are taught from an early age to become accustomed to think across disciplines, the cognizance of which proved essential in discerning social behaviour and the thoughts of a collective group. A lot of time was devoted to discussions with teachers and fellow students in an inquiring environment. Moreover, students were encouraged to become balanced individuals without having to excel at everything.

Breaches of conduct were sometimes tolerated. Getting into a fight was sometimes excused as long as it was one-to-one with bare hands. And, in such circumstances, it was the duty of prefects to step in to effect a truce between the combatants.

The ideal man was respected and had an important role in his community because he was essentially a balanced man. A straight-A's student who fawned over teachers, for instance, was the antithesis of balance, and was usually scoffed at. I would therefore have no qualms about debating with teachers, even if it sometimes left them red in the face. Was that a punishable offence? No, because teachers were fully aware that questioning those in power was an entrenched feature of British culture.

I once heard of a senior student named Hasheem who had initially taken a combination of subjects suited to the pursuit of the humanities. He then had a change of heart and wanted to study medicine. He self-studied the sciences intensely in order to fulfil the requirements to study medicine at university. Hasheem was an ethnic Indian who grew up in Africa. In the end he completed nine A levels, which was something no British student at King's School could accomplish. The other students were full of admiration, but grudgingly so.

"Trust an Indian to do such an outrageous feat", said one of them. Why? Because the prevalent stereotype for Indian students was that they were bookworms who studied and studied without thinking that balance in life was important. On the other hand, the Indians believed they were studying in the UK to take full advantage of what it had to offer.

"We have our own culture. White people don't need to understand that because they never will", an Indian friend once said, revealing his own ethnocentrism.

The great lesson here for me was that we all need to coexist amid pluralistic circumstances, develop empathy for diverse views and lifestyles, and at the same time preserve our own identity. Another lesson was that we must have enough resolve to achieve the best in whatever we do because achieving our best is the key to our existence.

Travelling through Europe

The first half of 1959 was spent waiting for our scheduled departure for home. We all stayed together in Belgrade, at the new ambassadorial residence in the Ljutica Bogdana district. Juwono and I used our waiting period to travel to different places in Yugoslavia, Austria and Italy, either by car or train.

We savoured the beauty of the Adriatic beaches with their adjoining centuries-old small towns like Opatija, Rijeka, Split and Dubrovnik. We also watched various concerts and soccer matches and caught up with our local Belgrade friends.

Juwono was always a competitive person. He created games for both of us to compete in, one of which was the grooming race. It would start with both of us having to wash ourselves and get dressed formally in a suit and tie in the least time possible. He won since he could do it in less than three minutes. Another game was when we raced from the first floor of the house to the roof, in which there was a hatch we could open so that we could sit up there. He also won that one since he was more athletic than me. Eventually, after days of packing, we made our way to Genoa, from where we would set sail for Indonesia. Our ship was the SS *Australia*, which belonged to Lloyd Triestino, and it was roughly the same size as the *Willem Ruys*.

Meeting Nini

Our fellow passengers included several Indonesian diplomats who had finished their postings and were on their way back home with their families. There was K.H. Zabidi, who had been our Ambassador to Saudi Arabia, with his rather huge family. There was Max Maramis, who was on his way home from the Netherlands with his wife and four children. Their boys, Budi and Maku, shared the same room with me. Their daughters, Nini and Rita, were in the next room.

There were also other passengers on board who would later become famous. There was the German author O.G. Roeder who went on to write the book *Soeharto, The Smiling General.* There was Dr Ma'rat, who would teach psychology at the University of Padjajaran. There were also a lot of Italians who were heading to Australia as immigrants.

"I wouldn't mess with Max's daughters if I were you", said Oom Son. "They are pretty, but they can fight, being black belt judoka."

I had no idea then that Nini would become my wife. Nor did I ever find out whether Nini was indeed a judoka, since she never tried to throw me or get me in a chokehold. At the time, we were just friends. We played a game once where Nini had to ask me if I wanted to marry her. She was a beautiful and educated girl. I wanted to say outright, "Yes, I do!" But my shyness had not completely left me, so I replied: "I'll think about it." Ten years later, we did get married.

The Sciences: Do or Die

Back in Jakarta I was once again reunited with Mimi and Ade in Sentiong. Mimi picked me up in a taxi from the hotel Oom Son was staying at, Hotel de Indes (located where Duta Merlin now stands). She was very pleased that I was back home and she took me for a drive around Jakarta, which had not changed much. I then remembered about her letter in English, so I tried to talk to her in English. But she only laughed and answered in Sundanese. "I'm just worried I'll make mistakes", she explained. "We need to get you reacquainted with Sundanese."

Ade was already in junior high school and was doing well academically. When she first saw me again she acted awkwardly and stayed away. Things had not changed much in the house, except that we had more boarders than before. They were students and office workers from different parts of the country, with different faiths. The atmosphere at Sentiong was definitely multicultural, and Mimi liked it that way.

I went to school informally at Yayasan Raden Saleh High School, where I ran into two of my old schoolmates from Perwari Elementary, Kusmartono and Surnatjahya. I cannot recall whether I was actually enrolled at that school, but I was allowed to sit in all the classes and follow all the lessons. My class was part of SMA (Secondary School) B, which specialized in mathematics, physics and the natural sciences. Aside from school, I spent my time housecleaning, repainting walls, windows and doors.

At school I felt so left behind in mathematics, physics, biology and chemistry compared to the rest of the class. In the UK I had not prioritized those subjects at all. By Jakarta standards, my knowledge of them was not even fit for junior high school.

What had happened earlier in the UK repeated itself: I was the most ill-equipped student in my class. As I quickly discovered, the exact sciences were highly regarded in Indonesia. An SMA B graduate could choose to go to any faculty at university, while SMA A graduates, specializing in languages and literature, were limited in their choices of faculty. This also applied to SMA C, the speciality of which was unclear, with some saying it was economics. A popular joke at the time was that A was for girls, B was for the naturally brilliant, while C was for idiots with no discernible talent.

It was probably not surprising that not only did I want to continue my education doing SMA B, but I wanted to do it at the best school in Jakarta. The first one I tried to crack was SMA 1 Budi Utomo State High School. I went to see its headmaster, Pak Sutedja, who interviewed me and assessed my knowledge of the exact sciences. Naturally, he found it wanting and he refused to admit me into the SMA A programme. He then took me out of his office and pointed to a classroom nearby. "That's 3A. There's a vacant desk at the back. You can sit there right now and be a student here", he said. "If you enrol now, you'll be able to go to university next year. If you insist on getting into B, you are far behind as it is and can only start next year ... in Class 1, and not at this school."

I was momentarily tempted to accept his offer. But I told him I would need time to think about it and consult with my mother.

"Of course, but I'm only giving you seven days to do that. You can start in 3A immediately if you want to." That was his last word on the matter.

I asked Mimi for her opinion and she said she thought B might be better for me. "We have a neighbour, Pak Budi, who teaches science in junior high. He can help you catch up with your studies."

Oom Son also agreed with Mimi. He even took me to the next prospective school on my list, PSKD High School, in Jalan Diponegoro.

We were met by Pak Soplanit, the headmaster. After going through my report from King's, he said softly that he could not admit me to his school. Oom Son tried to save the day by turning on his considerable charms and skills as a diplomat, but it was to no avail. Pak Soplanit merely smiled and waited for us to leave.

My Deal with Father Krekelberg

Some days later, as I made my way back home from Raden Saleh High, I spotted a Catholic priest sat reading a book at the front porch of Kanisius College in Jalan Menteng Raya. Kanisius was one of the best schools in Jakarta, run by Jesuit priests. It occurred to me it would be worth a shot to try to get in there. I introduced myself to the priest, who turned out to be Father Paul Krekelberg, the headmaster of Kanisius. He listened to me and then asked to see my school report from the UK.

"Your report says wonderful things about you, but the British are usually extravagant in their praises, so I would have to interview you. I can't just take what's said in your report on faith alone. If you want to do B, I will have to ask you questions to determine your knowledge of the sciences", he said. Then he started asking me questions in German and French. We then talked in those two languages. He proceeded to discuss literature and history with me in four languages alternately. He seemed pleased that I was able to accommodate him.

Then he gave me some mathematical problems to solve. I did not even try to. I told him outright that I could not solve them because my knowledge of mathematics was insufficient.

"Are you mad? You said you wanted to get into B, but you don't know your exact sciences. Why not just do A instead? You can start tomorrow", he tried to reason with me.

"It's possible I am mad, father. But I would like to be admitted into B with a trial period of six months in which I will do my catching up." I thought it could not hurt my cause to up my ante, since my admission into 3A was more or less assured.

"Very well, you can get into 1B", Father Krekelberg relented. "But, after two terms, if you still have substandard grades for any of your subjects, I will have to ask you to leave the school. I also don't want to get into trouble with the government, so you will have to get a dispensation from the regional office of the Ministry of Education." Still shaking his head, he then shook hands with me and gave me a handwritten note on a piece of paper to be given to the Ministry of Education.

It was already afternoon and government offices closed in those days at 2 p.m. But I very much wanted to sort out my dispensation that day, so I raced to the office on Jalan Hang Lekir in Kebayoran on my bicycle. When I got there, most of the civil servants were already outside getting ready to leave. Luckily, however, Pak Hutasoit, head of the office, was still there working. His staff told me he was busy and could not be disturbed. I decided to wait for him in the parking lot, sitting next to his white car. It was 5 p.m. when a man approached the car with a key. I was quite sure it was Hutasoit so I introduced myself.

"Oh, it's you who has some business with me. It must be important since you have waited for me for a while. What can I do for you, young man?" Pak Hutasoit asked. Decades later, I was told that Royandi Hutasoit, Chairman of the Peace and Prosperity Party (PDS), was his son.

I briefly explained to him my business there and presented him with Father Krekelberg's note. After reading the note, he opened his briefcase to retrieve a block note and his pen. He proceeded to jot down his approval for my transfer to Kanisius.

Things were simpler in those days. A school transfer was effected with handwritten memos. But, most importantly, there was no bribery or nepotism involved. There were no complicated forms to fill in. I am not saying there was no corruption within the government then—several corruption scandals were exposed and reported in the newspapers. But in those days there were still many niches in our society that were untouched by such practices.

Meeting Wimar Witoelar

The next day, I went to Kanisius to submit Pak Hutasoit's note. A few days later, I was informed that I was enrolled to start at Kanisius for the 1960/61 school year. On my first day, I found myself not knowing anyone at all in my class. I sat next to a student called

Wimar Witoelar, after moving from another desk. I sat next to him because I sensed no one else wanted to. Wimar was big with a deep voice and curly hair. His appearance was intimidating to most people because he fitted into the stereotype of what a brawler would look like. There was another student called Gasim Mar'ie who was big and tall with a Middle Eastern face. Even he refused to sit next to Wimar.

"I'd rather not sit next to him. He looks scary", Gasim said. He then looked at me and asked, "Why don't you sit next to him? Let's swap seats."

Among the alumni of Kanisius, several would become distinguished or famous. In my year, there was Wimar, Syarief Tando, who was to become a businessman and activist, and me. The more senior alumni included Ginandjar Kartasasmita, Nasrudin Sumintapura, S.B. Judono, Jusuf Wanandi and Sofjan Wanandi. Those who were my juniors included Akbar Tandjung, Marzuki Darusman, Fauzi Bowo and Chatib Basri.

My schoolmates came in a great variety. Urip Santoso, one of my classmates, was quiet and brilliant. He never seemed to study, was very laid-back, but always got top grades. He played the piano more often than he pored over books. He is now an expert on informatics.

There were those who were utterly delinquent but smart. Many of them later became professionals. Of course, there were also those who were conscientious and consequently did well in class. Not everyone was special though, because there would always be those who were simply unremarkable, unless certain idiosyncrasies that had nothing to do with formal education were taken into account. According to one teacher, the composition of the student population must ideally reflect society. "If all students were uniform in character and abilities, education would be sterile and uncreative", he said.

As it happened, Kanisius students were on average mischievous and rowdy. The teachers had their work cut out for them just to be in control of the classroom. The European priests and the senior teachers were usually in their element. There were even times when some senior teachers would create a ruckus rivalling those of their students. But the junior teachers were often out of their depth, and some female teachers sometimes ended up in tears.

As expected, I was also out of my depth—at least initially—with the onslaught of mathematics, physics, chemistry and biology. A teacher sardonically remarked that people could now get into Kanisius through having connections. I studied with Pak Budi every day and bought all the books from the junior high school level needed for my foundation studies in the exact sciences. I applied myself for at least four hours every day in this fashion. It was only in my language classes that I had any respite. Father Krekelberg, who taught German, would always ask me to leave class. "You don't need me", he said. "Just use the extra time to study what you need to study out there!"

I was pleasantly surprised to discover that my desk-mate, Wimar, was also good at languages. He turned out to be the exact opposite of scary. In fact, he was a gentle soul. His wit was acerbic, something that I felt I shared with him. He had also studied abroad, since his father was a diplomat. Once, we both got a hundred per cent for an English examination. For some reason the teacher suspected I had copied Wimar's answers. Accused of being a cheat, I was moved to another desk in the back. In the following examination, however, I once again scored a hundred. Moreover, the teacher's English was not as good as Wimar's or mine, so both of us would from time to time question him openly when he taught us something that was wrong. From that point onwards, neither of us ever got top marks again. Wimar and I made a pact not to make any concession to the teacher's ego. Even though that meant we would never get good grades in his class, we would continue to do what was right.

My school report for the first term was a disaster. My grades for the exact sciences were below par. But, thankfully, they improved significantly in the second term. I had managed to catch up with the rest of my classmates. Father Krekelberg asked to see me in his office, and he duly congratulated me.

Student Mischief Tolerated

Kanisius was a fun place to be. Although the students there were overall given to misdemeanours, acts of mischief within certain boundaries were tolerated. It was reminiscent of the way mischief was viewed at King's School. Expulsion only occurred when a student was caught red-handed cheating in examinations, being involved in a fight with weapons, or in a group fight. Pulling pranks on a teacher, on the other hand, was usually considered a minor offence and hence tolerated. In some cases when teachers lodged complaints with the Staff Prefect, Father Jan Bots, for having pranks played on them by students, they were ignored. Worse still, the complaining teachers might have their heads bitten off by Father Bots.

There was one famous prank involving a young priest called Father Thomas Huber, who had just arrived from Switzerland. He was fluent in proper and correct Indonesian. So we told Father Huber that his Indonesian was too stiff and formal, and that no one really spoke like that. Since that got him interested, we taught him a few new modes of "greetings"—which contained swear words—and he lost no time in putting them into practice, as we soon discovered. It was not long before local staff members spoke up about Father Huber's new "greetings".

"That new priest is very rude", a female staff member protested. "He's been here but a month and he already swears at people and says the most shocking things."

Father Bots then got involved. The students responsible for Father Huber's "mis-education" were disciplined by having to run around the school field. Father Bots oversaw our punishment with arms akimbo. But he was laughing as he shook his head repeatedly. That was light punishment indeed. Father Huber was furious, of course, when he found out he had been misled, but only briefly. We saw him red-faced, pacing about with his hands behind his back in distress.

Over time, Father Huber became like a friend to us. He later became the manager of Kanisius's soccer team. Our team captain was Soe Hok Djin, or Arief Budiman—Soe Hok Gie's older brother—who later became a cultural figure. He was an immensely talented individual. An all-rounder, he was intelligent and good at writing, painting and sports. We had two strikers: Wimar Witoelar and Rahmat. As usual, I was placed in a position no one wanted. Once, our goalkeeper did not show up for a match, for a game we were playing against the team from the Home Affairs Ministry. I ended up being the goalkeeper because no one else wanted the job. We lost 2-1. Indeed, the Ministry of Home Affairs was well-known for not losing much to anything.

Discovering a Blood Relative in Wimar

One day an unexpected event took place that led Wimar and myself to develop a closer relationship with each other. A family acquaintance turned up at our house to inform us Kang Otong had died. Kang Otong was a distant relative who had been an officer in the army. Father had often taken my sister and me to visit him in his house on Jalan Kebon Binatang when we were little. Mimi went to pay her respects to the deceased, but I decided to stay in and skip school.

The next day, I was summoned by Father Bots to be questioned about my absence. Wimar, to my surprise, was also there. When we entered the office, we were dumbstruck to see photos of three pretty Italian film stars—Gina Lollobrigida, Silvana Mangano and Sophia Loren—staring back at us from Father Bots' wall. The priest quickly clarified without being asked: "What are you staring at? I put up the photos of Gina, Silvana and Sophia because they are all good Catholic girls". I was thinking to myself there were probably better Catholics, like the Pope, but his photo was not there. I did not voice my opinion because I knew I was in trouble for having been absent from school without leave.

Father Bots started to interrogate me by asking why I had not come to school the day before.

"A relative of mine died. His name was Kang Otong", I replied.

"Who was Otong? How was he related to you? What did he do for a job? How did he die? Where did he die?" he asked thoroughly.

I then explained to him that Kang Otong was a distant cousin of mine, an army officer, and he had died of a heart attack.

"And why were you absent?" he asked Wimar in turn.

"My uncle Mang Otong died", he answered in a serious tone.

"Why, Sarwono went to Kang Otong's and so did you. Are they the same person?" Father Bots asked, mystified.

"Yes, we are both related. I should actually call him uncle", Wimar replied quickly, without having cleared with me how we were actually related, of course.

"All right. If you can't come to school next time, please bring a note from your parents", Father Bots said before dismissing us.

When we were out of his office, Wimar and I started exchanging information. We both verified that neither of us had gone to Kang Otong's, although it was true that we were both related to him, if only distantly. But in the Sundanese culture, blood relatives are all important, however distantly related. It was like the mini bus fare in those days; you paid the same fare whether you travelled far or near.

From that moment on, I felt a closer bond with Wimar, not just because we were related but also because we got on well and the two of us had the knack of picking up where the other left off. It was probably inevitable that both of us became the originators of so much verbal banter going round the school. We were good at word play and creating double-entendres, and our usual victims were the teachers.

The teachers' reactions to our banter came in roughly three types. The European teachers would take it in their stride and make their own verbal retorts. It was not unusual for us to banter back and forth with the Jesuit priests. Sometimes they would initiate it themselves. Most Indonesian teachers, however—although not all—would be offended if we tried a bit of banter with them, seeing it as insolence. The exceptions would be some of the senior teachers like Pak Sutaryo and Pak Wahab, who would at times outdo us in mischief. That was probably why they were also very effective teachers.

Politics Inflamed, the Economy Takes a Tumble

My second year of school back in Indonesia (1961/62) was marred by economic chaos and the political upheaval that beset the country. Inflation was high and basic staples were hard to come by.

Our old family habit of frequenting the local pawnshop, by necessity, was revived. I was also often asked by Mimi to borrow money from relatives and acquaintances. This was for me an odious experience that has left its mark to this day.

The government appeared incompetent in the face of our economic difficulties. It was busy tending to factional politics and carrying out megaphone diplomacy on behalf of the nations of the world that were still under the colonial yoke. Day in, day out we saw political action taken against Western imperialism and neocolonialism and heard calls for the liberation of West Irian, now know as Papua, which was still occupied by the Dutch.

In December 1961, President Soekarno, or Bung Karno as he was more affectionately known, declared Trikora (Three Commands of the People), which kick-started Indonesia's efforts to reclaim West Irian. After this, almost on a daily basis, a colossal rally took place at the Ikada Square (now Monas). The same people were paid to attend each time, and they were transported there in trucks, although technically the rallies were being held by different political parties, the ideologies of which would often differ markedly.

The situation would be different, however, whenever Bung Karno was about to make a speech. Masses of people would come of their own volition, even if they had to walk for hours to reach the event. All the parties tried to portray themselves as being close to the President, as they continued to disparage one another.

After the Indonesian Socialist Party (PSI) and the Islamic party Masyumi were both banned for disagreeing with the President, it seemed that everyone thereafter toed the line. The number of citizens detained for no clear reason was also increasing, with the most famous among them being Mochtar Lubis, Mohammad Natsir and Sutan Syahrir.

The grand plan to wrest West Papua from the Dutch by military force gave rise to the increasing militarization of the civilian sphere, including our bureaucracy. Mobilizations of "volunteers" dressed in military-style uniforms were a common sight. The political parties did not want to be left out, so they doubled their efforts in building their own bases within government departments.

Pak Sutrisno, the teacher of our citizenship class, was one of those who opposed the way the state was being run, and he often said so publicly. In his view, the government was busy with surreal policies and was neglecting the people, especially those at the bottom rung of society, whom he called in Javanese *kroco mumet* (*kroco*: Javanese for "small snail", often used figuratively to mean insignificant people with low standing; *mumet*: Javanese for "dazed", often used to indicate a mental state resulting from an impossible situation). Pak Sutrisno's vocal denunciations of government policy eventually landed him in trouble with the Supreme War Command (Peperti), which sent its people to our school to warn him against further transgressions. But this did not seem to daunt him.

"Yesterday, a colonel from Peperti tried to talk me into stopping what I have been doing here, which he called counterrevolutionary incitement", Pak Sutrisno said. We all held our breath to hear what he had to say next. "Maybe we have a snitch here. If that's true, please pass it on that Sutrisno will continue to do as his conscience dictates!" He then proceeded to expound his analysis of current events and his criticism of the government.

In the classroom next to ours was another citizenship class teacher, Liem Bian Kie, who is more commonly known today as Jusuf Wanandi. On account of his thundering voice, we could all hear what he said from the next room.

Jusuf Wanandi's high-decibel voice was only too real and well-known. Years later there was news that his pet parrot had died. People then started joking that the poor bird had expired while trying to match its master's yelling. Another account of what truly happened was even funnier, but its details are too sensitive to share. In short, the parrot was stressed out before it perished because Jusuf had been scolding it for imitating people's phone conversations and for often butting into discussions with sensitive topics.

"If you want to pass your exams, memorise your textbooks", Jusuf used to say. "But if it's the truth you are after, listen to me."

The state of affairs in the country puzzled us to no end. On the one hand, many people—including us, the young—admired Soekarno for championing independence for Asian and African nations. He was physically robust and he exuded confidence when he dealt with world leaders. He made us proud to be Indonesian. However, the economy had gone into free fall and our politics was full of intrigue and escalating conflicts, which, as time went by, became absurd.

We therefore also admired people who were critical of this situation, such as Pak Sutrisno and Jusuf Wanandi. For us, they were no less impressive than our national leaders because they had the courage to be anti-mainstream. Months later, Pak Sutrisno bade us farewell, saying he was resigning for "personal reasons". We never heard from or about him again.

If we look closely at that period of world history, all the developing nations, those which had just attained independence, could be seen to be in a state of flux. In Africa there were still several nations that were struggling to free themselves from colonialism. As these new countries emerged, their leaders tried to formulate a cohesive identity in economics, politics and culture. Each would come up with their own national ideology, which was the brainchild of their respective leaders. In Africa, socialism triumphed, while Indonesia birthed Soekarnoism, and in Yugoslavia, as we saw earlier, Titoism was born as a new version of communism out of the necessity to resist Soviet hegemony.

Following a collective instinct, the leaders of developing nations were averse to becoming involved in the "bipolar war"—better known as the Cold War—between the United States and the Soviet Union and their respective allies. This stance was then known as "non-aligned". To that end, newly independent countries gathered in Bandung for the 1955 Asia-Africa Conference, which led to the declaration of the Bandung Ten Points. The movement received a further boost with the convening of the 1961 Non-Aligned Movement Summit in Belgrade. Western countries, in particular the United States, did not welcome this development. The same could be said of the Soviet Union.

In the end, a combination of geopolitical wrangling and a lack of experience in governing drove many developing nations—Indonesia included—into internal political crises and economic difficulties, exacerbated by domestic interference from major powers.

In Indonesia, foreign interference was evident in the American involvement in separatist movements in the regions. This was then turned to advantage by the post-Stalin Soviet Union in propagating communism among the developing nations. Subsequently, the People's Republic of China under Mao Zedong stopped recognizing Moscow's lead and launched its Cultural Revolution. China began to spread its wings internationally, even at the expense of tens of millions of its citizens dieing of starvation as a result of the mismanagement of the economy.

Moving to Bandung

Economic hardship, along with other personal considerations, drove Mimi to put the Sentiong house up for sale and to move to Bandung. Mochtar had already found a new house in Bandung for us to live in. Since real estate prices were lower in Bandung, the difference between the funds generated by the sale of the Sentiong house and buying the new house was considerable. We decided to put the money in a term deposit, since the interest rate was high then, in line with the rocketing inflation. Mochtar had moved to Bandung first, to teach at the University of Padjajaran. So, in times of difficulty, our family could come together and help each other out.

For the schooling year of 1962/63, I attended Bandung's St Aloysius High School, which was widely known as TOP (To Our Pleasure) High School. Ade went to St Angela High School. After graduating from high school in 1964, Ade married Juzhar Tayang, who worked in the private sector. They had met years before in Jakarta. After their marriage, Ade moved back to Jakarta to be with her husband.

The move to my new school proved smooth sailing for me because it had a similar culture to that of Kanisius. Debating with one's teachers was not frowned upon. The teachers provided us with an education while allowing student-controlled outlets for mischief. Pak Banu, the science teacher, would interrupt his own lessons to sing with his lovely voice, egging us on to join him. Our Physics teacher was called Meneer Kho Djoen Sen. He had a little tradition every Thursday in which he would, instead of teaching Physics, conduct a free discussion whereby students could ask and talk about anything. The session was called "Sane Questions". As a new student, I chose to observe the proceedings without coming up with my own questions.

"The Jakartan student has so far kept quiet. Where is your Sane Question?" Meneer Kho asked me once out of the blue.

My bantering instinct was awakened, and on the spur of the moment I replied, "I haven't asked any question yet because I'm not sure of a sane response from you, Meneer Kho."

The whole class erupted in laughter. It then occurred to me that I might have crossed the line and uttered a gaffe. But, after a look of fleeting surprise on his face, Meneer Kho laughed so hard he was teary-eyed.

"Well, to uphold school rules, I'm obliged to give you punishment", he said, even though he was still laughing and obviously enjoying the whole thing. "Please leave the classroom and sit under that big tree."

My other memorable experience at Aloysius was when I wrote

an essay for my Indonesian teacher, Pak Sugito, on a free topic. My essay dwelt on the advances in science and technology and their impact and consequences. I argued, among other things, that inequality would develop between those with access to and understanding of technological and scientific advances—both as inventors or users—and those who did not. The divide would likely worsen and would surpass the existing social and economic inequality. I argued that the only way to avert this scenario would be to make quality education available to all. I qualified good education as one that would enable students to cultivate creativity, and not one that relied on slogans and speeches and the propagation of fear and division.

The essay earned me the highest mark possible. Pak Sugito was so pleased with it that he showed it around before returning it to me.

Mochtar Loses Tenure at University

The essay was inspired by the political clouds that were gathering over the country, and which also affected my family. In 1962, Mochtar was suddenly relieved of his tenure at the University of Padjadjaran (Unpad), after having receiving his doctorate in International Law of the Sea there aged 33—a tender age in those days to receive a doctoral degree. It was said that the order had come directly from the President, who had been incensed by Mochtar's criticism of his leadership. Another source claimed his dismissal had been planned long ago by those envious within the university of his achievements.

After Mochtar lost his job, Pak Ruhimat, a former colleague at the university, was good enough to lend him his garage in Jalan Supratman to serve as an office for him to practice law. I helped out by minding the office after school and keeping him company. We would play chess or bridge with dummies together. Mochtar still lectured at the University of Parahyangan. The only government agency brave enough to use his services was the Army Command Academy (Seskoad) under Lieutenant General Sudirman, with his second-in-command being Major General Suwarto.

Mochtar became a bit of a pariah. People tried to avoid being seen with him, and his legal practice hardly attracted any clients. Once, Mochtar and I were walking down Jalan Braga and he saw someone he knew in the distance. He waved his hand in greeting only to see the person scuttle away without returning the wave. I asked him who it was. He said, "Oh, an Unpad lecturer." But he was not without his supporters either. Posters and fliers defending him appeared out of nowhere. People could only guess who had masterminded them.

Incident of 10 May 1963

On 10 May 1963, the city was rocked by acts of vandalism and looting against the Chinese Indonesian community. It started with a fight between students of the Bandung Institute of Technology (ITB) over the use of facilities, which then escalated into rioting.

On a personal level, the incident was unsavoury for us as a family because there were rumours that the pro-Mochtar movement and the racial riot of 10 May were somehow connected. Our close friends did not believe this, of course. My Chinese Indonesian friends from St Aloysius trusted me enough to leave their motorbikes at our house. I myself learned how to ride a motorbike by using their bikes.

Mochtar and his family were facing dire problems. They had to sell their housewares and furniture just to get by. In the end, Mochtar told Mimi he could no longer help with my tuition fees. I had to start earning.

When Mochtar and his family had to vacate his faculty house in Jalan Tengku Angkasa, their belongings had dwindled to the point of easily fitting in the back of the Chevrolet pickup lent to them by Budi Soedarsono (who was then working at the National Nuclear Agency, Batan). These included a writing desk, books and a bookcase, a folding bed and two suitcases. Their other household appliances had already been sold.

Fortunately, Mochtar received a scholarship at the Chicago Law School, so he took his family with him to the United States. He had managed to secure a passport following an intervention from Seskoad, which had sent people to convince the staff at the Ministry of Foreign Affairs—in a fashion unique to the military—to issue a service passport for Dr Mochtar.

Mimi Becomes a Street Hawker

The yields from our term deposit at a foundation in Cimahi helped us to afford to run the household, even if only for a while. Once a month I was tasked with picking up our money from the foundation, along with the goods we had to buy. However, with the fast depreciating rupiah, our monthly yields were no longer sufficient. So Mimi had to take on supplementary work. By this time she was sixty, but she was young at heart. She bought groceries and cooked while humming tunes in Sundanese, Javanese and old Dutch songs. Washing our clothes was not a great chore, since we had so few of them. We cleaned the house together.

Mimi got up very early each day, at 3 a.m., to prepare various traditional snacks and cakes that she would sell by the roadside. Ade and I acted as her assistants in making *serabi* (coconut-milk pancakes), either from wheat flour or rice flour. It was also my job to look for banana leaves to use as cake wrappings. I also offered my services to catch rats and to debug houses. People said that rats and house bugs always increased when things were tough. I worked at odd jobs here and there, painting houses before Eid Al-Fitr, for instance. It was physically demanding, but because I worked alone the money I got was worth the effort.

Just before I finished secondary school, I managed to buy a bicycle, pay off the tuition fees I owed to the school, enrol myself at a university and buy new clothes. My whole wardrobe had consisted of two pairs of trousers and three shirts.

Because shoes were extremely expensive, I wore a pair of hand-me-downs from Mochtar, which were too narrow for my feet, resulting in a tear and my toes sticking out. To avoid looking ridiculous, I trimmed the torn parts of my shoes to resemble Indian slippers. The soles had worn out, so I added a layer of carton to fortify them.

A black sock of mine had a hole in it. To camouflage it, I applied some ink to the skin of my foot where the hole would show. The idea came from George Orwell, who did the same thing when he was destitute, as recounted in his book *Down and Out in Paris and London*. Now and then I got the travelling cobbler from Cibaduyut to mend my shoes as best he could to make them last. At the time, unfortunately, torn clothes and the worn look were not in vogue as they have been in more recent times.

2

Activism and Becoming a Politician

I finished secondary school in 1963 and, after passing the admission test, was admitted to the Bandung Institute of Technology (ITB). The prestige of ITB was my main reason for choosing the university. Why did I choose Civil Engineering? The answer was that the faculty was known for its "killer" lecturers. As my first backup in case ITB had fallen through, I also applied to the Medical School at Unpad and was accepted. On my mother's advice, I had in addition applied to the Textile Academy because the prerequisites were easy to fulfil. I was accepted there as well.

My choice of university major then, I must admit, did not reflect any clear life plan. Never did I envisage myself working as a civil engineer after completing my studies. I had indeed followed my urge to overcome a momentary challenge, while at the same time also making alternative arrangements.

My time as a university student at ITB was an important part of my life. It was a kaleidoscope of experiences for me. Between 1963 and 1965, campus life was as good as could be expected, but chaos reigned in our society. The volatile state of affairs affected our family, although I was fortunate enough to not have my studies interrupted.

Hazing at PMB

At the campus located in the Ganesha Complex that was ITB, I was reunited with my great friend from Kanisius College, Wimar Witoelar. He was studying electronics. Wimar and I became a team ever since we underwent the hazing rituals together at the Bandung University Students' Association (PMB) and the orientation period at ITB, known as *mapram*.

PMB was an organization for university students in Bandung. It was founded in 1948 on the premise that it was oriented towards societal harmony, nationhood and Pancasila (the Indonesian state ideology). Although it engaged actively in the discourse on political affairs, PMB was essentially a place of recreation, or as the youth of today would say, a place for students to hang out. Its members were students from the top three universities in Bandung: ITB, the University of Padjadjaran (Unpad) and the Catholic University of Parahyangan (Unpar).

PMB members were known for their creativity and independence. We planned and funded all our activities ourselves. Our gatherings— referred to using the Dutch word *kroeg* (get-together)—were recreational in nature. Most people knew about PMB on account of the hazing rituals for new members.

PMB's hazing rituals lasted for ten days and involved activities that were controlled and safe. In a state of physical fatigue, initiates were faced with orchestrated realities that were both shocking and frightening. Many students gave up. Those who wanted to proceed but admitted they were unable to complete the rituals were given the status of "red cross initiates". They were then given menial tasks such as minding parked bicycles, buying food for seniors and so on. Their "red cross" status placed them as second-class members of PMB.

By contrast, new students who made it all the way through the travails usually developed kinship and camaraderie both with their fellow initiates and with the seniors. Several of the seniors acted as mentors for new members, and as a new member I somehow received special attention from them.

During our hazing period, Wimar Witoelar and I once lined up in front of a booth in ITB's West Hall to complete some administrative requirements. From afar, a pretty young woman, who attracted a lot of attention, was walking towards us. Wimar suddenly thought to tease me. He challenged me to a bet by dangling a few candles before me, saying I would never work up enough courage to say hello to the girl. Since candles were the currency for the hazing rituals, it was quite a bet on Wimar's part.

To his astonishment, I walked up to the girl confidently and started talking to her. Wimar had no idea that I had met her before on the SS *Australia*. She was Nini Maramis. Nini was enrolled at the School for Urban and Regional Planning at ITB. I won the bet and Wimar begrudgingly surrendered a few of his candles.

"You cheated! You met her before", he whined. I countered that that was not a factor in the bet and I was entitled to the candles he had promised.

Our campus, I discovered, was in the throes of a political fever, so to speak. The student body was divided along the lines of being for or against communism. Each faction was busy recruiting students into their respective camps. Wimar and I were ripe targets, naturally. From the start, Wimar stood out like a sore thumb among the initiates. People just could not help but focus on him. He was even named General Initiate, which did not mean anything except by way of confirmation of his star status. His fame — or notoriety, depending on how you saw it — rubbed off on me as his closest buddy.

The hazing period at PMB became a recruitment arena for the seniors who were anti-communist. The pro-communist students, however, refrained from following suit because they saw PMB as part of the bourgeoisie, and its members as likely to be unsympathetic to their cause. Within PMB, senior students were on the lookout for new students with potential. They evaluated us through interviews and by giving us strange errands in order to get some insight into our basic character and levels of creativity. For instance, I was told — at midnight — to capture two bed bugs and to have them ready for a morning inspection at 5 a.m. Upon presenting them, I was asked which of the bugs was male and which was female.

"Wait a moment, Mr Senior", I replied. "We see the way they carry themselves, of course. The one in the front is female and the other in the back is male", I concluded.

"How did you make that out?" asked senior Deddy Krisna.

"These bugs are well educated. They are inhabitants of the city of Bandung and lived in houses", I began. "So, the one in the front is female. Ladies first. If these were rural bugs, the one in the front would be the male."

It was palpable that senior Deddy Krisna was dumbstruck and intrigued by my repartee. "Why do Indonesians tend to be skinny and shorter than Westerners?" he asked me next.

The question was interesting, given that senior Deddy, born and raised in Cirebon, was a strapping young man of 185 cm in height.

"Generally speaking, Indonesians have small postures because of nutritional issues", I replied, all the while anticipating his next question, which was bound to be about himself.

"I eat the same things you do; tofu, tempeh and salted fish, but I am big and tall. Why?" he asked. Under normal circumstances, his logic would have been watertight.

"I did say generally speaking, Mr Senior", I argued. "Mr Senior is obviously an anomaly. Anomalies are important because without them generalizations would not be possible."

"Well, well. Not bad, Initiate", Deddy Krisna said. "Smart like his older brother, I see. We should give you the special treatment; a future cadre. And by the way, screw you for calling me an anomaly! I am somebody, you know", he added, laughing.

As expected, the other seniors nodded in agreement to "give me the special treatment" and joined in the laughter after seeing how pleased Deddy Krisna was. If he had been infuriated, the initiate would have been punished by being made to do pushups or to leapfrog around.

Another "errand" that the seniors gave us was to acquire horse urine. There were several literal-minded initiates who patiently waited by the horses that pulled hired carriages at the train station with empty bottles, desperately hoping for the horses to pass water and to not mind having it collected in a bottle! The less literal of us brought our own urine from home and passed it off as horse piss.

The errand was just another test to grade future activists. Resourceful initiates ready with an answer were usually chosen to step up to activities of higher abstraction, while those that really collected horse piss were deemed suited for more practical tasks like moving tables and chairs at functions, distributing anonymous pamphlets, browbeating opponents and so on. These were nicknamed the "SS", after the notorious Nazi Schutzstaffel. I remember several seniors who acted as recruiters other than Deddy Krisna: Rudianto Ramelan, Ariono Abdulkadir, Udaya Hadibrata, Fred Hehuwat and Muslimin Nasution. They were all part of PMB's Mentoring Committee.

Initiates who made it to the next level were put into groups of five, each of which had a senior who acted as chief mentor. My mentors included Muslimin Nasution and Udaya Hadibrata. In our own group we were introduced to ideological issues, leadership, mass gathering techniques, making anonymous pamphlets, psychological warfare, stealing documents, and other arcane matters.

Friction between different student factions at ITB was fierce, and our seniors were engaged in a struggle to keep ITB as the only campus that had not been "Nasakomized" (Nasakom: Nationalist, Religionist and Communist was a state doctrine launched by Soekarno in the 1960s, supposedly to unify all the major ideological strains within Indonesia). As the government sought to impose the doctrine on the nation, university campuses were told to toe the line by ensuring all institutions within it—the chancellery, deanery and staff—were made up of people representing the nationalists, religionists and communists. The mainstream student body at ITB was against such segmentation. However, the pressure to conform from the proponents of Nasakom were considerable. I continued to keep abreast of the political events in Jakarta, although I now had a sceptical view of Indonesian politics in general. Politics was something to observe so long as it did not interfere with my studies. At this stage, my priority was to study until graduation and to earn a bit of money on the side.

Tutoring

My family's ongoing lack of money left me no choice but to start earning. Apart from helping Mimi out with her additional work, I needed to find another way that I could earn my own money. I thus became a private tutor for junior high school students. My main market was the children of the rich deemed by their parents to be stupid or lazy. In many cases this assumption was wrong. For a competitive edge, I agreed to collect my payment only after three months of tutoring, if I managed to ensure that the student's grades stabilized above the passing mark. The risk of not being paid motivated me to tutor my students as well as I could.

I taught English because I knew the language well. I also taught science in order to further inculcate it in my mind. I believed that teaching something I had not fully mastered was the perfect way for me to learn it as well. My willingness to forgo payment unless the students' marks improved also forced me to know my subjects well. In today's language, I adhered to a system of results-based payment.

I was also actively involved in PMB with the purpose of honing my social skills. The PMB set was known for partying hard. I tried to take it up, even if only as one of the organizers. I was in charge of party décor and the couriers we used to distribute and sell invitations. Even so, my social skills remained underdeveloped, especially when it came to PMB's female students, whose good looks were legendary. I felt I was in luck once when I was asked to be the DJ. But during the event my mischievous side got the better of me and I started putting on government propaganda songs. Our party was on the cusp of breaking up because people were outraged.

I soon developed a reputation among the seniors as a thinker. So it was not a surprise when they invited me to join them at the back of a party to discuss politics. In the end, I still did not find it convenient to socialize with many people.

My other activity of note was with the student press, to cover events around ITB. Once in a while I would also write an anonymous pamphlet, making a parody of society issues and turning the country's grandees into the butt of jokes.

Politics of Confrontation

In 1962 there was an important development in Indonesia's bid to take back Papua, known then as West Irian. The combined factors of military action and diplomacy eventually forced the hand of the Netherlands and it agreed to go to the negotiation table in New York, with a view to handing control of the territory to Indonesia. At the time, the Indonesian Navy, buttressed with the hardware of the Soviet Union, ranked fourth in the world. A military expeditionary force to

West Irian was being prepared, code-named Operation Mandala, under the command of Major General Soeharto. The American diplomat Ellsworth Bunker was to be the mediator between Indonesia and the Netherlands.

It would appear that the United States had changed tack in its approach to Indonesia. While it had helped separatists against Jakarta in the past, it now wanted to sway Indonesia away from the influence of the Soviet Union by applying pressure on the Netherlands to recognize Indonesian sovereignty over West Irian. For the transitional period, the UN went on to set up the United Nations Temporary Executive Authority (UNTEA).

Naturally, the news was greeted with delight in Indonesia, and many hoped that after the victory in Irian the government would turn its attention to diffusing the political tensions in the country and to begin fixing the economy.

Alas, this was not to be. A hitherto shrouded tinderbox ignited a conflagration when Soekarno vehemently opposed the plans of the federation of colonies formerly within British Malaya to form a new country called Malaysia. Indonesia therefore waged a campaign against what Soekarno saw as a "neocolonialist project called Malaysia". All our political and military energy was galvanized for the campaign. The Two Commands of the People (Dwikora) was declared. The slogan *Ganyang Malaysia* (Beat the hell out of Malaysia!) became a national greeting. The whole nation had the appearance of being united against a common enemy, but the reality was that internal bickering escalated and the economy slid further down the drain.

Our campus at ITB became a battleground for competing political camps. As of 1964, education per se took a backseat as political fever gripped the campus. Even the so-called bookworms had also embraced politics. The divide along political lines became more pronounced as each side tried to intimidate the other. Fields of work that had been solely moneymaking enterprises, such as tutoring and the sale of text books, became contested areas for political chicanery.

Rahmat Witoelar, who was elected as President of the Student Council for 1965/66, was greatly perturbed by this state of affairs. He duly appointed me the official organizer of the ITB tutoring programme under the auspices of the Student Council, as a means to end the conflicts in "welfare politics".

During Rahmat Witoelar's presidency, I took part in a journalism-training workshop for university students conducted by the Indonesian University Students Press Association (IPMI). Our instructors included Ismid Hadad, Lukman Isa and Alex Rumondor. At the end of our training, Ismid Hadad presented me with an award for being the best participant. Ismid and I have kept in touch ever since. Journalistic training was, in my view, important because the ongoing political situation meant the media were being employed to influence public opinion.

During this period, people tended to listen to hearsay more than to the press because news stories were often very contrary. On the one hand everyone wanted to be seen as supporting Soekarno, but on the other they actively took sides in the ongoing ideological war. In several regions, physical clashes had already occurred. In order to be in the loop, political activists sought to foster relations with political figures, sometimes openly but at times covertly.

In Bandung, two figures in the world of activism were often mentioned, not only as sources but also as the clandestine movers and shakers behind student activists. First was Suripto, who much later became a member of the House of Representatives (DPR) from the Justice and Welfare Party (PKS) and Secretary General of the Ministry of Forestry. Second was Rahman Tolleng, who went by the name Iwan Ramelan.

As junior students, we never saw either of the two. Nor did our seniors try to introduce them to us—the reason being that the two were wanted by the country's intelligence agency (BPI) on suspicion of being involved in counter-revolutionary activities. They were evidently "underground" entities whose existence was known only to a select few.

The reason given by our seniors may have been true, but it was also possible they wanted to monopolize relations with these underground figures. Had these hidden figures been exposed to many, the influence of our seniors would have been severely curtailed.

In our eyes, both Suripto and Rahman were mythical figures. Their names were often quoted as sources or as being in charge, but we could never verify this, and there was no way to control the flow of information. In Wimar's and my imaginings, Rahman Tolleng was a sturdy Bugis man with a sizeable moustache comparable to that of Andi Mallarangeng's, the former Democratic Party (PD) politician of today, and he would wear a bracelet of black coral (*akar bahar*). Bugis men in the old days were known for being fierce sailors. In fact, the English word *bogeyman* has its root in Bugis. We did not have overly wild imagination about Suripto, however, because Javanese men were commonplace in our environment and we had our own stereotypes about them.

Disappointment among "Soekarno's Offspring"

The most persistent rumour at the time was that Soekarno was very ill. Amid the ideological war, the lack of a succession mechanism and widespread economic hardships, everyone with a vested interest was preparing for a post-Soekarno era. The "analysts" among the students— myself included—agreed we were headed for an inevitable conflict. In essence, it would be a clash between those who were either for or against communism. Admittedly, we had no access to information on what each camp was doing. Because of this, all hope seemed to hang on the attitude and future of Soekarno. If the rumour of his grave illness had been false, many hoped he would be able to find a solution to the conflict and restore the economy to good health.

My fellow students and I had an ambivalent attitude towards Soekarno. We had admired him to begin with, but we were also exasperated that he seemed to ignore issues concerning people's welfare. We were also incensed that senior government officials appeared to live in a world of their own. Years later, a foreign Indonesianist wrote that Bandung university students were "Soekarno's offspring" whose disappointment then turned to anger. I think his observation was more or less accurate.

In many ways, we had always put Soekarno on a pedestal. We supported his international vision as expressed through Bandung's Ten-Points and Indonesia's distinguished membership in the Non-Aligned Movement. Every new class at PMB was named after one of Soekarno's speeches. However, the interpretation of his concepts was dominated by student organizations affiliated with the Indonesian Communist Party (PKI). Consequently, a lot of radical ideas circulated on campus, the application of which would have resulted in huge numbers of casualties, rather like Mao's Cultural Revolution or Pol Pot's genocide in 1970s Cambodia. We also heard that the various clashes in the regions were what the PKI called "revolutionary gymnastics".

The ideological polarization of society eventually found its way to our campus, stoking further tensions. Students often bickered with one another over politics. In dealing with the situation, we were inevitably forced to choose one side or the other. Left meant communist, while the others were automatically categorized as centrist or right. Over time the centrists became submerged, and what remained was either anti-communist or pro-communist.

In this regard, I was one of those alarmed at Soekarno's increasingly leftist stance. Within the student body, ever so gradually, the parodies and sarcastic jokes once reserved for high-ranking officials and political grandees became redirected towards Soekarno—something that had never happened before.

Quiet before the Storm

It was amid this unsettled period that on 1 October 1965 we heard Lieutenant Colonel Untung's radio announcement of the formation of a Revolution Council to prevent a planned coup by the Council of Generals. I vividly remember that day. At 10 a.m., Rahmat Witoelar and I were discussing what had transpired over bowls of mung bean porridge at Ganesha Park.

We were both of the opinion that the Revolution Council that had just been announced was highly irregular. For a start, it was chaired by an unknown middle-ranking officer who had to act as a superior to a member of the council who was a brigadier general. The general in turn had to be demoted accordingly because the council ruled that the highest rank in the military was now held by a lieutenant colonel. The council was said to hold the highest reins of power in government, but the exact position of the President was not specified. The cabinet had apparently been disbanded. The composition of the council was announced to give the impression it included figures of national stature, although these were referred to haphazardly.

Apart from adding that regional Revolution Councils would be formed shortly, Untung did not specify any other action. Rahmat and I speculated as to who was behind the stunt. In analysing the language used, we felt that it was similar to the tone and mode usually employed by the leftists.

The actual facts of what was happening at the time were unknown to us. We could only make educated guesses through what appeared to us as an impenetrable haze. Days later, however, sensational information started to come through. At that point in time we did not know the details of the kidnappings and murders of the generals in the incident now known as Gestapu, which is still highly controversial to this day. But we all felt that Untung's announcement did not bode well for the future. "If it is truly the wish of the Revolution Council that the highest military rank is lieutenant colonel, then surely it is the creation of the communists", surmised Rahmat.

Our next surprise came later that evening, with a continuous radio broadcast by Major General Soeharto, the Kostrad (Strategic Reserves) Commander, who refuted the veracity of the Revolution Council and appealed for calm from the public. He also mentioned that several high-ranking officers of the army had been kidnapped, and some killed.

Among the student activists there was a general agreement that the conflict was working towards its end. We were all restless and tense. I noted that there was no such sentiment among the masses. The general public assumed the whole thing was just the usual political kerfuffle that would eventually fizzle out. Only a few were aware that the sporadic events we heard about were part of an explosive situation that was about to detonate. The calm of the people was like the quiet before the storm.

Thus, between the end of 1965 and early 1966, Indonesia went through a period of transition. Soekarno was officially still President, but his position had been compromised by the events of 30 September, or the G30S incident. I will not elaborate further on this matter, since new versions and opinions of what happened are likely to keep appearing, as they have done recently. An intriguing development at the time for us the junior student activists was the persistent rumour that Rahman Tolleng and Suripto had abandoned their underground hideouts, so to speak, though they were still nowhere to be seen. We thought it possible they had spent so much time underground that they felt they missed coming up for a bit of air.

One day, Wimar came by my house in an agitated state. "Rahman Tolleng is at Odjak's house. Come quickly before he disappears again", Wimar said, hurrying me along. Of course I was elated at the prospect of meeting the legendary figure. Odjak Siagian was a senior student at

ITB as well as an army lieutenant in the Siliwangi Division. His house was located near Gedung Sate, not too far from mine. As we entered the living room, we did not see anyone who could be Rahman. Instead, we saw someone hunched over near the window as if he was too cold, a small-built man who was apparently sunning himself while smoking a Wismilak cigarette. He could not be Rahman Tolleng, we thought.

"Eweuh geuning si Rahman teh" (Rahman isn't here) Wimar said in Sundanese.

"I am Rahman Tolleng", said the small man in a thick Bugis accent.

Both Wimar and I were dumbfounded, as well as pleased, to be able to meet him at last. But there was also a niggling sense of disappointment that he was not at all what we had imagined him to be. The brawny Bugis man with a thick moustache turned out to be a figment of our imagination. Physically, Rahman Tolleng was just like an average Indonesian man, small and on the skinny side. Not only that. His front teeth were mostly missing. The possibility that they had somehow been knocked out during torture by the state apparatus was also small, given that his remaining teeth had bad nicotine stains. It was all too possible that he had lost his teeth because of excessive smoking. Heavy smokers were in the habit of using the gaps between their teeth to insert a cigarette, after all.

Rahman Tolleng as we met him in the house of Odjak Siagian. Photo by *Tempo*.

We started talking to Rahman, who knew a lot about the two of us. He was the clandestine man par excellence. He knew much, but so little about him was known. Our conversation with him earned him our respect and admiration. His eyes twinkled with intelligence and resolve. His analysis was spot-on, while his ethics were admirable. He was unpretentious. He was just as he was.

What pleased us most was that he had the same sense of humour as Wimar and I did. Some people said that Wimar and I shared the same sarcastic humour because both of us had been educated abroad, but there was Rahman Tolleng, an underground activist, locally bred, who had the same wit as we did. But not all clandestine figures were funny. On a later date we got to meet Suripto as well. He turned out to be equally impressive, but he was very serious in demeanour.

The Storm Gathers

Throughout October 1965—particularly after the exposure, on the 4th of the month, of the murders of the generals, a middle-ranking officer and a non-commissioned policeman—our seniors appeared to be extremely busy. We juniors were not roped into their activities, however. Instead, they told us to gather the next day—5 October 1965—to commemorate the anniversary of the Armed Forces.

At the time, the G30S incident, also known as Gestapu, was increasingly seen as a coup attempt by the PKI. The PKI leadership denied the accusation and instead declared that the incident of 1 October—Gestok, as it chose to call it—was an internal struggle within the army; a theory that it repeated time and again without further elaboration.

On 5 October 1965, about two hundred students gathered at Cibeunying Park. That day we saw for the first time several seniors whom we later came to know better: Sugeng Saryadi, Bona Siagian and the ones we already knew. From the crowd, I only knew people from PMB, including Erna, whom we later called Erna Witoelar following her marriage to Rahmat. She went on to become an environmental activist and, later, Minister of Public Works and Housing in the National Unity Cabinet under President Abdurrahman Wahid (1999–2001). All the participants were instructed to march across the city. Our numbers swelled with members of the public who decided to join our march.

Then, all of a sudden, some of the marchers started shouting anti-PKI slogans. We then stormed and occupied the PKI local headquarters, an office that belonged to the PKI-affiliated Concentrated Indonesian University Students Movement (CGMI) and the office of the *Warta Bandung* daily. People at those three offices looked surprised when we stormed in, but they did nothing to stop us, and most fled the scene. Several people then came in and carted off boxes of documents from the three offices and took them somewhere. Afterwards, we occupied the offices. Looking back, it is possible our action was the first public demonstration against the PKI in the aftermath of G30S.

At about the same time, newspapers, the radio and television were full of news about the murders of six army generals and a middle-ranking officer. Their bodies had been dumped into a well at Lubang Buaya. The retrieval of the bodies was televised. Army General A.H. Nasution had emerged from the incident unscathed, but his daughter, Ade Irma Suryani, and his adjutant, Captain Pierre Tendean, had been shot dead.

Newspapers and television news then churned out reports that singled out the PKI as having masterminded the murders, which had been carried out by members of the presidential guard, the Tjakrabirawa Regiment, aided by organizations affiliated with the PKI. Soekarno tried to belittle the incident, which he called "a small ripple in the revolutionary wave", and he promised a political solution. He then continued to wage his "confrontation" with Malaysia.

In the meantime, the PKI chose to weather the storm of accusations through inaction. Unexpectedly, its branches in West Java declared themselves disbanded almost simultaneously. This event received a lot of publicity. The PKI leadership kept repeating their defence that the incident of 1 October had been an internal issue of the army. PKI ministers were still seen at cabinet meetings.

The situation in Bandung was still calm, at least on the surface. It was a different story with the student activists. Wimar, Zulkarnain Yusuf and I spent a lot of time helping out Rahmat Witoelar in carrying out his duties as President of the ITB Student Council. We also kept an eye on the situation in the city and cultivated contacts within the regional military command (Kodam VI/Siliwangi), in particular with the Chief of Staff, Brigadier General H.R. Dharsono. We also made a trip to Jakarta to see fellow student activists there. In the capital, Rahmat, Wimar and I went to meet Pak Mashuri Saleh, who later became Minister of Education and Culture.

Pak Mashuri at the time was the secretary to the neighbourhood association in Menteng, which was headed by General Soeharto. He relayed to us a message from Soeharto that the general was in full support of the student movement, and that the Chief of Staff of Kodam VI/Siliwangi was the right person to contact.

We then heard that leading figures of various student mass organizations had held a meeting at the residence of Major General Syarif Thayeb, who was then Junior Minister of Tertiary Education and Science. At this meeting they agreed to form Unified Action of Indonesian Students (KAMI). KAMI acted as the umbrella under which the following off-campus student organizations coordinated with one another:

- Himpunan Mahasiswa Islam (HMI), the Islamic University Student Association
- Perhimpunan Mahasiswa Katolik Republik Indonesia (PMKRI), the Association of Catholic University Students of the Republic of Indonesia
- Gerakan Mahasiswa Kristen Indonesia (GMKI), the Indonesian Christian University Student Movement
- Pergerakan Mahasiswa Islam Indonesia (PMII), the Indonesian Islamic University Student Movement
- Ikatan Mahasiswa Muhammadiyah (IMM), the Muhammadiyah University Student Association
- Mahasiswa Pancasila, the Pancasila University Students

And local university student bodies such as:

- Perhimpunan Mahasiswa Bandung (PMB), the Bandung Student Association
- Ikatan Mahasiswa Jakarta (Imada), the Jakarta Student Association
- Gerakan Mahasiswa Surabaya (GMS), the Surabaya Student Movement
- Masyarakat Mahasiswa Bogor (MMB), the Bogor Student Society
- Corpus Studiosorum Bandungense (CSB)
- Ikatan Mahasiswa Pontianak (Imapon), the Pontianak Student Association

The local student bodies coalesced in the General Secretariat of Local Student Organizations (Somal) to enable them to take part in the KAMI Central Presidium. Local Student Councils were in turn interested in joining the KAMI Regional Presidium. As a result, our student activists interacted with each other on a scale never seen before, including with the founding organizations of KAMI.

Through our interactions with different off-campus student organizations, we discovered that their network of information and their political experience were far superior to our own at PMB. Our on-campus organizations were used to relying on information from mysterious figures who often communicated through cryptic means. So, all in all, the recent changes were an eye-opener for us student activists.

Peak of the Storm

Our economy, which was in tatters, took a turn for the worse. Inflation was at 650 per cent. In January 1966, the government devalued the currency, known in Indonesia as *sanering*. Thousand rupiah banknotes were to be exchanged for new one rupiah notes. Fuel prices increased dramatically, naturally causing a corresponding hike in transportation costs. This proved to be the last straw for ordinary Indonesians, who then took to the streets to protest. Waves of demonstrations took place across the country. Student activists under KAMI suddenly acquired a large number of constituents as more and more people joined our demonstrations.

The country witnessed street demonstrations day in, day out, especially in Bandung and Jakarta. In the same month, protesters declared Tritura (Three Demands by the People), which became the slogan for our struggle. General Nasution named our generation "the '66". Our activities in the early part of 1966 brought us into contact with fellow activists from Jakarta such as David Napitupulu, Mar'ie Muhammad, Cosmas Batubara, Taufik Ismail, Syahrir, Marsilam Simandjutak and Goenawan Moehammad.

Soekarno did not seem perturbed by the protests. Nor did we see any signs of his changing tack in his politics. He went on to form a new cabinet containing a large number of ministers, which came to be called the Hundred Minister Cabinet. This elicited even greater protests on the streets. A few of the ministers were then kidnapped. Mob attacks were launched against the Chinese Embassy and China's news agency Hsin Hua. China's partiality towards the PKI was obvious to all. Hsin Hua kept defending the PKI in its Indonesian language service through Radio Peking.

The Bandung students then decided to perform a long march to Jakarta during the fasting month. As we set off, people lined the streets to cheer us on and give us parcels of food. But in the end we turned back because the military command at Kodam VI/Siliwangi informed us of its opposition to our plan and that it was ready to intercept us at Padalarang.

The leaders of the student movement however chose not to reveal the real reason for our cancelled march. Instead they said that the ITB campus was now occupied by Soekarno loyalists who called themselves "Barisan Soekarno" (Soekarno Front). Many of us were in fact relieved that the long march had been called off because none of us could imagine what would happen if the march had reached Jakarta—an extraordinary mass reception to be sure. And we were not used to walking too long a distance—three kilometres maximum a day for most of us who, like me, had to walk to campus. My bicycle had been stolen by this point.

February 1966 saw the beginning of the court sessions of the Extraordinary Military Tribunal (Mahmillub) to try those implicated in the attempted coup: PKI figures, several ministers and military officers. The press reports from the trials seemed to confirm the PKI's involvement, at least at the party elite level. Protest rallies demanding Tritura continued to grow in Jakarta, amidst the government's seemingly non-existent presence in the life of the nation.

Our Bandung protest contingent was headquartered at the University of Indonesia (UI). We also witnessed student activism on the rise, with an ever-increasing number of student organizations joining our actions, such as United Action of Indonesian Students and Youth (KAPPI), United Action of Indonesian Students (KAPI) and United Action of Graduated Students (KASI).

Street protesters would congregate at different points in the city. We from Somal would meet up in Jalan Palem, at Djoni Sunarya's house. Other meeting points included the one at Margasiswa, PMKRI's office in Jalan Sam Ratulangie. Several friends set up a radio service, christened Radio Ampera, which broadcast news and updates on student activism. The atmosphere had changed completely from that of the previous year, in which revolution-themed propaganda and mass agitation were the order of the day. Our actions were not without their casualties, such as the death of Arief Rahman Hakim in Jakarta and Julius Usman in Bandung. They became icons for our movement.

After the Storm

March 1966 ushered in an event that would mark the next phase of change in the country. President Soekarno signed an order that would later be known as the Decree of 11 March (Supersemar) in which he fully authorized General Soeharto, then the Army Chief of Staff, to take over the day-to-day running of the government. The very next day, the government officially disbanded the PKI, and the members of the cabinet were declared demissioned. The public breathed a sigh of relief, and the military parades held in Jakarta turned into street parties. Two of the three points in Tritura had been fulfilled.

As a consequence of Supersemar, although Soekarno was still President, he no longer governed the nation. Soeharto, appointed Chair of the Ampera Cabinet Presidium, made all the decisions, albeit in Soekarno's name. Soeharto's own reputation skyrocketed. He came to be known by the public as someone who could run the government effectively, and in due course he won the support of the people.

Mass protests stopped after the formation of the Ampera Cabinet Presidium. Life returned to normal as people went back to their lives, and politics became once again the domain of the elite. The Bandung university students also headed back to the campus and resumed their studies, although campus life was different from the pre-G30S period. Our university chancellor at ITB, Kuntoadji—an army colonel—had to deal with a student community fresh from a victory.

Rahmat Witoelar's own tenure as Council President came to an end. An HMI activist, Purwoto Handoko, known as Pungki, was elected to succeed him for the period 1966–67. To cast a vote to elect the Council President, a student had to be a member of the Student Consultative Assembly (MPM), the members of which in turn were elected by their respective faculty. Each faculty was allotted a number of seats on the MPM commensurate with the size of its student population.

A number of things at that time were happening simultaneously. First, students and staff members deemed to be pro-communist by the chancellery were being penalized. Among the lecturers, those who were members of the Indonesian Graduates Association (HSI) were sacked or at the minimum suspended.

For the students, membership in organizations such as CGMI, the Indonesian Student Movement (Germindo) or the Indonesian Student

Association (Perhimi) meant expulsion from university, as their names were erased from the registry. In many cases the expulsions took place without the respective students being present or notified, because they were not seen anywhere. No one knew where they were or what had happened to them.

Second, a process of de-Soekarnoization was in full swing. Students who had previously declared themselves part of the Soekarno Front were suspended. But the move against the Front was largely symbolic because most of its members were sociologically and politically close to the anti-communists. Therefore, both students and staff proceeded to help the suspended students to keep up with their studies, if only covertly. Their academic achievements were soon recorded, as their suspensions, which only lasted a few months, ended. Many of them even went on to graduate sooner than the '66 activists, who were still kept busy.

My friends and I often engaged former Soekarno Front students in discussions. We concluded that our previously polarized stances owed more to the information that was accessible to the respective camps rather than any significant ideological differences. As a foreign academic once observed, Bandung's youth started out as "Soekarno's offspring" who became disappointed and then angry at the way things had developed. As such, our friendships with former members of the Soekarno Front were still intact, and we all realized we were often the products of circumstances that were out of our control.

Third, the euphoria after our victory also produced its own side effects. In the years before 1965, the PKI was vociferous in its efforts to root out those it called "reactionary", "counter-revolutionary" or "the enemies of the revolution". One of its targets was HMI, which PKI campaigned to have disbanded. Consequently, as of 1964, HMI was under extraordinary political pressure. Many sympathized with its travails, but most were too afraid to have any contact with HMI at the time.

By default, after PKI was disbanded, HMI was well placed to recoup its former vigour as support started flooding in. In 1966, HMI in Bandung admitted 1,500 new members. As an HMI figure, Pungki— Rahmat Witoelar's successor as President of the Student Council—however, remained unaffected by the sudden reversal of fortune and unchanged in his demeanour.

Nevertheless, increasing sympathy and support for HMI led to the rise, within HMI itself, of a sectarian group that proceeded to launch an ideological offensive, one aspect of which was their campaign against "Westernized" on-campus recreational activities such as dancing. They also started recording the names of people who did not participate in Friday prayers at the Mosque in the Western Hall. They then started pointing fingers at others for being "secular", mystifying many who felt they should not be accused of being secular as if it were a bad thing. Many of their concepts were exclusive in nature, and put people into boxes.

Another triumphant group comprised student activists who were close to the military. They subsequently became members of the Mahawarman Regiment and were known at ITB as 1st Battalion. They were fond of such "masculine" activities as trooping in formation, parachute jumping, conducting basic infantry exercises and so on. Although they were an exclusive lot, they did not bother others. When not in uniform, they mingled with the other activists and were involved in various activities with them. I do not know why Nini joined the Mahawarmans, but she did look stunning in her uniform.

Making up another grouping was the mishmash of activists with independent characters, many of whom came from student off-campus mass organizations such as PMB and PMKRI. Included within this group were the residents of certain prestigious boarding and lodging houses, one of which was the Bangbayang Clique. Some of the members of this clique, such as Arifin Panigoro, became famous. I myself belonged to this loose and diverse group, as one of the Gang of Four; named after Mao's inner circle. The four of us were Rahmat, Wimar, Zulkarnain Yusuf and myself, and we were so named because we were always together.

Outside the groups I mentioned were the great many who were unaffiliated, the so-called silent majority, who were in essence uninterested in activism. They did not belong to any organization and could hardly bear on-campus activism. They believed it was high time students devoted their time to learning. At first they did not do much to voice their opinions on the matter, only complaining occasionally. However, when the competition between the groups intensified and had the appearance of being influenced by outside forces, they became more vocal and initiated a "back to campus" campaign, with the mission of depoliticizing the campus.

At the national level, great changes were afoot. Soekarno's position was on a knife-edge, while Soeharto's had gone from strength to strength. The 1968 General Session of the national parliament (MPRS) appointed Soeharto as an interim president. Soekarno was only given the chance to present an accountability speech, which consequently was rejected by MPRS. He was in the end replaced by Soeharto. The new cabinet had its fair share of technocrats, picked from our educated class, giving the impression that the government was a coalition between the military and the technocratic class. Still, as far as we students were concerned, the political events in Jakarta were too remote to elicit any reaction from us. We were too busy balancing our studies, activism and earning money.

Death of Soekarno

Amid the great changes, Soekarno, now deposed, was more or less forgotten as he retreated from the national consciousness. He spent his last years away from the public gaze at Wisma Yaso. After he died in 1970, he was subsequently interred in Blitar. It was only years later that the public learned that Soekarno's last days had been spent in misery. He was accorded a state funeral with military salutes, attended by President Soeharto. But, at the time, the sense of national loss was not universally felt.

As the decades passed, nostalgia for Soekarno surfaced. With the long span between 1966 and the post-Soeharto era, Soekarno's image underwent some rehabilitation as Indonesians started to view him and his legacy in a more balanced way.

Tamblong Group

Rahman Tolleng had abandoned his underground hideaway and had started to be seen more often. He even had a base in Jalan Tamblong from where he published the West Java edition of *Mingguan Mahasiswa Indonesia* (The Indonesian Student Weekly). The newspaper was well-known and it sold well because of its influential opinions. We often congregated at this base. University students from different campuses came to ask Rahman Tolleng to become their mentor, a distinction he has retained to this day.

So we all came together on 10 November 1967 to form the Indonesian Student Study Group (Kelompok Studi Mahasiswa Indonesia), later better known as the Tamblong Group. It is probably safe to say that, at the time, the only window we had into national politics was through the discussions at Tamblong. Further down the timeline, in 1968, to accommodate the interest shown by non-students in joining the group—including bureaucrats, lecturers, military officers, entrepreneurs and officer workers—the name was changed to the 10th November Study Group.

President of the Council

During the early part of 1967, several friends and I took part as candidates in the upcoming student elections at different faculties for MPM. Pungki's term as President of the Student Council was also coming to an end. Many of the newly elected MPM members turned out to be non-activists who had no discernible affiliation with any student organization. Candidates who were members of off-campus national organizations had suffered major electoral setbacks, partly caused by the growing popularity of the "back to campus" camp. There were also more independent activists who stood as candidates and won. Wimar and I were elected into MPM.

Two among the independent activists were nominated as candidates to become President of the Council, Hindro Tjahjono and Bangun Sarwito Kusmulyono, known as Bus. But the rules required that there be three candidates. So I was entered into the race, with the consent of the other two preferred candidates, and with no expectation whatsoever to win. I was just another activist on campus and was known to very few students. My role was behind the scenes, supporting the campus bosses through things like ideas for speeches and providing analyses. Wimar was more of a public face than I ever was, and he had just been elected Speaker of MPM.

When the time came for the candidates to present their visions, Hindro and Bus carried themselves very well, elaborating the slogan "back to campus" fluently through attractive promises. I, on the other hand, was their antithesis. Friends later told me that my eyes were on the floor while I was addressing the students and that I mumbled a lot.

It was therefore to my great surprise when I learned I had garnered the most votes. Evidently, many MPM members had changed their minds by voting for me. They had apparently been dissuaded by the fact that a few on the campaign teams of the other two candidates had gone over the top in their efforts. I also believed that other MPM members had voted for me because they wanted to see me fail as President of the Council, something they could easily use as political capital to win the next election. My unexpected victory, however, distressed me greatly. I at first thought that Wimar and Zulkarnain had masterminded my election, but both denied it and were visibly shocked to learn of it.

"Why would I do that? I had sooner get myself nominated rather than plot your victory", Wimar replied to my accusation. He did in fact go on to win the presidency in the next election

When the election results were posted on the university announcement board the next day, I was there to watch and listen to the reactions from my fellow students. "Sarwono? That's strange. Which one is he?", asked a female student, whom I later learned was called Karlina. I of course stayed silent and savoured their ignorance of me.

Even Mimi was taken by surprise at my election. "I thought you were just the errand boy", she said with her usual candour.

The composition of the new student council was drafted by Hindro, Bus and myself. Around about the same time, a rumour circulated that I had dealt in horse-trading by offering seats on the council, right, left and centre, for my own benefit. Consequently, for the purpose of keeping an eye on me, several MPM members offered to "help" with the formation of the council. I welcomed their presence because I had nothing to hide. Our programme was mainly drawn from the campaign promises made by both Hindro and Bus.

During our discussion of prospective personnel, Hindro came up with an interesting idea. "I have just the perfect candidate to head the Seminar and Discussion Department."

"Who is that?" I asked, not knowing what I was about to hear.

"Nini Maramis, from Urban Planning. She would go anywhere to take part in any public discussion, even on foot, if need be", he said enthusiastically. I responded by saying I needed more background information on her.

"She's smart. Her English is good. She knows about a lot of things and always carries a book or two wherever she goes", he continued.

"She sounds interesting. All right. I second your idea", I finally said. Hindro of course did not know why I found Nini to be of interest.

The Student Council was duly formed and was a solid team because it was not built on compromises. We were all on the same page and wanted campus life to be as comfortable and useful to the students as possible.

My term as Council President proved to be amenable to most students since together with the other council members we managed to create a memorable campus atmosphere based on merrymaking, freedom and usefulness.

Once a week we gathered in the West Hall in the evening. Everyone would bring with them any game paraphernalia that they had: chessboards, cards for bridge, dominoes and so on. To participate, students only needed to buy a very affordable ticket. Our West Hall weekly always saw a full house because students had long been starved of normal life for young people. The organizers responsible for the weekly event—christened the Iota Tau Beta (ITB) Night—were Bus, Arifin Panigoro and Aburizal Bakrie.

Students who were in music bands of any genre—whether pop or jazz—were invited to play. We also invited street-food hawkers to come into the hall and open their stalls there so that students could get food and drinks easily. We set up an English Conversation Club and a Centre for Sociological Studies. We also planned for the construction of a Student Centre, which was an idea that Bus had. For my part I began to put our finances in order because I had developed an obsession with leaving the next council some money in the treasury.

My term as Council President coincided with a most unhappy event. When our new students were gathered for their orientation period, we discovered that around thirty per cent of them were ethnic Chinese Indonesians, which was a first for ITB. Things quickly took a turn for the worse, as racial sentiments were at play. I felt alarmed because I was, for better or worse, the students' leader. The terribly destructive event of 10 May 1963, when I was still in secondary school, which I have referred to earlier, was still fresh in my mind.

Racial prejudice against Chinese Indonesians had always existed. Proponents of this form of discrimination often sought to justify it by using geopolitics and local incidents that always seemed to place ethnic Chinese in a bad social light. In what was essentially a transitional period—in both ideology and regime—Chinese Indonesians were again put on the spot because Radio Peking was still fiery in its defence of the PKI.

Sometime before the admission of the 1967 student intake, a short-lived incident of the same strain took place at the Bandung Commisariat of KAMI. When it was PMKRI's turn in the periodic chair of KAMI Bandung, it appointed Djoko Sudyatmiko, an ITB student and an ethnic Chinese. The decision elicited protests from several other organizations within KAMI that demanded he be replaced by a *pribumi* (indigenous) student. In the end, after heated debate—a highlight of which was the creative intervention by Marzuki Darusman from the University of Parahyangan—and strong support by Rahman Tolleng for Djoko, he was accepted as chairman. Marzuki eventually became Attorney General within President Abdurrahman Wahid's National Unity Cabinet.

Our orientation period became a provocative arena because of the racial prejudice mercilessly directed towards Chinese Indonesian prospective students. They were confronted with mental terror that was difficult to rein in.

As Council President, I took two immediate steps in response. First, I strongly criticized the chancellery for admitting new students based merely on their admission test results. In preceding years, the university had always taken social considerations into account in its policy of student admissions so that pluralism within the student body was ensured. Second, I undertook to prevent violence or racial rioting, which was all too real a danger.

I was fortunate that my actions received the full support of the Student Council, the members of which actively sought to keep a lid on the already tense situation. I was also indebted to fellow activists from PMKRI, particularly Bernard Sadhani and Djoko Sudyatmiko. The chancellery also showed a generosity of heart by admitting that its new admission policy had been misguided.

Many of our prospective Chinese Indonesian students eventually chose to cancel their applications and move to private universities.

Many others chose instead to study abroad. There were of course those who still stayed on at ITB, but only by trying to suppress their fear and sensibilities. As the orientation period came to an end, things reverted to normal.

ITB Student Council Shies away from Politics

The politics of the nation remained vibrant, with various new ideas for reform being thrown into the public discourse. However, being sworn in on the "back to campus"' pledge, I kept my distance from politics. The Assistant Chancellor for Student Affairs, Dr Midian Sirait—who was also a KASI figure—repeatedly urged me to be more vocal in responding to political affairs. Probably to his disappointment, the only political act by the Council during my term was a declaration of dissent against the appointment of a member of the House of Representatives specifically to represent university students. I signed a statement to that effect with our General Secretary Istanto Oerip. We did not believe that university students were a separate social enclave that needed to have its own representation in parliament.

My own personal contribution to politics took place when Fikri Djufri—a reporter with the *KAMI Daily*—interviewed me in my capacity as Council President, asking my opinions on reform of the political structure. My interview then became the main story in which I was depicted as someone consummate in political theories.

I was quite taken aback when I saw the interview in the *KAMI Daily* because what I had told the reporter was not purely my brainchild. Rather, it was a distilled version of what I had heard from the discussions at the Tamblong Group by my seniors such as Rahman Tolleng, Midian Sirait and Djamal Ali.

An off-campus activity I was a part of in 1968 was the National Congress of Indonesian Student Councils, organized by the University of Indonesia's Student Council. Its President at the time was Hariadi Darmawan, who later became Inspector General of the Ministry of Forestry. The chief organizer of the event was Akbar Tandjung, who would become Chairman of the Golkar Party during the Reform Era. At the congress, the "back to campus" platform became a dominant theme and it was unanimously adopted.

ITB's Student Council of 1967–68 under my leadership was generally perceived to be a success. Our accountability report was accepted by MPM at the end of our term. The coffers were in surplus and we were able to leave the next council some funds. The bookkeeping was carried out under the guidance of a public accountant, Pak Sudarman. As I mentioned before, Wimar Witoelar was elected President for the period 1968–69.

Not wishing to rest on my laurels after a successful run as Council President, I began visiting Jalan Tamblong again and applied to become a reporter with the West Java edition of *Mahasiswa Indonesia*, the Indonesian student magazine, under Rahman Tolleng. I resumed my participation in discussions on political and social affairs there, after a year's absence. I duly joined the organizing committee of the 10th November Study Group.

Cibaduyut Shoes

While activities at Jalan Tamblong kept me busy, I started to notice that I had not seen my usual shoe cobbler from Cibaduyut village for almost a year. The thought occurred because I needed him for some shoe repairs. I had long discarded Mochtar's old shoes and bought myself a new pair, but wear and tear meant I had to have them mended from time to time. As it happened, my shoes had started to cause my feet some discomfort and my cobbler was nowhere in sight.

Worried he might be ill or in trouble, I went to see him in his village. His name was Pak Singgih, an unusual name for a Sundanese man, so it was easy to recall. As it turned out, he had stopped repairing shoes for a living. When I met him, he was in the process of starting out as a shoemaker. "Shoe cobbling is on its way out. The country is developing now and people can afford new shoes", he reasoned. He related how he had been trained to make shoes by a businessman in Bandung. His friends from the village received the same training.

I thought such a venture should have support to have the best chance of succeeding. So I decided to see Pak Rusdi, the Village Chief of Cibaduyut. Many of his villagers called him "Village Chief of the

World" because he had often met and spoken to various government officials, including the Minister of Home Affairs. Pak Rusdi was a unique individual. From my conversations with him, I was under the impression he could not read or write, but it was obvious he was far from ignorant. For me, that was the most important thing. He had ambitions for his village, and I gathered he might need some support.

Back at Jalan Tamblong, I discussed the matter with Kusnaka Adimihardja, a lecturer at the University of Padjadjaran. We worked out an advisory scheme for the Cibaduyut shoemakers. Accompanied by some of his students, we went to the village and had a discussion with the villagers and the young people there. After several meetings, Kusnaka and I set up the Cooperative of Indonesian Shoemakers. We also started programmes for the rest of the villagers in chicken farming and agriculture.

Our efforts were eventually taken over by LP3ES (the Institute of Research, Education and Socio-economic Information) under Ismid Hadad. It was a project that ran for decades before Cibaduyut was transformed from an underdeveloped village into the well-known centre for shoemaking and other leather goods that we know it as today. Unfortunately, I have heard that the Cibaduyut shoemakers are now struggling with some new issues, chief of which is the difficulty in sourcing good quality leather locally. They have therefore had to start importing. Other factors have also caught up with them, decreasing the competitiveness of their products.

On the ITB front, things on campus continued to evolve. While the "back to campus" programme that Wimar and I championed was an unqualified success, there were some rumbles among the silent majority of the student body. Not content with having kept politics off the campus, they now started to demand that on-campus organizations like MPM and the Student Council be free from students affiliated with off-campus organizations, including PMB, which had been instrumental in the "back to campus" campaign. They said that the campus should be run by "pure campus" students. Wimar and I jokingly referred to this group of students as "Indomilk", after an advertisement of the day proclaiming that Indomilk products are "pure milk".

"Killer" Lecturers

The academic side of campus life was also noteworthy. I did well in all my subjects except one, which, curiously, was not due to my lack of mastery. ITB, particularly its Civil Engineering faculty, was known for some of its "killer" lecturers who would go out of their way to make some students fail for purely non-academic reasons. For tests, they would devise trap questions designed to ensure failure on the part of the student.

Therefore, in order to ensure I would pass the subject, I would study and analyse their traps in order to prepare myself better. That usually did the trick, except in the case of lecturers who were probably certifiable and who went for certain students with a vengeance, often for reasons of a personal dislike.

The power resting with lecturers in those days was so absolute that they did not have to explain themselves to anyone why so many of their students did not pass. On the other hand, students' time was also unregulated: we had the right to demand an examination any time of our choosing, and attendance at lectures was not compulsory. Years later, the system known as "free study" was replaced with "semester-credit (SKS)", so both lecturers and students became bound by certain rules and schedules. The new system resulted in a sudden repentance by many killer lecturers, and lecture halls were filled with students.

Because I was busy earning and dabbled in politics in a small way as an analyst, I had to resort to certain strategies to keep abreast of lectures while not attending them too often. My usual trick was to befriend conscientious students who formed study groups. I brought them snacks and cakes—the ones Mimi could not sell in the morning—and made them coffee, all the while commenting on their studies as if I was not sure they were doing it right.

I was able to absorb and assimilate the gist of lectures that way. The more sceptical I was, the more enthusiastic they were in explaining things to me. There were times when we were having examinations where some of these goody-goody students flunked their tests because they had sudden mental blackouts from fatigue brought about by consecutive all-nighters. I, however, was always fresh-faced for tests and almost always managed to do well, even though the face of the lecturer often looked unfamiliar to me.

It took me a long time to graduate from ITB because, on top of studying, I was busy earning money and being an activist. My old formula for life remained unchanged: study and earn. My activism at this point was limited to the 10th November Study Group. For the most part, this arrangement suited me, except that the pre-graduation certificate I should have received did not materialize because one lecturer always failed me in his subject. I had, by this point, passed most of the other subjects required for graduation.

I was informed by one of the assistant lecturers that the lecturer in question would pass me if I apologized. But I did not know how I had offended him and, consequently, what I would be apologizing for. In the end I sent my informer a message: "Let's see who has the longer staying power".

The lecturer's course subject, Foundation Technique, was not difficult at all. I even helped some friends with the subject and they all passed.

The impasse lasted until Professor Doddy Tisna Amidjaja replaced Colonel Kuntoadji as the new ITB Chancellor. He proceeded to reorganize the academic side of campus life with a determination to ensure quality education. Known killer lecturers were duly asked to explain themselves. Some of them had their subjects transmuted to become non-compulsory. My own killer lecturer of Foundation Technique must have found himself in a spot because he suddenly changed my grade to a seven, which allowed me to pass without sitting for an examination.

That was the old ITB whereby academic life was often strange, only made rational and fair in 1969 by instituting the new credit-based system. Previously, good lecturers went unrewarded, while the bad ones carried on with impunity.

The year 1969 was also a memorable one for me because my application to the East Asia and Pacific Student Leaders Exchange Program was accepted and I spent two months in the United States. The scheme was open to applicants from thirteen countries in East Asia and the Pacific region. It had been recommended to me by Soe Hok Gie, who completed it in 1967.

I obtained many precious lessons during the trip, which would take too long to tell if I were to recount them all in this book. Suffice it to say the scheme allowed participating students to meet and get to know a diverse range of people in the United States, including the trendsetters of the time, known as the Flower Generation, for their peace-loving philosophy. We stayed at campuses and with ordinary Americans in their homes.

I had the chance to meet people who held different views to mine, such as the racist John Birch Society, the socialist Students for Democratic Society (SDS), the Black Panthers and so on. Many of the participants, myself included, condemned American involvement in Vietnam, and we were all free to debate the matter with US government officials while we were there.

What struck me most was the ignorance of the average American about the outside world, something that has not changed much since. While I was talking to a group of Americans, I even got away with an outlandish tale that I was the heir apparent to the Prince of Jakarta, that I journeyed to school on the back of an elephant with my personal guards tagging along, and that I was fluent in English because I had a private tutor flown directly from England. Unbelievably, perhaps, they bought the story and appeared impressed.

Getting Married

Back in Bandung after my American trip, I cultivated a new activity, which was to try to get a girlfriend. Rahmat Witoelar showed every sign of marrying Erna before long, which was soon confirmed through an unexpected event.

One day I was about to head back to Bandung on a chartered vehicle service, known as Suburban, where the vehicle is shared with six to nine other passengers. Unlike the common practice of travel today, where passengers sitting close to one another will be busy on their mobile phones, we actually talked to one another. On that particular trip, I struck up a conversation with a Bugis man called Daeng Tata Maladjong, although I never saw him again afterwards. Daeng Tata told me stories about his niece called Erna whom he obviously thought highly of. He also told me about her friend called Rahmat Witoelar, and that they were to be married. "Both will become successful people", Daeng Tata predicted.

Although he knew I was also an ITB student, he did not ask me whether I knew either of them. Perhaps he thought I looked too ordinary to mingle with the top students at ITB. It did not help that I kept asking him questions about Rahmat and Erna as if I knew nothing of them. As we arrived at my drop-off point, which was in Jalan Ciumbuleuit, Bandung, I casually said to him, "Rahmat and Erna are good friends of mine. This is Rahmat's house." I shook his hand and got out of the car. The Suburban then left me on the side of the road while Daeng Tata looked surprised, smiled and touched his head with his hand.

Rahmat, Wimar, Erna and I were indeed close and we often went on trips together in a decrepit Fiat sedan made in 1948, which we named Oskosh. Rahmat would be at the steering wheel with Erna at his side while Wimar and I sat in the back, with the duty of helping start the car by pushing. Because I was skinny and could move faster than Wimar, I was the one expected to go up to the front of the car if needed, usually to open the hood and pour petrol into the carburettor to keep the engine going.

Once, as my motoric dysfunction crept in, I mistakenly poured petrol into the radiator. The engine, not surprisingly, went kaput and Oskosh had to be towed to our regular repair shop in Jalan Cihampelas. Alas, we had to wait for a few days because the shop's owner was still looking for a new mechanic. He told us that the mechanic who usually tended to Oskosh had fled and gone into hiding because some people accused him of being "orang Gombinis dan Markis". What he meant, of course, was "Communist and Marxist".

After this incident, Wimar and I separately decided to find our own partner so that we would not have to be involved in the goings-on caused by the antics of an old car. Wimar had a few female friends, while I had less luck than him. Attractive girls ignored me, while those who showed interest tended to be plain-faced, which did not suit me.

Then I received word from a reliable source that Nini was interested in me. It was a great surprise for me because Nini was a campus star and could have anyone she wanted. Emboldened by the news, I started to try to get close to her, and the two of us proved compatible.

I started with an activity that appealed to us both: reading books. But, as time went by, we got carried away with heady activities that did not require literacy at all.

Wedding Photo, January 1970.

With the extended family at our wedding.

Friends celebrate our nuptials.

It then occurred to me that I had to act fast before she changed her mind and was wooed by someone else. I wrote a letter to her father, Max Maramis, who was at the time posted as ambassador in Moscow, and related to him my intention to marry Nini. I also paid a call on Nini's mother, Ina Rumbayan, in Jakarta, who was divorced from her father, but she disapproved of our match. My own mother, Mimi, was fond of Nini. So was my brother, Mochtar, who supported my decision to marry her.

My close friends then learned of my plan to marry Nini. On hearing the news, Syarief Tando sought me out, took off a gold ring from his finger and gave it to me. "You have it cut in halves. There should be enough there for two wedding rings", he said. I was very touched by his gesture, and the ring was reworked to make two rings, but we kept the original design. I still wear my half, even though Nini passed away in 2011.

I received a reply from Max Maramis who gave his right of guardianship for our wedding to his close friend in Bandung, Dr Kamarga. In early 1970, Nini and I were married in a very simple ceremony. I posted an invitation to all and sundry at ITB's Speaker's Corner. Some students thought my invitation was a prank. They only turned up at the event after first conducting a reconnaissance patrol.

ASEAUS

Immediately after my wedding, a new activity presented itself: ITB and Unpad were due to host the second conference of the Association of Southeast Asian University Students (ASEAUS). The first was con- ducted in 1969 in Manila, where it was decided the second conference was to be held in Bandung the following year. Unpad, however, was lukewarm to the idea of hosting the event, so it was up to ITB to step up to the mark.

If my memory serves me right, the only people from Unpad actively involved in the preparations for the ASEAUS conference were Nugraha Besoes and Noke Kiroyan. Nugraha would later become Secretary General of PSSI, while Noke became Director of Kaltim Prima Coal and now practices as a renowned consultant. Wimat Witoelar, who had just served his term as Council President, was asked to chair the conference's Organizing Committee by the new Council President Syarief Tando. But Wimar had to decline because he was about to leave for the United States, having applied for the same exchange programme that I had the previous year.

Consequently, everyone, including people from Unpad, urged me to take on the role myself. We at ITB discussed the matter and agreed that the conference was important in the long term as it had the potential to strengthen ASEAN, which had just been created. It was heartening to see ITB students discuss regional geopolitics. Holding the conference also had an additional benefit for our university: it would serve as further momentum for a fundraising campaign to speed up the construction of our Student Centre, which had already begun thanks to a donation from BNI, the National Bank of Indonesia.

We duly formed the Organizing Committee, which proceeded to work out the budget, which came to around 7.5 million rupiah. We doubled the figure in our proposal to be on the safe side because it was customary for sponsors to grant only half of what was asked for.

We then heard that the state-owned oil company Pertamina might be willing to be our sponsor, so we tried to find out what would be the most appropriate channel we could approach the company through. Our findings indicated we would have to see Pak Ali Moertopo, who was at the time the most influential person within President Soeharto's inner circle, as his Personal Assistant. He also wielded wide-ranging powers as head of Opsus, which was only answerable to the President.

Syarief Tando and I then contacted Jusuf Wanandi, who was close to Ali Moertopo. Jusuf Wanandi in turn suggested that our funding proposal include a conceptual framework that argued the role ASEAUS had in supporting ASEAN, the recent creation of which was a crucial regional forum for Indonesia's foreign policy.

I duly wrote up a conceptual framework for the conference, putting all my thought into the task. Next we went to the Opsus Headquarters in Jalan Raden Saleh, where we met up with Jusuf Wanandi, and an hour later we were received by Ali Moertopo. Pak Ali Moertopo welcomed us warmly and went on to praise the conceptual framework we had written. He, Jusuf Wanandi and I discussed the future of ASEAN. In the meantime, Pertamina had been ordered to foot the entire bill contained in our proposal.

When the meeting was over, we felt overwhelmed and stunned to realize that we had secured the whole 15 million. We then set out for Pertamina where, as suggested by Pak Ali Moertopo, we asked to see Pak Sjarnubi Said. It did not take long before Pak Sjarnubi came out of his office with a cheque in his hand. After receiving the sponsorship money from Pertamina, we did not feel the need to seek additional funding.

Our committee set to work immediately to prepare the conference, which was slated to be held in May 1970. The movers and shakers on behalf of our committee were fellow students from the Bangbayang Group and Battalion 1 Mahawarman led by Arifin Panigoro, Djoni Saleh, Bus Kusmulyono, Sjahril Anwar and Pande Lubis. Everything was neatly done, and our Student Centre was finished well ahead of time for the conference. The real hurdle proved to be the fact that our students were poorly informed about regional issues.

When participants from other ASEAN countries finally showed up at our campus, we realized how lopsided things looked. They came from our much smaller neighbouring countries—Malaysia, Singapore, the Philippines and Thailand—and the numbers making up their contingents were small compared to how many local students were attending the conference. This led to an awkward start, which was not helped by the raging debates between Indonesian students. Language also proved to be a barrier, since not many Indonesian students could speak English. But their desire to communicate was great, and this overtaxed the interpreting mechanism we provided.

As the host country, we had assumed that an ITB student would be elected as Chairman for the conference, as was the international norm. However, it was T.T. Durai of the National University of Singapore who was elected as Chairman. Our own ITB Student Council Members, now consisting of non-activists, looked ill at ease. The senior students, who were busy organizing the whole event, in the end felt they had to step in. It was very exhausting. Nini could not take part with the preparations because she was pregnant with our first child, although she did help out in the last days before the conference.

In the end, the grand idea to persist with ASEAUS faded away from lack of interest. Substantially, the conference did not achieve much. However, for our campus, it was a great success, mainly because we now had a new venue, the Student Centre, which had been envisioned by Bus Kusmulyono back in 1967. Our campus also saw some repair work, although it was limited in scope. Our budgetary accountability report was also shipshape, thanks to our public accountant supervisor, Pak Sudarman.

In a state of total exhaustion and dejection over the failure to achieve substantial progress with ASEAUS, I was taken out of the conference room by Djoni Saleh to be examined by a doctor. Apparently, I could be persuaded to rest only through medical intervention.

While brooding over how stupid I felt because the contextual framework I had devised failed to find its target, I received news that my father-in-law, Max Maramis, had just died shortly after returning home from Moscow where he had been ambassador. Nini and I naturally wanted to pay our respects, and we were full of regret that we had not seen him in years. Arifin Panigoro came to the rescue by lending us a car driven by Joy Rotinsulu, a famous car-racer then. Our journey to Jakarta by car took under two hours, which was extraordinary.

In September 1970, our first child was born, and we named him Rezal Ashari. Nini and I decided to live in rented accommodation in Gang Titimplik, at the pavilion house belonging to the family of Pak Nadisah. He was a lecturer at the Sports University (STO). Nini and I decided to catch up with our studies because we needed to graduate as soon as possible.

Our firstborn, Rezal.

Rezal (being held) with the three children of Nadisah: (from left) Achmad Nurfadillah, Endang Widyati and Rini Widyantini. At the time of this book's publication, Rini was the Deputy at the Ministry of Administrative and Bureaucratic Reform.

When the two of us returned to campus, we left Rezal in the charge of the Nadisah family, who very kindly agreed to babysit him. Pak Nadisah's youngest daughter, Rini Widyantini, was the most involved in taking care of Rezal. She is now a high-ranking government official, the Deputy at the Ministry of Administrative and Bureaucratic Reform.

Mimi accepted our decision to move out to a rented house with good grace. She thought it only natural that a young couple would want to do that. She then replicated her Sentiong way of life by taking in boarders while still selling snacks and cakes. My mother remained happy-go-lucky, healthy and an incurable optimist.

1971 Election

I thought a new phase in my life could now begin: going to university, graduating and then life as a professional. Activism could now have a supporting role, in the sense it would allow me to continue to broaden my horizons and network of contacts. As for political affairs, my position in the 10th November Study Group would keep me amply apprised of the latest developments. I was also a freelance journalist at the time, writing for *Mahasiswa Indonesia* weekly and the daily newspapers *Pikiran Rakyat* and *Indonesia Express*.

In 1969, I was riveted by President Soeharto's decision to hold an election as soon as possible, followed by his move to transform the Joint Secretariat of Golongan Karya (Sekber Golkar) into a new socio-political force alongside the existing political parties. Sekber Golkar was intended to become a partner for the military in the political sphere.

An incident that took place in Bandung in mid-September 1970 became for me a sign that the trajectory of one's personal life would often not go as planned. A massive wave of student protests ensued after an ITB student, Rene Coenrad, was shot dead in the confusion of a group fight between ITB students and cadets from the Police Academy. Soccer teams from the two sides had just finished playing against each other when the fight broke out. Rene happened to pass by on his motorbike as the fight was in full swing; he got caught up in it and someone shot him.

Ironically, the soccer match had been designed to mend fences between ITB students and police cadets following an earlier incident in which the latter, apparently as part of an off-campus training programme, had stopped young people in the streets for having an inappropriate appearance. Young men with long hair were subjected to impromptu shearing, leaving them bald. Youngsters wearing jeans had their trousers cut off. It was unclear why the powers that be at the Police Academy had sanctioned such an absurd operation. Young people and university students were naturally outraged to be treated like this, and protests took place through the media.

Rene Coenrad's death added fuel to the fire and gave rise to unexpected and unforeseen anti-military sentiments. The Regional Military Command VI/Siliwangi weathered the incident with restraint and wisdom, which in the end left the students with no bone to pick, and the protests subsided.

A military tribunal was held to try the case. What the prosecution produced as a suspect was an NCO from the Brimob division by the name of Djani Maman Suryaman. The public, however, was convinced of Djani's innocence. Hence, a movement to defend him by collecting donations to be given to his family was initiated by ITB student Pontas Pardede. We, the senior activists, however, were not involved throughout the Rene Coenrad affair. The movement was purely the initiative of a new generation of activists.

The student protests were a wake-up call for the Regional Command as to how potent student activism could turn out to be and how it needed to be contained in order to safeguard the 1971 election. At the same time, the transformation of Sekber Golkar—Golkar from this point on—into a contestant in the election as well as a partner of the military (ABRI) had just begun, with key positions within Golkar being taken over by the military. At the provincial level, the highest post within Golkar was *ex officio* held by the Regional Military Commander, while the Chairman of the Provincial Governing Council was the Assistant V to the Commander, who was in charge of territorial affairs.

As of 1966, our campus activists were on good terms and interacted with the Regional Military Command VI/Siliwangi, starting when Brigadier General H.R. Dharsono was Regional Chief of Staff. He went on to become Regional Commander, succeeded by Major General A.J. Witono. It was on General Witono's watch that the Rene Coenrad incident occurred. We also saw a lot of Colonel Maman Darmawan, who was Assistant V of the Regional Command VI/Siliwangi, and we had good relations with him.

We also often ran into Pak Witono, who was known as Bang Gapleh when he was interviewed on Radio Mara. The private radio station was owned by student activists, one of whom, Muhammad Sulaeman Hidayat—better known as Belo—was to become Chairman of Real Estate Indonesia and later Minister of Industry in President Susilo Bambang Yudhoyono's United Indonesia Cabinet II. The previous Regional Commander, H.R. Dharsono, was also a regular interviewee on Radio Mara, with the code name of "Kalong".

Herded into Golkar

Pak Witono invited Bandung's student activists to a meeting in the Regional Command's Main Hall, where he asked activists, students and campus scholars to join Golkar's camp by becoming its legislative candidates at both the provincial and national levels. He argued that activists had the responsibility to build the future of the nation alongside ABRI. The alternative was, he suggested, to be on the other side of the fence and face the consequences.

Pak Witono related this to us in a relaxed and humorous manner. But the effect was more than convincing. If he had done it through blatant intimidation, the assembled might have taken it as a bluff. I then put up my hand and asked him a question. "What is our fault that we need to face the consequences if we refuse to be nominated as legislative candidates?"

Pak Witono answered by saying the Regional Command had enough notes on every activist to decide on what sort of treatment would suit us. "Please consider becoming our brothers-in-arms instead. Think about it. I will give you a week to make up your mind", he said, concluding our meeting.

We then gathered in Jalan Tamblong to discuss the Commander's offer. People were divided on the issue. Rahman Tolleng advised us to "get into the system and work from the inside". At this point, he, along with Jakob Tobing, Rohali Sani and Sugeng Saryadi had indeed served as members of the House of Representatives (DPR Gotong Royong) through direct appointment. However, most activists in my age group, like Djoko Sudyatmiko, tended to be against taking the political path.

I was also in two minds. Rahmat Witoelar was on the verge of graduating as an architect and had started designing buildings. I often helped him by acting as a technician and had earned some money that way, though not much, admittedly. Our discussion failed to reach any conclusion, so everyone was left to think for themselves.

I found out next that an Unpar student, Awan Karmawan Burhan— we usually called him Mang Awan—had been tasked by the authorities to lobby all the student activists. Mang Awan was renowned for his powers of persuasion. He was also good at finding solutions to any problem, however complicated, that his friends might have. So Mang Awan went on to do his rounds of visiting each of us, carrying the nomination forms. One by one my friends eventually signed the forms, and I did too.

My own line of thinking at the time was that Golkar, as a newcomer in politics, would probably fail to attract voters. Political analysts of the day—no public survey involved—predicted that Golkar could only hope to get 35 per cent of the vote at best. As young candidates, we would probably be put at the bottom of the list at any rate, in which case we would not have much chance of getting into parliament.

Another consideration was that if we had been deemed as being at cross purposes with ABRI, we could have been implicated in the anti-military movement following the Rene Coenrad incident. The New Order regime under Soeharto shared one attribute with its predecessor, the Guided Democracy regime of Soekarno: both were authoritarian. To be out of step with the powers that be meant going to prison. An individual could be detained or released without explanation.

I conducted an inquiry into the conditions at the military prison in Jalan Jawa. The guards were composed of friendly old soldiers on the cusp of retirement. But the cells were full of mosquitoes, cockroaches and other creatures and were far from pleasant. At this stage in my life, I was unfamiliar with the importance of biodiversity and had not developed an appreciation for those crawling creatures.

I consulted with Nini as to what I should do, but she left it to me to decide my next course of action. In the end, believing my chances of being elected into the DPR were slim, and to avoid a confrontation with the Regional Command, I, too, signed the nomination form. To my surprise, the Regional Command did not make token candidates of us. Campus activists from KAMI, KASI and young figures from the Siliwangi Young Generation (AMS) were allotted middle positions on the list.

At the top of the list were well-known figures in society. Some were vote-getters, those who would resign once elected. Activist friends of mine who made it on to the list included Rudianto Ramelan, Rahmat Witoelar and Djoko Sudyatmiko from ITB; Ida Ayu Utami Pidada, Kusnaka Adimihardja, Nugraha Besoes from Unpad; Awan Karmawan from UNPAR; Tjetje Hidayat Padmadinata, Tatto Pradjamanggala and Taufik Hidayat from AMS. There was also a veteran politician, Sumarno, who brought his own retinue, all of whom made it into parliament.

In the preparations for the campaign, the senior activists had a prominent role. Golkar set up Bapillu (The Agency for Electoral Victory and Control). Senior activists like Rahman Tolleng were already in it, engaged in such activities as drafting television texts for the campaign. I was asked to do a television campaign with the available text. Other Golkar figures who got to campaign on television were Sultan Hamengkubuwono IX and Mrs Nani Ali Sadikin.

During the campaign, we first-time candidates only had peripheral roles. Our vote-getter was Pak Mashuri Saleh and we were in his retinue. Pak Mashuri gave a speech in front of teachers to outline policies regarding education, and he had a warm reception from the audience. We, the first-timers, only wished for the election to be over soon so we could all go back to becoming professionals in our fields.

When the election results were counted and announced, we were astounded. Golkar had won 62.8 per cent of the total national vote. What was even more surprising was that in West Java Golkar had done better than the national average, at 76.1 per cent.

From these results it was natural to assume the electorate had been coerced and were too afraid to vote for other political parties. However, as we investigated the matter further, by asking many people, the overwhelming response was that political parties had lost credibility among voters as they were seen to have been involved in the political chaos and economic ruin of the past.

One opinion I heard on the matter was "Golkar brings hope because it isn't a political party." Another factor that ensured Golkar's victory in West Java was that the Regional Command VI/Siliwangi was adept at cultivating good relations with the people through their doctrine of a territorial approach. Consequently, the presence of the military in West Java was not felt as repressive, but rather it was seen as being protective of the people. This special characteristic of the Siliwangi division was present everywhere its troops were deployed, enabling them to subdue various rebellions with the support of local people.

Being a Member of Parliament

After a week of orientation, we were sworn in as members of the DPR. The state of affairs at the DPR then could not be more different than it is now. Apart from the impressive Plenary Hall and the storeyed buildings used by the DPR Secretariat General and the party leadership, the rest was rudimentary. The rooms for commission sessions were like typical classrooms in a secondary school.

Our work there amounted to almost nothing, except for members who were in the previous DPR. They worked in teams formed by the leadership of their respective faction. We would of course be asked to approve of legislation at the plenary session, but, since we lacked any reference on which to base our opinion, we simply said yes.

As I quickly learned, formulating a political stance as an independent activist was far easier than as an MP. As activists, we developed ideas based on a set of basic values and our commitment. As a politician, it was far more complicated. We were faced with various parameters that we had never encountered when we were free agents.

We also came face to face with the reality that the opinions and thoughts of an MP were inevitably moderated by stratified organizational authority and the complexity of public policy. To conduct oneself effectively and maturely in politics was not easy, especially for those independent in spirit, since they would inevitably clash with authoritarianism. Sobered by these considerations, I also had to come to terms with the fact that an MP in those days did not receive the support he or she should have been given to carry out his or her task effectively.

An MP's salary did not in fact amount to much. Members from the provinces had to find their own accommodation, since it was not provided. It came as no surprise that one room would be occupied by three members. I stayed at Ade's house in Rawamangun and got around by public transport. Just as weekend was about to start, or even before, I would head back to Bandung on the train using state-issued coupons.

One day, whilst I was at home, the ITB Chancellor, Professor Doddy Tisna Amiddaja, sent word he would like to see me. At the chancellery he told me that the rules of the university stipulated that I must finish my studies in 1973. "I understand you are an MP now", Professor Doddy said in a most polite manner. "But I must uphold the rules. If you don't make the deadline, respectfully, I would have to terminate your status as a student here."

As it happened, Nini was facing the same problem. All students who enrolled at ITB in 1963 were given an ultimatum to finish their studies in 1973. We were both determined to do so. Graduating meant more choices in life. Starting a professional life would also make more sense with a degree.

I duly went to see the Chairman of the Golkar Parliamentary Wing (FKP), Pak Sugiharto, to tell him about Professor Doddy's ultimatum. Pak Sugiharto supported my decision to finish my studies, and told me he understood that my presence in Jakarta as an MP might be curtailed because of my studies. In the DPR there was no official leave, so what I needed was the consent and understanding of the Chairman of FKP. "Go ahead and finish your studies, but if there is an urgent matter we need your help with, please come to Jakarta", Pak Sugiharto said.

Break from Politics

Hence, as of mid-1972, Nini and I concentrated on our studies. I limited any other activity in order to make finishing university my priority. When our rental of the house in Gang Titimplik was over, we went back to Mimi's, occupying a room that a boarder had just vacated.

The Sentiong ambience was evident at Mimi's. There were a few boarders whose diversity reminded me of being in Jakarta. Economically, Mimi was doing well, as befitted the new economic stability under Soeharto. Her small business of selling traditional snacks and cakes had increased in volume, necessitating her to hire a domestic maid to help around the house.

In March 1973, our second child, Nino, was born. Rezal was overjoyed at the arrival of Nino because he now had a brother. He had disliked being alone and had often asked to be taken to play and sleep over at the Nadisahs'. Now he wanted to sleep over at the Nadisahs' with Nino in tow.

I seldom went to Jakarta anymore. If I did it was only to fulfil requests by friends to help with the consolidation of Golkar through drafting new organizational rules, including regulating relations between the central board and its provincial counterparts. Meetings at Golkar's central board were chaired by Cosmas Batubara and Pak A.E. Manihuruk.

In my eyes, these two were special individuals. Cosmas was very meticulous, patient and consistent in tackling complex problems.

Pak Manihuruk was a feisty character, but he had an eye for detail in formulating guidelines for programme implementation, using the most plain and clear language and impeccable step-by-step instructions.

Nini ended up graduating first. My graduation presentation took place at the end of 1973, so I finished my studies during injury time, so to speak. The two of us were able to graduate together in February 1974, after which I went back to Jakarta and assessed the political situation. Among other things, I tried to find out about the 15 January (Malari) incident that had taken place a few months previously.

Rahman Tolleng Arrested by the Military

A number of events that occurred before Malari only registered cursorily on my mind. My distinct impression was that there was great dissatisfaction with the presence of Presidential Personal Assistance (Aspri) because it was deemed to have influenced policymaking in a negative way. Moreover, the predilection for Japanese investment meant that Japan was uncommonly dominant in the Indonesian economy, causing worries about the derogation of national sovereignty.

Behind the waves of protests that took place was the seeming rivalry between the Commander of the Operational Command for the Restoration of Security and Order (Pangkopkamtib), General Soemitro, and General Ali Moertopo, Personal Assistant to the President.

Massive rioting broke out on 15 January 1974 during a state visit by the Prime Minister of Japan, Kakuei Tanaka. Japanese-made cars were vandalized by the rioters, who clearly were not students, although their demands were an exact match to the concept expounded by student activists and scholars, especially those from the University of Indonesia.

The protests and rioting were confined to Jakarta. I later learned that there had been attempts to induce Bandung activists to take part in the Malari movement, but these overtures had been ignored. What took me by surprise was that Rahman Tolleng had been placed under arrest at the military prison in Jalan Budi Utomo, alongside Marsillam Simandjuntak, Syahrir and Adnan Buyung Nasution.

I visited them at the military prison, taking my son Rezal with me. It was a warm and friendly meeting. Our conversations then and after they were released failed to identify the reason for them being detained.

The aftermath of the Malari incident saw a number of magazines and newspapers having their permits revoked by the government, including the Indonesian Student Weekly (West Java). Rahman Tolleng was also recalled from parliament and he was no longer an MP, but he was duly released from prison. Our 10th November Study Group became dormant because most of its activist members had been co-opted into Golkar, while the new generation of students were an apolitical group, largely kept busy with academic requirements under the stringent credit-system.

Mochtar becomes Minister

Just before the 15 January 1974 riot broke out, Mochtar told me that he had been summoned by President Soeharto. At the time, Mochtar was the Chancellor of the University of Padjajaran. The President asked him to become Minister of Justice, replacing Professor Oemar Senoadji, who had been sworn in as Chief Justice of the Supreme Court.

Mimi with her three children: Mochtar, Ade and myself, in 1974, at the time Mochtar was appointed Minister of Justice.

Mochtar came back from his studies in the United States in 1967. Upon arrival in Indonesia, he was immediately asked by Bandung activists to join the '66. Mochtar however was steadfast in keeping to his own plans, unlike myself, who became engaged in all manner of things at the same time. He chose to practise as an expert on international law, both law of the sea and investments.

Moreover, he also developed new concepts on the role of law in social engineering and environmental law. In his efforts, he collaborated with Professor Otto Soemartowo and Professor Emil Salim. Their new ideas were then disseminated in society and within the central government, as well as having the concepts integrated into his lectures. Mochtar then became chancellor of Unpad before receiving the summons from President Soeharto to become a minister.

His appointment came as no surprise to me. From the time he was young, many believed Mochtar would make something of his life. His unceremonious dismissal in 1963 now gave him a social advantage in the post-Soekarno era.

Mimi's New Venture

Mimi was naturally pleased to have a minister for a son. But, for the person who brought up Mochtar well, and given that Mochtar's exceptionality was evident from a young age, Mimi did not make a big deal out of his exalted position. Her lifestyle barely changed. She kept selling traditional snacks and hosted boarders in her house, albeit she only took in three now. Her roadside stall venture, however, had started to attract criticism, often to her face.

"Her children are all married and aren't poor. One is a minister and another is an MP. She should be ashamed of herself for selling snacks on the roadside", was the general commentary of her neighbours and competitors.

Mimi, however, was not one to be cowed by criticism. "My son is a minister, not me. And what does his being a minister have to do with how I earn my money? Selling snacks is *halal*, so what's the problem?"

Mochtar and I discussed the matter and we both agreed that Mimi was getting on, at seventy, and that it was high time she cut down on her activities. So it was not for a matter of family prestige that we tried to dissuade her from running her roadside stall. "Please find a way so that Mimi can stop selling", Mochtar said to me.

I thought hard how to best present my case to her. Then I thought I knew what to say. "Mimi, you have the stall going because it's been a habit. But in our circumstances today, you are competing with those who need the income from their stalls just to get by. Your own economic situation is much better than theirs. It seems to be an unhealthy competition there", I said. Her conscience pricked, Mimi relented.

However, when I returned from Jakarta a few days later I found her busy in the kitchen with two "assistants". But, on querying her, I found that she was making snacks for her former competitors to sell. Apparently she had worked out a profit-sharing deal with them in which she continued to make snacks, which they would proceed to sell. It was such a characteristic of Mimi to find a solution that satisfied everyone.

Jalan Prof. Kusuma Atmadja No. 1

After graduating, Nini applied for a job at the Ministry of Public Works and was accepted. Consequently, our family had to move to Jakarta. By coincidence, Mimi's mother, Ina Rumbayan, had been wanting to make amends to us, and she offered to let us live with her at her house. We had known her address to be Jalan Tosari No. 1, but the street had been renamed, and now the address was Jalan Prof. Kusuma Atmadja No. 1.

I need to clarify that it was pure coincidence that the street name closely resembled my last name. Professor Kusuma Atmadja, after whom the street had been renamed, was the first Chief Justice of the Indonesian Supreme Court, and he was quite unrelated to us. Nevertheless, many did not know this fact and continued to assume that the house belonged to our family.

When she filed her report of relocation to Jakarta with the local council in Menteng, Nini brought with her a letter of reference from Bandung. The clerk at the sub-district office was mystified on two fronts: First, he thought Nini was a Chinese Indonesian by the name of Nini

Kusumaatmadja Maramis; Second, the said Mrs Kusumaatmadja had moved to Jalan Kusuma Atmadja No. 1. While finalizing the registry, the clerk could not help himself and commented, "Ci (a mode of address for a Chinese Indonesian woman), how on earth did you have your name changed to match the name of the street you live in?"

Professional Life as Civil Engineer

Not long after we moved to Jakarta, Rudianto Ramelan came to see me and offered me a job as assistant consultant at Widya Pertiwi, Ltd, a company owned by Ariono Abdulkadir. The company had secured a tender from the state's logistics agency (Bulog) to design and construct rice storage facilities. The colleague in Bulog who signed off on the tender was Muslimin Nasution.

Here, the PMB connection was obvious. Rudianto Ramelan, Ariono Andulbakir and Muslimin Nasution were my mentors at PPA PMB. Naturally, I was gratified by Rudianto Ramelan's offer. I thought my path towards professional life had been laid before me, a state of affairs comparable to my life as a rookie politician in DPR, which looked all too uncertain.

As an assistant consultant, my task was simple, which was to design large warehouses for the purpose of storing rice, on the condition that the design for the construction had to be simple. I also designed supporting facilities for the warehouses, such as access roads, bridges and retaining walls. After finishing my designs, I submitted them to the senior consultant for checking and approval. It was not difficult.

At around about the same time, Rahmat Witoelar formed a construction company named ATRIA, Ltd, with him as its director. Wimar was the finance director, and I became technical director in the company. There was ample work, starting with the house renovation projects in Kemang and Kebayoran Baru, involving bringing old houses up to standard to serve as accommodation for foreign investors coming to Jakarta. As a result, PT ATRIA found it easy to find work partners. With the three of us being fluent in English, PT ATRIA soon developed quite a reputation among the house owners and their foreign clients.

Looming Eviction

My improving fortune emboldened me to ask for a loan from Mochtar. Although the loan came with very few conditions, Mochtar was very business-like in giving it to me. He had worked out a detailed repayment plan for me to follow. The loan turned out to be timely, since we soon found ourselves having to move out of my mother-in-law's.

The house in Jalan Kusuma Atmadja was occupied by my mother-in-law on the basis of a permit issued by the mayor's office, known still by its Dutch name, Vergunning Bewijs (VB). The permit had recently been revoked by the Central Jakarta Mayor because some prerequisites within the permit had not been satisfied by my mother-in-law. In due course the house was sold by the municipal government to someone else, who came knocking on our door and told us to vacate the building immediately.

Nini and I were dismayed at this turn of events. My mother-in-law's legal position was weak, and we could have been evicted by force. In the meantime, Nini gave birth to our third child, Devyandra—Adja to us—in November 1974. The new owner of the house was in no mood to compromise. An idea then occurred to Nini to request the help of the law firm Mochtar, Karuwin and Komar (MKK) to negotiate with the new owner. MKK was a prestigious law firm in those days, owned jointly by my brother Mochtar, the senior lawyer Karuwin and Komar Kantaatmadja, a law lecturer at Unpad, who was also the husband of Mieke Palar, a friend of Nini's. Mieka Palar went on to become a Supreme Court Judge.

Upon hearing our family was represented by MKK, the new owner changed his tune and was respectful and conciliatory. I do not know how MKK conducted the negotiation, but in the end the new owner agreed to pay my mother-in-law fifty per cent of the market value of the house and we were given six months to vacate the premises. With such a windfall, my mother-in-law was able to buy a decent house in Ciledug, a new car, a trip to Paris and still have some left over in the bank.

With the loan from Mochtar, Nini and I moved to a rented house in Jalan Cidurian, Kebayoran Baru and became neighbours with Abdullah Zaini, a fellow member of the House of Representatives from Central Kalimantan. I also bought a plot of land in Kalibata and a second-hand car, a red Honda Life, which my DPR colleagues called "helicopter".

The Pertamina Case

As I mentioned earlier, as a rookie politician I at first did not have sufficient points of reference on which I could make a political stance, so I tended to agree with what my colleagues decided. I subsequently had to divert my attention to my studies, which meant I was unable to devote much time to important political events such as the 1973 fusion of political parties, Law No. 1/1974 on Marriage, the Law on Political Parties and Golkar, and the Malari incident. But by the end of 1974 I had enough time to be able to make a contribution in parliament. Activities within assessment teams formed by the Golkar parliamentary leadership increased in both frequency and intensity.

In this respect, my young colleagues and I started to be counted. For those of us who came from Bandung—many of whom had been part of the 10th November Study Group (Tamblong Group)—the training we received there now came in handy as we sifted through legislative drafts to refine the concepts our leaders were working on or to pick out problematic areas in a draft bill. We also contributed to various debates on the concepts of the right to express opinions, on the right to question government policies, and real-life issues that affected society. So, finally, young parliamentarians were seen in a new light by their seniors, not only those from the Tamblong Group but also other young MPs such as Oka Mahendra who represented Bali and Rivai Siata from Southern Sulawesi.

The Chairman of our Golkar Parliamentary Group (FKP), Pak Sugiharto, and other seniors like Pak Sumiskum, Pak Djamal Ali, David Napitupulu and Moerdopo were very fond of engaging us in discussions, which were always lively. These discussions were not always serious in tone and they were often interspersed with biting humour.

The role of young MPs in working sessions with the government became increasingly significant, as did the parliamentary working visits to the provinces. Our presence had started to be noticed by the press, who were always eager for stories on DPR activities.

Our usual meeting place was the office of the FKP Secretary, Pak Soemarsono, who was always delighted to see us there. With members of the media, we even liked to give them ideas for stories, especially to test the public's reaction to certain topics.

Aside from the public activities I mentioned earlier, FKP also had closed-door activities in its position as the government's fraction in parliament, together with the ABRI Fraction. We had code names for such activities. If FKP held a meeting with the government, it was called a "quarter-chamber" meeting. If FKP met with F-ABRI, it was known as a "half-chamber". Such meetings were used to find solutions to sensitive situations, and they were always informal and off the record.

Overseeing the government's interactions with us was the Office of the President, particularly the State Secretariat. The Minister of the State Secretariat at the time was Pak Sudharmono, who entrusted the meetings and their results to Moerdiono as Deputy Secretary of the Cabinet and Hamid Attamimi, Head of the Legal Bureau.

The standard mechanism could lead to other informal meetings in which Moerdiono often spoke to a few of us alone; that is, Rahmat Witoelar, Djoko Sudyatmiko, Rivai Siata, Oka Mahendra, myself and sometimes Pak Sugiharto. Such meetings often saw intense debates that then led to solutions to the matters at hand. Equally important was to show the public that FKP was capable of voicing public aspirations by making policy suggestions to the government.

This particular role of FKP was fully tested in the resolution of the Pertamina Scandal. It was discovered in 1975 that Pertamina was suffering from liquidity problems, chiefly because it had worked up huge debts to the tune of USD 10 billion to its foreign contractors. The underlying reason for the mess was mismanagement.

Investigation showed that the state-owned oil company had been using its revenues from oil exports to invest in new products and schemes beyond its core business. The reinvestments were carried out in a most wasteful manner and utilized inappropriate and reckless funding schemes. The company should not have suffered such huge losses because oil prices were dramatically on the rise as a result of the action of OPEC members, of which Indonesia was one. In reality, the country was expecting a windfall from the rising oil prices.

The government sought to control the situation through corrective actions by Pertamina's own Council of Commissioners and coordinated efforts involving several ministries. In the House of Representatives, lines of communication on the matter with the government remained open and conducive. The situation seemed to be under control when Piet Harjono was appointed as Pertamina's new Managing Director.

Just as we thought the worst was over, a new, related, scandal came to light, known as the Tahir Case. Before his death, Tahir was a high-ranking director in the old line-up of Pertamina. In the wake of his death, a feud broke out among his family members over a deposit account of almost USD 100 million under the name Ahmad Tahir at the Sumitomo Bank in Singapore. An investigation to determine whether the money had been embezzled from Pertamina was under way, and it turned out Pertamina could legally file a lawsuit to secure the funds.

In response to the developing case, Pak Sugiharto requested a mandate from FKP's Plenary Session to oversee the government's efforts in resolving the case, and if necessary to use the parliamentary right to question the government on the matter. The full mandate was duly granted. The FKP leadership then proceeded to form a team to prepare questions for the government, drawn from the relevant commission members, as well as to satisfy regional representation. The team members included Rahmat Witoelar, Djoko Sudyatmiko, Oka Mahendra, Fahrin Ilham, Nocian Kaman, Johnny Simandjuntak and myself, all of whom were rookie parliamentarians. Our team was supervised by another MP, Warsito Puspoyo, who was a senior expert on public law.

The team was formed in circumstances whereby we were informed, through the "Moerdiono channel", that the government was in the process of enacting steps to resolve the Tahir Case. FKP's right to question was then incorporated into the government's scenario in tackling the case. Thus, FKP asked the President questions. Essentially, we expressed our distress over the Tahir Case, especially when parliament and the public had been led to believe that the Pertamina Scandal was well behind us, as reported by the government to the DPR. FKP asked the President what steps the government planned to take in order to resolve the case.

The questions elicited diverse reactions within the House. Within FKP, many saw the move to question the government as overly brave. Some even saw it as sedition. On the other hand, among the political parties, our questions were deemed too lame. Many of our colleagues accused us of insubordination, forgetting that we had secured a full mandate from FKP. There were those who predicted the President's fury and our eventual removals from parliament.

We did not have to wait long before a response from the government presented itself. The Minister of the State Secretariat, Sudharmono, appeared before the DPR in a Plenary Session on behalf of the President to answer our questions. It was interesting that, out of the many ministers the President could have chosen to appear before parliament, it was the Minister of the State Secretariat whom he eventually selected. In his statement before the House, Sudharmono, in a flat tone, gave out signals that the chain of events that constituted the Pertamina Scandal was being dealt with and he implicitly indicated that the Tahir Case was one of them.

Subsequently, the Indonesian government, through its legal team headed by the Intelligence Assistant to the ABRI Commander, Lieutenant General L.B. Moerdani, worked alongside Pertamina to file a claim for Ahmad Tahir's deposit account with the Sumitomo Bank. As with most legal battles, it took a long time before Pertamina finally won the case.

Nevertheless, the appearance of Minister Sudharmono before the House showed the government's responsiveness in the face of the deep concern enshrined in FKP's questions. The swift action by the government in resolving the Tahir Case stunned members of FKP. Most were not aware that what had transpired was a public relations exercise in which all the institutional formalities were observed but, simultaneously, behind-the-scenes coordination through the "Moerdiono channel" was also made.

It was amid such circumstances that we faced the next legislative nominations for the 1977 General Election. The Bandung Group received Golkar nominations again, except for Rudianto Ramelan, who chose to go back to the professional world by leaving for West Germany to do his post-graduate studies. Djoko Sudyatmiko moved to his new constituency in West Kalimantan. So we saw new candidates from a generation younger than myself, such as Akbar Tandjung and Marzuki Darusman.

As a result of the fusions of political parties, there were only three contestants in the General Election: the Indonesian Democratic Party (PDI), Golkar and the United Development Party (PPP). The results of the 1977 election did not differ much from the one in 1971. There was, however, a shift in the nature of the Golkar campaign, which saw the inclusion of celebrities who performed live music or shows, so that the campaign trail was full of merrymaking. Perhaps it was this phenomenon that gave rise to the idea that an election is essentially a fiesta of democracy.

Unlike the 1971 election, I had a bigger role to play now, and I started appearing as the main speaker at small campaign forums, usually referred to as face-to-face sessions.

The events surrounding the 1977 General Election had a profound impact on the direction I was about to take in my life. After graduating from ITB in 1974, I lived my life in two different streams—as a novice civil engineer and as a rookie politician. It was around this time that I truly felt more at home in politics. It made good sense because I was raised at Kramat Sentiong in the atmosphere of nation-building social activism that my parents consistently cultivated.

During my teenage years in Europe, I was very much taken by humanities subjects. My decision to enrol at ITB was, to a greater degree, motivated by the desire to prove myself able to overcome challenges. When I worked as a novice civil engineer, I realized my heart was not in it. My role as an assistant consultant and technician in small building projects was perhaps not challenging enough for me.

Not that there is anything wrong about being a civil engineer. My senior, Rudianto Ramelan, for one, resolutely chose his profession over a life in politics. I instinctively understood his choice because I knew him well. His steadfast character was evident when he led the Bandung contingent in Jakarta to set up radio Ampera, and when he organized the student movement in Jakarta. While he lived his life as an activist then, he never wavered from his archetype as a man of science. Among his juniors like me, he was known as "Mr Principles".

By contrast, someone like me finds the intricacies of human nature fascinating. Social interactions with other fellow human beings often reveals more than just black and white, but also degrees of shades not always immediately visible to the eye. So, as the 1977 election drew closer, I felt that my life's calling just might be in politics after all.

3

Full Time Politician and Outsider

Political Structure Reform Agenda

In the lead-up to the 1978 MPR General Assembly, as a full-time politician, I started pondering upon issues worth pursuing as an MP in order to make my presence in the DPR/MPR meaningful. Not championing any cause would have rendered my presence ineffectual.

To that end, my colleagues and I revisited the political ideas that had once been dissected in the 10th November Study Group since its inception in 1968. Some of the ideas emanating from the group had found their way into the 1966 MPRS General Assembly. One idea that stood out among the rest was on political restructuring, leading to the creation of new settings with which the New Order would differentiate itself from Soekarno's Guided Democracy.

High-ranking government officials often pontificated that, "The New Order isn't the Old Order minus PKI. Rather it is a regime that implements the 1945 Constitution and Pancasila in their pure and consistent form." The agenda to reform our political structure arose from the search for that format. Discussion of this idea was not confined only to those of us from Bandung, but it was also widely debated among the '66 activists.

There were essentially two elements to the agenda: First, quantitative reform, which would ultimately empower sociopolitical forces with the largest representative basis so they could play their maximum roles. It would also act to limit the number of sociopolitical entities taking part in the General Election. Consequently, the political instability that a multiparty system tended to bring about could also be avoided.

Second, qualitative reform, to be carried out by entrenching Pancasila as the only ideological basis permitted in the public sphere. As a result, political rivalries could only be competition between programmes within the boundaries of pluralistic values as represented by Pancasila.

Rejection

These concepts found favour with the '66 community. But the question remained of how we would put them into action. The means with which we could restructure Indonesian politics was never going to be easy to find. That was why, after General Soeharto was sworn-in as President at the 1968 MPRS General Assembly, it was suggested that the plan should be an initiative by the executive. The idea received widespread support from the '66, scholars and high-ranking military officers. The motivation for change was so strong that many supported the idea of setting up a military regime first—with the election not held until a new political structure was in place.

President Soeharto, however, rejected the last idea unequivocally. "If we did that, we'd never have an election, even when our hair has already turned grey", he said, as quoted by several sources.

As if to emphasize his point, the President wanted an election as soon as possible, which was duly held in 1971. The New Order's first "fiesta of democracy" was at the very least meant to neutralize aspirations to alter Pancasila or the Constitution. To that end, a new mechanism to redress the composition of our parliament was introduced by the appointment of a hundred members of the DPR-GR, twenty-five of whom came from the military. Contestants in the election were the existing political parties, coupled with Sekber Golkar as the political partner of the military.

As previously explained, Sekber Golkar, which was to undergo another transformation before turning into Golkar, went on to win the 1971 election with a margin that defied expectations. This meant that not only did the government achieve its minimum target but the prerequisites for a stable government were also fulfilled. Hence, with the result of the 1971 election, the New Order government secured strong political legitimacy. It also ushered in an opportunity for Indonesia to work towards economic stability, which would benefit the population as a whole. This was the difference from how life had been under Soekarno's Guided Democracy.

A year later, President Soeharto repeated his theory. According to him, the existing sociopolitical forces in the country needed to be categorized into three groupings: First, those who prioritized spiritual development without neglecting material progress; Second, those who prioritized material development without neglecting spiritual progress; and Third, those who strove for balance between spiritual progress and material development.

No one could really contradict the President's theory, which was articulated based on common sense and without intellectual pretensions. Political actors at whom the categorization was aimed knew where they stood respectively, without being able to come up with a retort because of the stigma of failure that tainted the previous eras of Guided Democracy and Parliamentary (Liberal) Democracy.

Early 1973 therefore saw the fusions of political parties, whereby Islamic parties merged into the United Development Party (PPP), while the National Party of Indonesia (PNI) and the rest merged into the Democratic Party of Indonesia (PDI). Meanwhile, Golkar positioned itself as the "middle force".

As a rookie politician, I was faced with a changing political landscape. As an aspiring full-time politician, I had to be able to navigate the changes to the political structure that were taking place. However, while quantitative reform had been accomplished by reducing the number of political parties, a qualitative problem remained; which was how to establish Pancasila as the only prevalent ideological basis in the public sphere.

What was needed was a new modality through which Pancasila could have its values elaborated as a living ideology in the midst of changing times. This question was answered by President Soeharto, who came up with the idea of formulating P4, or Pedoman Penghayatan dan Pengamalan Pancasila (Directive for the Realization and Implementation of Pancasila), also known by its Sanksrit name of Eka Prasetya Pancakarsa.

P4 was duly enshrined through an act of MPR at its 1978 General Assembly. The act further empowered and complemented the ongoing Pancasilaist education in schools through the subject of Pancasila Morality Education (PMP), furthering its outreach in the most comprehensive and fundamental way. Prior to this, PMP received very little weight in the education curriculum as drawn up by the Ministry of Education and Culture, leaving it vulnerable to political whims as cabinet compositions changed.

Consolidating Golkar

The consolidation of Golkar was the next point of concern. Our ultimate goal was to turn it into a resilient organization thriving on regeneration. The future we envisioned for Golkar was as a volitional body made up of motivated individuals working towards a common goal for the country, as mandated by Law No. 3/1975 on political parties and Golkar.

After the 1997 General Election, Golkar was still essentially the federated body consisting of its original founding organizations in addition to professional functional organizations using Golkar to channel their aspirations. The military acted as a unifying force through policy initiatives and even interventions, ostensibly as part of the military function of sociopolitical pacification.

In 1971 such interventions were conducted *ex officio*, but they were subsequently carried out informally through retired ABRI officers who had either access to the ABRI headquarters or to those who were in charge of the sub-organizations under Golkar, such as Kosgoro, SOKSI, MKGR and Gakari. The shift from direct influence took place after the Minister of Defence and Security/ABRI Commander, General M. Yusuf, sometime after the 1978 MPR General Assembly, forbade active serving officers from being involved in political organizations.

The proposal to turn Golkar membership into one based on active individual volition—by the mechanism of personal declaration in applying to become a member—was essentially democratic in nature. If realized, it would have eliminated group political manipulation and created a political sphere in which political activism was the result of individual awareness through a process of self-conviction. But the plan ran aground because of strong opposition from the founding bodies of Golkar, especially from the Trikarya bloc (Kosgoro, MKGR and SOKSI).

The main argument against the plan was that it would decimate political participation since most citizens would prefer to belong to the category of the "floating masses". This supposition gave the impression of a huge group of voters who were apolitical, undecided and with no aspirations whatsoever. One Trikarya figure who was most vociferous in his opposition to the plan was *Mas* Isman, the Executive Chairman of Kosgoro. I had the impression that his hostility was the result of his perception that there was no potential democratization in the nation's political life through individual membership of political entities.

Isman's viewpoints motivated me to accept the invitation by Mas Soeharto and Jouke Wowor to attend the Kosgoro National Convention in Semarang in June 1978. I was struck by how such an important event was conducted in a very informal way. I remembered how our old house in Sentiong was visited by various people to discuss politics. The atmosphere at the convention was something similar, which then reminded me of my beloved father.

The Kosgoro convention proceeded like an informal gathering— a far cry from the formally organized event it should have been. Those who attended came from various backgrounds, from the Kosgoro seniors who founded the organization—most of whom were former Indonesian Student Soldiers—to the junior members. I had the opportunity of meeting people who represented a wide spectrum of political beliefs. They all talked to one another with openness and warmth.

There was another important event for Golkar happening around the same time as the convention, which was the inauguration of a new body called the Indonesian Young Reformers (AMPI), in Pandaan, East Java. But I was more interested in understanding what Kosgoro was all about. In my attempt to get to know it, I was trying to discern the lines of thinking and activities of one of Golkar's founding organizations, and to also predict, if I could, where such organizations were going. It then occurred to me that Kosgoro was akin to a powerhouse of activism, capable of generating many ideas. Moreover, it also functioned as a vessel for charitable deeds and empowerment for the people, for instance in the fields of education and economics.

Having listened to various ideas and opinions on democratizing our politics, I started to believe that even the "floating masses" could benefit from a dose or two of democratization. Naturally, there were prerequisites that had to be satisfied first, which was that Golkar needed — at some point in the future — to shed its dependence on the military and bureaucracy. If the existing dependence was to be allowed to continue unchecked, Mas Isman's dire prediction had every opportunity of coming to pass. In other words, Golkar needed to manifest itself as an independent political organization that relied on its own ability to generate new cadres for its survival.

In line with Golkar's own doctrine on functionality, it was these new cadres who were supposed to take the lead through Kosgoro and the other founding organizations of Golkar. Each individual member had to cultivate his or her own work for the good of others, aside from Golkar's collective functional endeavours.

Actually, the Board of Patrons' Secretariat had drawn up a document known as Kirka, which sought to predict and extrapolate future conditions and circumstances for Golkar. Kirka was the source of Golkar's long-term strategic plans. Many of these plans worked their way into the country's legislation and they were also implemented through Golkar's own programme.

In an environment where the means of communication was strictly controlled and its circulation limited, the mechanism for the management of ideas was not readily transparent. Consequently, there was always information to which not all Golkar activists were privy. Nevertheless, debates over strategies concocted by the Board of Patrons — involving the three major streams within Golkar's "extended family of golongan karya" — were sufficiently intensive but friendly.

The three major streams I just mentioned were, first, stream A: the ABRI Inc., encompassing retired military officers with access to the active military; second, stream B: Golkar and ABRI figures who occupied important government posts; third, stream G: established civilian politicians from professional-functional organizational and '66 backgrounds and other influential figures.

I referred to this extended family without using capital letters because the group was too diverse to be lumped into one identity since it encompassed a large community. The first letter of the name Golkar is capitalized because it is the generic name for an organization. This would have been the assessment of Pak A.E. Manihuruk, who was known within Golkar for his linguistic precision. He was a retired ABRI officer who served as a chairman in charge of organizational affairs on Golkar's Central Governing Board for three consecutive terms. His forte lay in producing guidelines that were semantically clear-cut, detailed and easy to understand.

Stability and Political Dynamism

Apart from the management mechanism of new ideas on changes to the political structures, another internal issue of note was the mechanism for power management in maintaining political stability.

In practice, there were two red lines that could not be crossed as they were deemed to be detrimental to national stability. First, the taboo on tinkering with the 1945 Constitution and Pancasila. To ensure this, the composition of the MPR included those who were appointed rather than elected. The presence of the ABRI Fraction, Regional Representatives and Golkar within MPR nullified the possibility for constitutional amendment, even if Golkar's electoral performance ever became seriously challenged. The desire to amend the 1945 Constitution and Pancasila was considered a latent danger posed by proponents of liberal democracy, the sectarians and communists.

The second red line was national succession. If ever there was any serious attempt to replace the President—by anyone or with any means—swift action would be taken to neutralize it. The issue of succession in the national leadership was seen as a credible threat. This was evident in the political representation within parliamentary bodies like the MPR and DPR. The political system had been designed as if to ensure that President Soeharto's rule would continue no matter what, rather than to protect the Constitution.

However, as future events proved, such a political paradigm would only lead to bigger problems for the nation, which is what happened during the transition from the Guided Democracy era to the New Order. One of the reasons for the 1965 political crisis was the non-existence of a succession mechanism for the national leadership after President Soekarno was declared President for Life by the MPRS.

The Middle Course

Between the two red lines was a narrow passage in which everyone could hope to voice their opinions or criticisms. To be in this passage, characterized by freedom of expression, one needed to take the middle course, a pathway taken by several non-governmental organizations (NGOs) such as the Cipayung Group.

The middle course was navigated by certain people with critical minds and a characteristically strong conscience. But they typically lacked political access and limited themselves to issues that had no potential of crossing the red lines. Succinctly, they had no desire to change or modify the Constitution or Pancasila, and they had no design on the presidential succession.

In the lead-up to the 1978 MPR General Assembly, in January 1978 to be exact, a movement sponsored by the ITB Student Council reared its head out of nowhere. They released a strongly worded statement condemning the government and calling for members of the MPR to not re-elect Soeharto as President.

In my view, it was out of the question that a group of student activists were serious about such a declaration, since they had no political means whatsoever to make it happen. However, as far as the government was concerned, such an expression meant crossing one of the red lines. For security officials, the ITB student movement was to be monitored, as it involved mass mobilization. It is possible that government officials had been informed about this group of student activists who tended to be recklessly confrontational.

The next thing to occur was that the university's chancellery was shot at by unknown gunmen. The ITB's Chancellor at the time was Professor Dr Ir Iskandar Alisjahbana, the designer of the Palapa telecommunication satellite, which had been launched in 1976. Was Professor Iskandar involved in the students' declaration? I can confirm that he was not. But the Chancellor represented the whole campus and, as it happened, he was close to student activists. The shooting incident was fuel for the fire of the student movement. Faced with this growing student movement, the Regional Military Command VI/Siliwangi under Major General Himawan Sutanto took steps to pacify the students in a characteristically Siliwangi manner. The central government thought the approach was too soft, especially after my close friend, Wimar Witoelar, who was then a lecturer at our alma mater, declared himself ready to be nominated for President.

Was Wimar really serious about becoming a presidential candidate? I knew his typical sense of humour when I saw or heard it. His so-called nomination was an act of parody. The managers of security for the New Order might have understood Wimar's attempt at humour, but they had been trained to see calamity in any unscripted succession scenario, however trivial. For them, here was a student movement that had steered away from the Middle Course and crossed a red line. In response, a military contingent was dispatched from Jakarta—a unit that had just come back from East Timor (now Timor Leste)—to occupy the ITB campus and discipline the students. The soldiers ended up behaving violently. Perhaps for soldiers hardened in East Timor, what they did was nothing harsh, but several students were physically injured in the process.

Wimar and leaders of the student movement were promptly arrested and jailed without trial, although they were released later after things had cooled down. Wimar did not appear to have been overly affected by what happened to him. After being released, he spoke a lot about his experience and he saw it as something to have spiced up his life. But he did not even try to use his arrest as a means of projecting himself as a figure in the world of activism.

The January 1978 incident, like its antecedents in the annals of the student movement—the Rene Coenrad incident of 1970 in Bandung and the Malari incident of 1974 in Jakarta—was a sign of the re-politicization of the movement. This was clearly a blowback from the "back to campus" movement, which in turn had been a reaction to the excesses of campus politicization during the Guided Democracy era.

In the aftermath of the ITB incident, the Minister of Education and Culture, Professor Daoed Joesoef, enacted the NKK-BKK (the Normalization of Campus Life and the Student Coordination Agency) policy for campus life in the country. The policy aimed to bring campus politicization to an end and to return it to its original function as a place of learning.

The transformation of universities in the direction desired by the government naturally would take a long time. After all, the trend of politicization had started as early as 1966. However, Minister Daoed Joesoef managed to do it eventually. The NKK-BKK saw the Student Council disbanded, and student activities were subsequently regulated by the chancellery. The policy elicited protests from students, albeit not in any significant way, given how repressively the January 1978 incident had been dealt with.

As a direct result of the new policy, off-campus activism became stronger among university students, evident in the increasing prominence of the Cipayung Group, which had been founded in 1972 through the Cipayung Accord. The new group was the direct successor to KAMI, which had naturally faded into oblivion as the political conflict of 1966 came to an end. Even though the Cipayung Group would face sporadic government pressure, its dexterity at communication was more than sufficient to ensure the group's survival. The student organizations that were members of the Cipayung Group were HMI, PMKRI, GMNI, GMKI and PMII. Former Cipayung activists who later entered politics included Akbar Tandjung and Nurcholish Madjid from HMI, Soeryadi from GMNI, M. Zamroni from PMII, Binsar Sianipar from GMKI and Chris Siner Key Timu from PMKRI.

At the ITB, students worked around the NKK-BKK policy by forming groups through which they could communicate with each other beyond the scope of the chancellery. One of these groups was the Salman Mosque Community. A key initiative was the implementation of appropriate technology in the villages through the Mandiri Foundation. The students who were the pioneers behind the various initiatives were known as the 73 Forum (Fortuga), named after the year they entered ITB. They were also the students behind the January 1978 incident who served as politicians, NGO activists and even ministers in the period after 1998, such as Indro Tjahjono, Rizal Ramli, Al Hilal Hamdi, Jusman Safei Djamal, Heri Achmadi, Sugeng Setiadi and Hatta Rajasa. The next generation of activists was made up of students who started at ITB in the 1980s such as Pramono Anung, Sahganda Nainggolan and M. Djumhur Hidajat.

Golkar National Congress, 1978

It was in such a lukewarm atmosphere that Golkar held its National Congress in Bali in October 1978. Most of the objectives of the congress were achieved. Individual voluntary membership was accepted alongside organization-based membership comprising Golkar's founding organizations and others founded by individual Golkar members, as long as they chose to channel their aspirations through Golkar.

Trikarya decided to accept this formulation after an intense dialogue, of which I was involved through Kosgoro, following its Semarang convention, as explained earlier in the chapter.

During the Congress in Bali, the younger cadres, including myself, sat on the Steering Committee in supporting roles, a position not unlike at Sekber Golkar following the 1971 election. Those in charge within the committee were our seniors, like A.E. Manihuruk, Cosmas Batubara, Jusuf Wanandi and Moerdopo. A.E. Manihuruk was a likeable organizational overseer. Apart from his admirable and unique linguistic prowess, he was also very thorough when formulating the legal construction of a document. Not only did he make sure it was consistent with our organization's rules, he also saw to it that it was in line with our national law.

Had Golkar's regulatory output been measured by the country's existing laws, it would have easily passed. We even held simulations to this effect. What was special about Manihuruk's output was its simplicity. Golkar's internal rules were so easy to understand that cadres right down to the local level needed no facilitator or instructor to discern them.

Mang Awan is Stunned

Towards the end of the Golkar National Congress, a meeting was convened to determine the composition of the next Central Governing Board (DPP). The meeting included senior Golkar figures from the Board of Patrons: General (Rtd.) Maraden Panggabean, General (Rtd.) Darjatmo and Mashuri S.H.

As my younger colleagues and I were sitting and discussing things at the canteen of Hotel Patra Jasa in Nusa Dua, Pak Mashuri came out of the meeting room and started talking to us. He said that the Bandung Group was under consideration of being admitted into the DPP. However, because we lacked seniority, it was decided that we had to play roles as leaders of FKP in the House of Representatives first. "If there's anyone more senior than you, let me know his name. I will present it to the board", he said. We then suggested Awan Karmawan Burhan or Mang Awan. Pak Mashuri asked us further questions about Mang Awan and he said he remembered him.

In the afternoon, news was leaked to us about the names that made it into the DPP, and Mang Awan was named Deputy Secretary General. We looked for him immediately but found he had gone to Ubud in search of a painting to buy. So we decided against telling him of his appointment.

The following day, the results of the meeting were announced in the plenary session by General Panggabean. We were seated in the back and saw Mang Awan in the centre of the hall. We waved to him and he waved back. Names were being read out one by one, starting from heads of department and working the way up. Every time someone's name was read out, people almost always clapped their hands and or shouted in celebration, which was a good sign. Then Pak Panggabean read out Awan Karmawan Burhan as Deputy Secretary General. Mang Awan was stunned, got up and looked back towards us, asking loudly in Sundanese, "Eta dewek euy? Nyaan?" (Is that me? Really?). The whole room erupted in applause and laughter.

Secretary of the FKP

From the day I joined Golkar, never did I feel truly at home until I became Secretary of the Fraction Karya Pembangunan in the DPR (FKP), following the Bali National Congress. I felt comfortable because I had finally found a niche I could work within, which was to steer a Middle Course in politics, something that a group of us pioneered before the 1977 election.

To keep us on course—unlike many other new generation politicians —my colleagues and I made a conscious effort not to get too close to members of the New Order's political elite. The only exception to this rule for me at least was my close relationship with Moerdiono, whom we all knew better in his role as Cabinet Secretary. There were two reasons for my association with him. First, we both loved to play tennis. Second, I felt a cultural affinity with him, especially his egalitarianism with those he thought to be his intellectual equals.

My access to Moerdiono was also important because, as I explained earlier, the Minister of the State Secretariat, Sudharmono, had placed his ministry's dealings with the FKP in Moerdiono's hands. The fact was, colleagues of my age group within the FKP and I were able to discuss, debate and at times bicker with Moerdiono over policies without prejudice, bitterness or intrigue. "We all work hand in glove", as Moerdiono once said.

My task was essentially to provide policy support for both the FKP and Golkar. This encompassed work to achieve internal targets or to carry out legislative duties. I also had to gauge public opinion on various matters and to pass this information to the relevant bodies within the DPR to be used as consideration in policymaking.

This approach—that is, to empower the secretariat as a policy support unit that dealt with matters of substance rather than merely providing administrative support—became a cornerstone policy of mine, in politics and later on in government. This was a departure from the normal practice at the time, which emphasized the administrative role of the secretariat. Naturally, administrative support remained crucial, and I designated it as the main job of the Head of the Secretariat, not the Secretary of Karya Pembangunan. In functioning as a policy support system, we aimed at ensuring maximum policy integration and coherence so that the public could accept it as a comprehensive package benefitting the maximum number, not just a few.

The side effect of this approach, however, was that my office was always crowded with people coming and going, most of whom came to discuss various issues with a view to finding solutions together. The atmosphere was always friendly and informal. Eventually, my office became a reception room for representatives of different groups in society.

Camaraderie with Newsmen

The journalists with whom my colleagues in FKP and I were acquainted well before I became Secretary were among the first regular guests in my office. They did not just come to find news but often worked together with us to create news. My friendship with them started when we were young men—most of them are even younger than I am—and it has remained strong to this day, where they have become senior figures in the journalistic world and decision-makers in various leading media.

One of the first newsmen I was introduced to was the late Helmi Khodyat, who then worked for the daily newspaper *Kompas*. Many of the stories Khodyat wrote were engineered. Often the two of us would hold a dialogue, and then he would treat it as an interview and write a story based on the transcript because he thought it newsworthy. Other newsmen who used to frequent my office were M. Sjafe'I Hassanbasari, Joseph Osdar, Karni Ilyas, Yusuf Suroso Eko Suksmantri, Padmono S.K., Derek Manangka, Bruno Kaka Wawo, Oemar Samsuri and Sugiyanto. Some of these are no longer with us.

My relationship with the press was not confined to work alone. My FKP colleagues and the journalists we knew often played soccer together. This was no doubt very enjoyable for all concerned. The position of keeper was entrusted to the Head of FKP, Sugiharto. Moerdopo specialized in executing penalty kicks, a privilege he had as a member of the Central Governing Board of Golkar. I played in left midfield, in tandem with Rani Yasin, an MP from West Kalimantan and a fellow left-handed person, who was our left-winger. On the right side were Aloysius Aloy from West Kalimantan and Derek Manangka. Rahmat Witoelar, who had played in the same team as I had at Kanisius College and who once played for Persidja Junior, acted as playmaker in the central position. Others who played with us included Nugraha Besoes, a former Persib player, journalist Padmono S.K., who played all over the place, Djoko Sudyatmiko and Albert Hasibuan.

Sugiharto, or Mas Giarto, Head of FKP, also held *gamelan* (Javanese percussion instrument) practice at his residence regularly, which saw the participation of our reporter friends and FKP members. Once a year, around Independence Day, Mas Giarto would always host a cultural show in the evening.

The Angsana Case

A delegation of people who came to us in March 1979 became a focus of interest for both domestic and international media. The delegation came from the village Angsana, in the regency of Pandeglang, Banten. Dressed simply, they came to express their grievances in Sundanese. I received them accompanied by other FKP colleagues—Oka Mahendra, Deputy Chairman of Commission II DPR, which oversees domestic affairs, and two individuals from Commission III, which dealt with legal affairs, Dr T.S. Sihombing and Anindya S. Boedisoesetya, who used to be a prosecutor. I acted as interpreter since my colleagues did not speak Sundanese.

Our guests turned out to be farmers who brought with them a petition signed by six people addressed to the Speaker of the DPR and Head of the Central Disciplinary Operation (Opstibpus), which was the operations wing of Kopkamtib. They came to petition us over a local case of abuse of power in the form of land grabbing and extortion by their village chief. This action implicated local government officials of the Regency of Pandeglang from the civil service and the municipal council to the military and the police. The villagers came to us, as members of the national parliament, as a last resort since they had exhausted other measures.

Our petitioners appeared genuine and without guile, relating to us occurrences in the countryside that most of us were unaware of. After they returned to their village, our six guests were detained by the local authorities, but they were later released after the Angsana case was widely covered in the press. This story led to other similar ones being reported from several other villages.

In early April 1979, the FKP released a statement to the press concerning the Angsana case, announcing that we had despatched an investigative team to Pandeglang, which subsequently concluded there was strong reason to believe that injustices had indeed been committed. We also made it known that the Village Chief of Angsana had been penalized. The statement was signed by R. Soekardi, Deputy Chairman of the FKP, and myself as Secretary.

We formed the impression that the Angsana case was being handled by the local elite in the regency, the military and the police in a most awkward and surreptitious manner, like someone who had been caught red-handed doing something inappropriate.

Admiral Soedomo as Pangkopkamtib publicly stated that he had taken over the investigation of the case. Initially, however, he did not give a clear indication of how he planned to tackle it. To the surprise of many, including myself, in early May, Kopkamtib confirmed the veracity of the allegations made by the six villagers. Moreover, Soedomo instructed the Police Chief and Commander of the Regional Command VI/Siliwangi to punish the police and military personnel involved in the abuse of power. Punitive action was also handed out to the Speaker of the Pandeglang Municipal Council, who was a military officer.

Relations between Golkar and ABRI

An interesting feature of this period was the personality and policy of the Minister of Defence and Security/Commander of ABRI, General M. Jusuf. Hailing from Bone, South Sulawesi, the general held several portfolios in the cabinet, including industry, making him more civilian than military because of his longevity in the cabinet. As one of the earliest ministers of the New Order, he was known to be loyal to President Soeharto, as well as a general who stayed away from internal rivalries within ABRI. As former Commander of the Regional Command XIV Hasanuddin, South Sulawesi, he—along with General Amir Mahmud and Basuki Rahmat—was part of the trio that went to see President Soekarno at Bogor Palace back in 1966, which led the latter to issue the 11th March Decree, effectively making General Soeharto ruler of the country.

Because of his long absence from active military duty, General Jusuf's activities became a subject of considerable public interest. As it turned out, the general had taken a surprisingly popular path by positioning himself close to low-ranking soldiers. He devised initiatives to improve their welfare, built new dormitories for them and revamped existing ones, as well as ensuring adequate military exercises. Interviews with M. Jusuf in the media were eagerly read by the public because he always used easy-to-understand language. The general also launched

Buku Saku Prajurit (A Soldier's Pocket Book), which detailed both a soldier's rights and duties.

In explaining his policy as the Minister of Defence and Security/ Commander of ABRI, he emphasized the importance of greater professionalism within the military and better welfare for the soldiers. The general was also at pains to stress that ABRI was above political and group interests, something he would repeat time and again. Early on in his tenure, he forbade serving officers from becoming functionaries in political organizations, which we saw in a positive light in terms of encouraging Golkar's maturity. However, his overly frequent pronouncement of ABRI being above politics gave rise to a sense of confusion within Golkar, especially because the usual Three Stream coordination was still functional and, in our communication with the ABRI Fraction, the policy was never mentioned.

Then something sensational broke out when, on 15 December 1979, *Tempo* magazine reported a purported meeting between Golkar's Governing Board and the Deputy Commander of ABRI/Pangkopkamtib, Admiral Soedomo, in which a declaration that "ABRI was Golkar" took place. It was also reported that visits to regional centres were being planned to consolidate Golkar's special relationship with ABRI. It was also claimed that a document detailing shared programmes between ABRI and Golkar existed. These claims became the basis of questions by A.J. Mokoginta from the Constitutional Awareness Foundation when they came to FKP for a dialogue. The allegations of a meeting and political partnerships between Golkar and ABRI did not sound outlandish to us. But the claim that the meeting produced a written document was extremely odd. As previously explained, the political communication between ABRI and Golkar was conducted through the Three Stream mechanism, which was informal in nature and off the record.

The media exposé of the meeting was anathema to both ABRI and Golkar because it seemed to go against the policy of the Minister of Defence and Security/Commander of ABRI, M. Jusuf, who had repeatedly said ABRI would prioritize professionalism by staying above politics. When he spoke of ABRI being above politics, the general did so in the context of ABRI's main function within Indonesia's doctrine of universal defence and security.

It was this main function of ABRI that was in the process of being enshrined in a new law known as the draft bill on the Defence and Security of the State (Hankamneg). Bodies such as Kopkamtib were not mentioned in the draft because Kopkamtib was outside the defence structure and it owed its existence to a different legal foundation. ABRI's dual function was also regulated in a different law on the composition of the legislature. The Deputy Chairman of Golkar's Governing Board, R. Soekardi, who was also the Deputy Head of the FKP, in the end redressed the mistakes in the media report and denied the existence of the Golkar-ABRI document.

KOMPAS - SELASA, 5 MEI 1981 HALAMAN 12

Dialog Lagi, YLKB dengan F-KP

Jakarta, Kompas
Sekretaris Fraksi Karya Pembangunan, DPR RI, Ir Sarwono Kusumaatmadja mengungkapkan bahwa Selasa pagi ini, F-KP akan menerima tamu dan berdialog dengan anggota-anggota Yayasan Lembaga Kesadaran Berkonstitusi.

Dialog ini merupakan permintaan dari YLKB bulan Maret yang lalu, yang baru bisa dipenuhi F-KP sekarang ini, sebab DPR belum lama ini menjalani masa reses panjang. YLKB ini terdiri beberapa bekas tokoh kawakan pemerintahan dan ABRI, dan sebagian di antara mereka yang kemudian turut menandatangani Petisi 50 yang terkenal itu. Beberapa di antara mereka adalah Dr Azis Saleh, AJ Mokoginta, Prof Soenario, Jenderal Pol (purn) Hoegeng, Letjen Marinir (purn) Ali Sadikin dan sebagainya.

"Sebetulnya bisa saja kita penuhi permintaannya pada masa reses, tetapi kami sulit mengumpulkan tokoh-tokoh F-KP dan mereka 'kan bukan orang sembarangan," ujar Sarwono.

Enam orang
Menurut dia, F-KP sudah meminta agar mereka datang cukup enam orang saja. "Tetapi kalau mereka datang lebih dari itu, kami sebagai orang timur tak akan mungkin bisa mengusir mereka," tambahnya.

Dari F-KP, akan bertindak sebagai tuan-rumah adalah Ketua fraksi Soegiharto, Wakil Ketua F-KP bidang politik Sukardi, Sarwono, Albert Hasibuan SH, Jamal Ali, Sudarko dan Warsito Puspoyo SH.

Menurut keterangan, anggota-anggota YLKB itu datang ke F-KP untuk menyampaikan pokok-pokok pemikiran tentang Pemilu mendatang.

Ketika wartawan bertanya apakah pertemuan itu boleh diliputi oleh pers, Sarwono mengatakan saat pertemuan itu terbuka. "Namun kalau kehadiran para anggota YLKB itu berhubungan dengan konsensus yang kalian orang pers buat dengan Pemerintah, kami nggak ingin ikut campur," ujarnya.

Juga hasil pertemuan itu dimuat atau tidak, itu bukan urusan F-KP. "Saya ndak mau campuri urusan kebebasan pers," tambahnya pula sambil tertawa. (hw)

My press briefing on the proposed meeting between the FKP and the Constitutional Awareness Foundation was carried by *Kompas* in its Tuesday edition of 5 May 1980.

The leader of the Development Work Fraction (right row) held a dialogue with members of the Constitutional Awareness Foundation (YLKB), whose members included Ali Sadikin and Hoegeng Iman Santoso, 5 May 1981. Photo by Kompas/Oemar Samsuri.

Petition 50

As mentioned, in the aftermath of the *Tempo* report, on 5 May 1980, a delegation from the Constitutional Awareness Foundation paid us a visit at the FKP, led by the former Governor of Jakarta, Pak Ali Sadikin. Among his delegation were Pak Hoegeng Imam Santoso and Chris Siner Key Timu. The FKP decided to meet them with our full team, from our Head, Sugiharto, to our commission heads in parliament.

Apparently, the media eagerly awaited the proposed meeting between the FKP and the Constitutional Awareness Foundation. In my capacity as FKP Secretary, I informed the press our meeting would take place on 5 May 1980. It is said that Petition 50 was also signed on this very same day.

I told the press that the meeting was public in nature. Moreover, the FKP had no intention of censoring the meeting for the media. But the extent to which it might be reported had to be a matter between the media and the government, not the FKP.

As it happened, the delegates proceeded to criticize the way governance was carried out in Indonesia, particularly the role of ABRI in politics. Naturally, the FKP disagreed. Even though the dialogue was tense in places, with fierce debates between the two sides, it was by no means acrimonious. With bantering and joking at the expense of the other side, we exchanged ideas in a most congenial manner, even if we eventually agreed to disagree.

It was said that after visiting all the parliamentary fractions, Ali Sadikin and friends went to see the house leadership to convey their profound concerns about the state of affairs in the country. The petition they presented was signed by fifty national figures that were members of the Constitutional Awareness Foundation. From this point onwards, they were better known as the Petition 50 Group.

The controversies surrounding the issue of ABRI's disproportionate role in government was one of the catalysts for the declaration of concerns by the fifty national figures that signed the petition. Essentially, they took issue with the personification of Pancasila and the 1945 Constitution and the exploitation of our military to buttress the President's power. It was no surprise that, given the political paradigm of the day, President Soeharto came to view the petition as a grievous offence.

Upon further scrutiny, the Petition 50 Group was seen to be made up of public figures of glaringly distinguished track records and stature. While Ali Sadikin was Governor of Jakarta, he transformed the capital city phenomenally into a metropolis with his gentrification of the kampongs through a programme called The Muhammad Husni Thamrin Project (MHT). The Ancol Beach was spruced up to become a popular recreational centre known as Taman Impian Jaya Ancol. The city zoo, which was located in Cikini, was moved to Ragunan. The old Cikini site was turned into the Ismail Marzuki Cultural Centre. The city's infrastructure went through an upgrade, including the construction of bypass roads, after the completion of the Semanggi Interchange during the Soekarno era. Ali Sadikin was known for his coherent communication style employing a linguistic clarity that appealed to many people.

The next notable among the petitioners was General A.H. Nasution, a highly respected retired high-ranking army general with an outstanding service record. Born on 3 December 1918 in South Tapanuli, North Sumatra, he was widely known and revered for his strategic thoughts on defence and security issues, as well as his role in the military. Accolades for the general even came from international military circles. On the very early morning of 1 October 1965, he luckily evaded assassination, but his daughter was killed.

Another eminent Petition 50 figure was General of Police (Rtd.) Hoegeng Imam Santoso, Indonesia's fifth Police Chief from 1968 to 1971. Possessing an extraordinary personality, he is still remembered for being an honest, principled and professional man who lived a simple life. The image of how an honest policeman should act is the legacy of General Hoegeng. In addition to his role as a policeman, the public also knew him for being a consummate musician, through the group the Hawaiian Seniors, who performed regularly on TVRI. Whenever I saw Pak Hoegeng, I was always impressed by his winning smile, his warm and firm handshake and his authenticity as a person.

Other prominent names among those to have signed Petition 50 included former Prime Minister Burhanudddin Harahap and senior statesman Muhammad Nasir. Given the calibre of the figures that signed the petition, they were probably not natural "Middle-coursers". Neither were they a group of people with limited access to politics, nor were they socially marginalized. In fact, what they did was take a stance diametrically opposed to that of President Soeharto. In the eyes of the New Order's grandees, they might have been seen as an alternative source of power or, worse, a threat with the potential to trigger the question of political succession.

In his autobiography, *Soeharto: My Thoughts, Words and Deeds*, Soeharto made no secret of his displeasure at the political statement made by those who signed the Petition 50. The manifestation of the President's displeasure took the form of restrictions of the civil rights of the petitioners. They also faced social sanctions applied by the state apparatus. The government took this course of action instead of having them arrested since they were deemed too influential. Making them pariahs became the preferred way of containing them. The national press was also pressured against reporting anything on them. The public only learned about what they were doing through the international press.

The contrast between the way the government and the FKP reacted to the petition could not be more palpable. The government considered the petition seditious, whereas the FKP saw it as a divergence of opinion that was still open to being harmonized. Aptness in political communication is one of the benchmarks of success for any parliament, and in this case the FKP did its utmost.

The perceived success of the FKP in conducting itself was illustrated in an analogy by Sudarko Prawirojudo, a Golkar MP representing Irian Jaya—now two provinces called Papua and West Papua. In the spirit of laughing at oneself, we the vocal ones in the DPR were analogized as flying lizards, or, in Javanese, *cleret gombel*. This particular reptile glides from one twig on a tree to another. It hugs the twig and, every now and then, it relaxes its hold and glides away. The trees the lizard inhabits were likened to the political jungle. A flying lizard politician was, to the untrained eye, one who was capable of shaking tree twigs, while in fact he or she simply glided here and there on his or her own. The twigs were moved by the wind, which, like events within the political jungle, blew in the most unexpected directions. We took to this analogy because the ability to laugh at oneself is healthy and keeps oneself on one's toes, as well as being an antidote for self-importance, arrogance and being out of touch.

Looking for New Challenges

In short, I managed to carry out my duties as Secretary of the FKP with considerable success, given all the systemic restrictions at the time. Consequently, my colleagues and I decided to break new ground by exploring new parliamentary output. In order to find that niche, we reviewed and researched all the laws and regulations concerning the functions and prerogatives of the DPR.

Our thorough checking of all the available legal products revealed that the DPR had the right to carry out a wide range of powers, including initiating new legislation, drafting state budgets and conducting a supervisory function of the government. So we came up with an idea to initiate a draft bill on a safe issue to effect increased parliamentary participation. We chose to legislate a new law on the National Library, an idea that was discussed internally within the FKP and was received favourably.

We subsequently tried to gauge the reactions from the Three Streams. To our great surprise and dismay, the reaction by the government was downright hostile. The FKP, or any other parliamentary group, was apparently forbidden to initiate any legislation, no matter what the substance was. It would appear the government believed that a parliament-sponsored bill was akin to straying from the Middle Course. It was for the government alone to initiate legislation. Parliament may have been able to amend the draft bills tabled by the government, as long as it did not seem to be imposing its will, but to sponsor a new bill was tantamount to an outrage!

"So the flying lizard who feels that it can move the tree twigs now wants to shake the branches. Impossible!" Sudarko said, exploding into laughter.

Moerdiono, who was already Cabinet Secretary, was among those who thought the government's harsh response to be out of proportion. However, he could not breach the government's collective responsibility and thus could not support us publicly. The question that arose was why such an initiative on a banal matter like the National Library should have elicited such resistance. Our conclusion was that, innocuous as our initiative seemed, it could well become a precedent for something of greater significance.

As far as the government was concerned, if allowed to go unchecked, such a precedent had the potential to spiral out of control since parliament could be tempted to stray from the Middle Course and interfere with the prevalent management of power. Such attempts at interference did take place in 1974 as the government and parliament were in the middle of passing the draft of the Marriage Law—in the form of mass demonstrations. A second case was the passage of the Law on Political Parties and Golkar, which, although it did not see mass protests, was rough sailing, to say the least.

The State Defence and Security Bill

Although we at the FKP were disappointed with the ban on initiating a bill, the period between 1978 and 1983 was a busy and productive one for the FKP. A new initiative—within the permitted boundaries— was launched by the FKP's deputy chairman for finance and economics, Johnny Simandjuntak, who published a prognosis of the National Budget, which was accurate and well received by the government. The prognosis came with policy recommendations. Various ideas in the fields of energy and infrastructure were also discussed in the public sphere on the initiative of the FKP. Consultation with the government became more frequent and productive.

The deliberation on the State Defence and Security Bill was plain sailing, facilitated by General M. Jusuf's open and egalitarian style of communication. The controversies about the relationship between ABRI and Golkar had receded into the background. At the very least, they did not feature in our meetings. What puzzled me was the general's special attention to Arnold Baramuli, an MP from North Sulawesi, and myself.

Perhaps the attention towards Pak Baramuli was understandable since it was obvious the two had known each other for long. But the general's attention towards me was puzzling. I reminded myself that I was a Middle-Courser and therefore did my best not to react to his attention. Besides, my role in the deliberation on the bill was confined to content harmonization, even though I was a member of Commission I, of which specializations included defence. I was also seldom present at many of the meetings, except for the half-chamber ones.

All of a sudden, towards the end of the deliberation on the State Defence and Security bill, I received a phone call. It was 11 p.m., but we at the DPR were still busy at work, preparing our Statement of Response for the next day. The caller was General M. Jusuf. "Sarwono, I want you to read the FKP's Statement to approve the draft of the State Defence and Security tomorrow", he said without beating about the bush.

"Pak Jusuf, that task was given to Pak Nasrudin Hars", I replied.

"No. It must be you!" he said with finality and hung up.

I had no choice but to work on a statement overnight as best as I could. If I had known I had to do it earlier, I would have been better prepared. In the morning, I contacted Nasrudin Hars and explained the situation. He did not mind the fact I would be the one to deliver the statement, and he handed over to me his own draft statement.

When it was my turn to read out the FKP's Statement of Views, I walked up to the podium and spoke. What I said was a mish-mash of Nasrudin Hars' draft, my own hastily written one and on-the-spot improvisation. But it went quite well.

After the Plenary Session concluded, Minister Jusuf shook hands with MPs. Then quite suddenly he said to me, "Hey, Sarwono. You must take the Lemhanas regular course." I immediately replied, "Minister, I'm still under 40, so I'm not allowed to take the course."

"I will give you dispensation", he insisted. But I think he eventually forgot about the course.

Foreign Policy

In our interactions with the government in the House, I naturally paid special attention to my brother, Mochtar Kusuma-Atmadja, who was the Minister of Foreign Affairs for two terms of cabinet, or ten years, until 1988. Mochtar's appointment to the post had been predicted by many, since he had the track record and reputation to excel at it.

What somewhat surprised me was the views of a few cabinet members I knew on foreign policy. I conveyed these views to my brother, who responded, "Let them be. It'll get them nowhere." I initially thought that my brother either did not think my report important or interesting, but I could not be more wrong. I certainly did not expect him to share what I had told him during his work session with Commission I of the DPR.

"My brother told me that there are in fact six foreign ministers, including myself", he jested, provoking much laughter from the assembled MPs.

At the time, Indonesia's foreign policy was dominated by the issue of the Vietnamese "boat people". These were refugees who had fled Vietnam on boats after the 1975 war to avoid living under the victorious Communists. They wanted to start new lives in either the United States or Australia. In their flight on makeshift boats, around forty thousand Vietnamese entered Indonesian waters and became stranded in the Riau Isles, around the islands of Batam, Bintan and Galang. They received help from the Indonesian Navy, fishermen and sailors on commercial ships. The Indonesian government also provided humanitarian assistance for them.

Relaxing with my brother. Mochtar was Minister of Foreign Affairs
at the time I was Secretary of the FKP.

The issue of boat people created a stir within the cabinet. As
Foreign Minister, Mochtar was of the opinion that Indonesia needed
to provide temporary refuge within an international framework.

The contention surrounding the topic subsided when President
Soeharto supported Mochtar's stance. Not long after, the Prime Minister
of Vietnam, Pham Van Dong, visited Indonesia in September 1978
and promised that his country would be part of the solution. In

early 1979, ASEAN convened a foreign ministerial summit in which Indonesia declared itself willing to provide temporary refuge for the boat people until they could be sent somewhere permanent. The scheme was conducted with the support and cooperation of ASEAN, involving the United Nations High Commission for Refugees (UNHCR). Vietnam eventually repatriated those who wanted to go back home. The island of Galang became a processing station for the refugees.

The operation did much for Indonesia's international standing and revealed an interesting side to Indonesia-Vietnam relations. I sensed this while attending the reception to welcome the PM and his delegation at the residence of Pak Sudjono Humardani. A Vietnamese official there said that they needed to learn a lot from Indonesia about economic development. They modestly added, "We are only good at war, but we don't know how to build yet."

The Vietnamese displayed such modesty in seeking to befriend ASEAN countries, including Thailand, which had been an ally of the United States in making war against Vietnam. The charm offensive was launched, as we later learned, because they were having difficulties with China. In February 1979, China invaded Vietnam "to teach them a lesson". However, in the span of just a month, the Chinese forces had been beaten back with casualties reportedly amounting to eighty thousand. To save face, Beijing declared it was pulling back its troops because it had successfully taught Vietnam a lesson.

Misuse of Diplomatic Passports

Another matter on which I had dealings with Mochtar was the practice of misuse of the diplomatic passport. According to international convention, the holders of diplomatic passports should be high-ranking officials of a country with special rights and extraordinary privileges, including diplomatic immunity, a waiver of customs rules and any criminal investigation. Consequently, diplomatic passports are issued for high-ranking government officials with specific tasks who satisfy certain criteria.

On this very issue, Mochtar telephoned me to ask if I could speak with his Director General of Protocols and Consular Affairs, Joop Ave, because the Foreign Ministry had been having difficulties with a number of DPR members who apparently demanded to be issued with diplomatic passports. As it happened, I knew of instances of abuse of the diplomatic passport outside the DPR, including by those in the private sector. I told Mochtar that the Director General was welcome to contact me anytime.

Soon after, Joop Ave got in touch with me and related how a number of DPR members were about to make overseas trips and had demanded diplomatic passports. He said that the Foreign Ministry could not comply with their requests because, owing to the prevalent rules, the diplomatic passport could only be issued for the Speaker of the DPR if he or she is on state duty. The ministry, however, would be happy to issue service passports instead.

I replied that the government had two options. One, to stick to the prevalent rules about the diplomatic passport; or, two, to come up with new looser rules to accommodate requests for diplomatic passports by government officials. Joop Ave said the government had no intention of making new rules in this respect, and asked me to speak to the DPR members that had applied for diplomatic passports and request them to desist.

In response I also asked the Director General, as the enforcer of the rules, to set a good example by rectifying the misuse and abuse of the diplomatic passport by those connected with officials at the Ministry of Foreign Affairs. When I mentioned a few names, Joop Ave was taken aback and promised to address the matter swiftly and to in the future ensure that only those meeting the criteria would be entitled to the diplomatic passport. After we concluded our conversation, Mochtar was back on the line and I told him what had transpired between Joop Ave and me. He seemed to be in agreement with what I had said.

For my part, I also invited the said DPR members to come and see me. As it turned out, they were quite ignorant of the rules on the diplomatic passport. However, they said they had seen people outside government show off their diplomatic passports. I explained to them about the misuse and asked them to report any such instances in the future.

Meeting Benny Moerdani

For readers who did not live through the New Order era, the name Benny Moerdani may sound unfamiliar. He was an important figure during much of Soeharto's presidency. Although he later receded into semi-retirement before Soeharto's fall from power, he remained a figure of great influence. Many have written about his relationship with Soeharto.

Benny Moerdani's life story has been told through a number of books, such as those written by Julius Pour and Salim Said. The latest book on the subject is a biography entitled *Keputusan Sulit Adnan Ganto* (Adnan Ganto's Difficult Decision). Adnan Ganto was an Acehnese who featured in Soeharto's relationship with Benny Moerdani. Adnan knew much about the dynamics between the two. I was acquainted with Adnan, though our introduction took place after I really became a politician, not during my early engagement with the New Order.

Around mid-1980, I received an invitation to accompany a delegation from Jakarta's Centre for Strategic and International Studies (CSIS) to visit South Korea, where Chun Doo-hwan had just been elected President.

Juwono Soedarsono.

"Pak Benny wanted to meet you", Jusuf Wanandi said. Someone else outside CSIS joined us on the trip—my own cousin Juwono Soedarsono. In the evening, after we arrived in South Korea, we gathered for dinner. Everyone who was somebody at CSIS was there, such as Professor Daoed Joesoef, General Ali Moertopo, Harry Tjan Silalahi, Jusuf Wanandi and Hadi Soesastro. Benny Moerdani sat between Juwono Soedarsono and me.

I could not just pass up the prospect of getting to know Benny Moerdani, who was both charismatic and controversial, not to mention his capability in managing a number of things, not just intelligence-gathering.

"So, you are Sarwono", said Benny Moerdani by way of introduction. He had obviously met Juwono earlier. We then got to talking about general things, but nothing in particular. The following day we all made for the Presidential Palace, where we only spoke in broad strokes with President Chun Doo-hwan about several bilateral issues, especially economic cooperation. We left South Korea the next day.

Election 1982

Time flew by whilst we were busy. Before we knew it, it was time to prepare for the 1982 General Election. Golkar's Governing Board started to draw up a list of suggested candidates from the regional chapters for consultation. I discovered that I had not been nominated by the West Java Golkar Provincial Board. The Angsana incident of 1978 and my role in it had obviously left their mark. The West Java political elite felt they had been humiliated by the stringent punitive actions by Kopkamtib against officials of the Pandeglang regency who had been found guilty of corruption and collusion. In their eyes, I was partly responsible for their shame.

I decided not to react to what had happened. I thought to myself that politics was indeed a path full of uncertainties. Even steering a Middle Course did not preclude any risks. I did not feel threatened economically either since I had my own house built on the plot of land I had purchased in 1976 in the Kalibata area with another loan I had secured from Mochtar.

As I made clear previously, Mochtar was in the habit of making a written agreement about any loan, even with me, his own brother. It came naturally to him as a man of law. However, in practice, he was very lenient. With the second loan he gave me, I was able to have my house built gradually, albeit in a thrifty manner, because most of the material used in its construction had been cannibalized from the houses demolished by PT ATRIA, where I was the Technical

Director. Because much of the house was built from re-assembled bits and pieces from different houses, it looked slightly odd in places. But because of that the house looked unique and aesthetically pleasing. With the housing question already sorted out, I was not overly worried about not being an MP. There were other career choices.

Just as Golkar was about to finalize its list of legislative candidates, I unexpectedly received a telephone call from the Secretariat of the Central Governing Board who informed me that my papers as a candidate representing Jakarta were to be delivered to my house. I subsequently filled in all the required forms, signed them and returned them to the DPP Golkar. When the verified list of candidates was announced by the Electoral Commission (KPU), I went to the office of the regional board of Golkar Jakarta. At the time, the chairman of Golkar Jakarta's DPD was Achmadi. I had met him before when he was Director General of Village Development in the Ministry of Home Affairs.

My name was really on the list of candidates. I had no idea how I had come to be a candidate for Jakarta. By pure coincidence, I then heard that a Kosgoro figure, Mas Edardono—commonly known by his nickname Mas Bendol—had said that he was willing to forgo his own candidacy if I were to replace him. In preparing for the campaign period, I ran into Mas Bendol and asked him if he had helped me become a candidate and I thanked him for it. He merely smiled broadly and hugged me. But he never answered my question.

My colleagues at DPD Golkar Jakarta and I immediately set to work on a campaign to win the 1982 election. The approach to the campaign was to work our way up from the smallest locality, something that Pak Achmadi liked to emphasize for our benefit. He likened the campaign to a *tumpeng* (a rice dish shaped conically like a mountain that Indonesians use in celebrations).

"We make a small *tumpeng* at the village level—a residents' get-together perhaps—and then on to a bigger *tumpeng* at the district level, and ultimately the biggest *tumpeng* will be at the provincial level, just before the quiet week", Pak Achmadi explained.

All present at the meeting agreed to the plan. A bonus to the plan was, according to Pak Achmadi, that the people we would be campaigning with this time around would be familiar to us in the next election. By knowing the voters, we would be able to prioritize which areas could be mobilized based our experience with the respective areas in the previous election.

In the next phase, we mapped out our constituents with predictions where our strongholds and weak points would be. We also made a list of speakers for campaign events and local issues to be featured in our campaign. All the work on campaign preparation was carried out enthusiastically, with the view to reaping the most votes in Jakarta for Golkar, which had not happened in the previous two elections. I had a vested interest that Golkar should come in as number one because of my own unsafe threshold on the list. The only way I could hope to enter parliament again was if Golkar performed better. Naturally, I did not publicise this fact.

Bared Teeth at the 1982 Campaign

The pre-campaign period in 1982 was no different from that of the previous election. "The political temperature is on the rise" was the oft-said prognosis. In anticipating the worst-case scenarios, the security forces had taken steps to keep the rising temperature under control. In early March, in the first round of the campaign by the United Development Party (PPP) at Banteng Square, a fantastic crowd numbering 150,000 attended. They were in high spirits to the point of being agitated, and according to the observation of our teams, the Iranian Revolution and Ayatollah Khoemeini were mentioned by speakers at the rally. These speakers condemned Golkar and likened its members to several kinds of animal that are neither adorable nor usually found in the company of people.

We at Golkar immediately carried out our own evaluation of what had happened and how to respond to it. Based on reports from the field by our local chapters, an atmosphere of belligerence towards us was palpable even before the PPP rally. We discussed what steps we should take in response. Pak Achmadi believed we should not allow our political rivals to easily bait us and we should proceed with our campaign as previously planned. A review team was also formed to formulate measures necessary to counter the unusually high tensions we were witnessing.

The Iranian Revolution

Since the Iranian Revolution had become a hot topic in the PPP campaign, it was probably necessary for us to revisit the event. Before the Ayatollah returned to Iran from his exile to head the Islamic Republic of Iran, the country was a monarchy under Shah Reza Pahlevi, commonly referred to as the Shah of Iran. Reza Pahlevi had declared himself emperor. He was obviously a megalomaniac because he claimed that his empire was the successor to the great ancient Persian Empire.

The Shah came to power with the help of the United States and Britain, which had vested interests in monopolizing Iran's oil. After a power struggle, Iran became an absolute monarchy. Iran under the Shah purchased the most modern weapon systems of the day, and its navy became the world's third largest after the United States and the Soviet Union.

The Shah's delusion of grandeur was showcased through extravagance to convey the image of the mythical glories of the ancient Persian Empire. He was also a repressive ruler, with his secret police, the Sazeman-I Ettelaat va Amniyat-I Keshvar (SAVAK), acting as his attack dogs. The ruling elite also adopted the Western lifestyle in the extreme, to the extent they started to behave very strangely. They were both feudal and oppressive, but they clothed themselves in the modern fashion and were inimical to religion. Scholars and the ulema were arrested and tortured, and many were murdered.

Ayatollah Khomeini, who lived in exile in France, did not merely become the symbol of resistance against this repressive regime but he also effectively directed the movement from afar. Resistance to the Shah gradually increased, starting with the Bazaari movement, initiated by business owners in urban shopping districts. The supporters of the regime in the end were split, and there was upheaval in the Iranian Army, which led to the armed resistance by the militia known as the Revolutionary Guard.

The rule of the Shah collapsed suddenly like a tower of cards in the wind. The Shah, his family and his closest aides fled abroad. The Ayatollah returned home from Paris in February 1979 and became Iran's new leader in an event known as the Islamic Revolution, or the Iranian Revolution. Subsequently, the Ayatollah and the mullahs, who had formed their own hierarchy, set up a government and rooted out the remnants of the Shah's power structure. Hence, from Iran came the call to export the Iranian revolution.

Major Disruption to Golkar's Campaign

Against such a geopolitical background, Golkar was gearing up for its turn to campaign. Our meeting was not held at the Golkar headquarters in Pegangsaan Barat since the Jakarta Governor Tjokropranolo invited us to meet at his residence. I went as part of the DPD Golkar team. When we arrived, Ali Moertopo was already there. He was to be our chief campaign speaker.

Ali Moertopo wanted to outdo the PPP's recent campaign. The impression we had was that he wanted our first round of the campaign to be a merrier event that drew larger crowds than the PPP had achieved. Achmadi, however, still wanted to put into action our original plan of starting small, with the largest event to close off. So he argued his corner, quite convincingly, I thought.

It was at this point that Pak Ali Moertopo became emotional, and he then told Tjokropranolo to take over the planning of the campaign. He then left the room. Tjokropranolo proceeded to instruct his under-lings to mobilize as many people as they could for the event. Achmadi interjected to say that it was risky to do so, but was then reminded that he was no longer in charge of organizing the campaign. I was dumbstruck that a senior government official like the governor would make up his mind without considering all the factors involved. What they wanted was a way, within two days' time, to muster a greater crowd to top their competitor.

Achmadi duly went home and concluded that since the first round of the campaign had been taken out of our hands, the DPD Golkar Jakarta did not need to take part in organizing the event. I concurred with him that we should just sit it out. The other functionaries did the same.

On the day of the event, 18 March 1982, I was at the DPD Golkar office, which was almost deserted at the time, to formulate the next phase of the campaign while talking to a few colleagues by telephone.

At around 2:30 p.m. a police unit arrived. Its commanding officer informed me that they had been instructed to secure the DPD Golkar office, other government buildings and public facilities. The officer kept checking with his headquarters to monitor the situation and to be prepared for any eventuality.

Gradually the office was filled with Golkar activists, all of whom looked anxious. We then talked about what had happened at the Banteng Square. Achmadi soon turned up and the gathering became a meeting. What had transpired, according to our best sources at the time, was that our stage at the rally had been vandalized. The action started as soon as the main campaign speaker, Ali Moertopo, took to the stage to speak to the crowds. The stage collapsed and was set on fire. The perpetrators of this had been standing around the stage wearing the jackets and berets of AMPI, but had been the last to arrive. The genuine AMPI members standing guard around the stage thought that the ones that arrived late were reinforcements.

The perpetrators then took off their AMPI jackets to reveal they were wearing PPP T-shirts. They proceeded to shout out the Takbīr and then attacked any vehicles nearby. There were government cars and buses in the area, used to transport rally goers. These were vandalized and set on fire. In the ensuing chaos, Ali Moertopo was taken to Hotel Borobudur. The situation deteriorated quickly. Vandalism and looting spread like wildfire.

Prior to the incident, crowds had been filling up the square slowly. Celebrity entertainers like Elvy Sukaesih had been unable to calm the masses, and when Ali Moertopo turned up at 2 p.m., they were restless, tired and thirsty.

Just after Ali Moertopo walked on the stage amid yells of campaign slogans, the fake AMPI members simultaneously took out their saws and bottles of petrol from under their jackets. They used them to bring down the stage and to set it alight. It was chaos all around in no time.

Golkar's Political Machine Paralysed

At that moment, I wanted to find out more about what had happened from the Golkar leadership. It was evident that unknown actors had masterminded the incident—to what end, we did not know. I then remembered that the closest Golkar headquarters was the Board of Patrons' Office at 29 Jalan Teuku Umar, Menteng, Central Jakarta. I decided to go there on foot because it was close-by and I thought it was safer to walk, especially in the midst of a riot. As I walked, I could not help feeling tense and circumspect.

As I entered the office courtyard, I saw a number of sedans parked neatly by the side of the road. It was quiet. A watchman told me that a few members of the Board of Patrons were assembled in the office of the Executive Chairman. I let myself into the office without knocking first, something I did not think of as being wrong at the time. In Golkar's hierarchy, the Secretary of the FKP was second echelon, while those gathered in the office were members of the Board of Patrons, an institution whose position was strategic and influential. Looking back, I should perhaps have knocked at the door first and requested their permission to enter.

Inside the room were Sapardjo, who was previously Secretary General of Golkar's Governing Board and who was known to me, and Colonel Harisugiman, a staff member of Pangkopkamtib who later became Director General of Social and Political Affairs at the Ministry of Home Affairs. There was also a number of others that I did not know. They were all seated in silence. I then asked why they were not doing something in a situation like this.

"We are all waiting for information. Something is happening inside the government", Sapardjo replied.

I said that while that might be true, what was happening was rioting and vandalism. I then asked to speak to Pangkopkamtib. It was probably the first time I tried to get in touch with the Admiral. "Mas Hari, please put me through to Pak Soedomo. I would like to talk to him", I said firmly to Harisugiman.

"Yes, Pak Sarwono. Right away!" replied the Colonel.

Within moments, I was speaking to Pangkopkamtib Soedomo. We both discussed what had happened at the Banteng Square. Pak Domo only gave me a general idea of what had happened. He claimed that the security forces were trying to get things under control. He added that he was still gathering information on who was behind the incident.

My observation informed me that the public was waiting for an official account of what happened. There were confusing accounts of what truly happened at the Banteng Square. "But the public needs to hear from Kopkamtib about the Banteng Square incident. We need to show them that we have taken firm action to restore law and order. Whoever was behind it, what happened afterwards was rioting and vandalism", I reasoned with him.

Then Pak Sudomo said, "Please give me some material to work with through Colonel Harisugiman."

I immediately passed the handset to Colonel Harisugiman, who then listened to Pak Sudomo's order. Harisugiman nodded his head several times and accepted his orders. "Yes, sir!" he said several times. Next, the colonel asked me to convey a statement point by point, which he jotted down on a piece of paper. He then made a telephone call in which he related my message point by point to Kopkamtib. There was no reaction whatsoever to what was going on from the assembled company, who were clearly happy in their silence.

As I made my way out of the Golkar office, I touched the hoods of the cars parked outside and they all felt cold. So it was true that they intended to stay put and wait for further news. It was fair to assume they never turned up at the Banteng Square.

Restoring Communication

I got back to the DPD Golkar office on foot and was informed that rioting was still taking place. Golkar's campaign banners had been taken down and burned by youngsters wearing PPP T-shirts. While rampaging, they were shouting religious slogans. At that point in time it was as if Golkar had vanished.

In the evening, I was busy communicating with members of Golkar's leadership, such as Pak Sugiharto, Head of the FKP as well as Deputy Chairman of DPP Golkar. The other members of the DPP were, as it happened, out of town, having gone to the provinces to campaign. Sugiharto told me that he had spoken to the leaders of both PPP and PDI and there was a consensus that they would together condemn the vandalism against Golkar's rally.

The next morning, a few colleagues and I went to the DPP Golkar office in Slipi, West Jakarta. The city had the air of being deserted. Military and police personnel stood guard conspicuously at the office.

They were on high alert. I went into the Secretary General's office and tried to reach other colleagues.

I managed to get in touch with a few, such as Iman Taufik, Arifin Panigoro, Rohali Sani, Jakob Tobing, Ida Ayu Utami Pidada and Marzuki Darusman. We all agreed to meet up at the Athletes' Housing Estate of the Senayan Stadium, at the office of PT Heintorisa, a company that belonged to Jakob Tobing, the Deputy Head of FKP for Industry and Development.

Throughout the day, while talking to different people, I kept thinking about what action we could take. It felt at the time it was not going to be easy to find a way out. Then I thought of a piece of advice once given to me by Pak Soekardi, the Deputy Chairman of the DPP Golkar as well as the Deputy Head of the FKP. He said this long before the Banteng Square incident. In facing a thesis, he said, we did not need to come up with an antithesis. What we needed to do was to take a leap by developing synthesis. When interpreted in the context of dealing with the consequences of the Banteng Square incident, it meant Golkar needed to come up with both a stance as well as action. The formula for these needed to be outside the framework of conflict, which seemed to be the intent of the masterminds behind the riots, whose identities still remained shrouded at this point.

Soaring with the Red and White Action

The night-time meeting at Senayan took place in an atmosphere of warm emotions. We exchanged ideas as to what needed to be done. The synthesis according to Pak Soekardi's way of thinking was eventually found. It would have been unwise for us to react to what happened in a confrontational manner. There was no need to formulate an antithesis, but we needed to come up with something unexpected. We then agreed to respond with a Red and White Action; that is, by flooding Jakarta with the national flag.

We lost no time in planning for it by working out the logistics, and all present pledged some money to fund the operation, among other things, by having Red and White stickers printed in different sizes. Ida Ayu Utami Pidada was tasked with fundraising. According to our estimate, we needed 15 million rupiah, to which everyone was committed. We raised the cash in three days.

I saw Pak Achmadi the following day and related to him the plan from the meeting at Senayan. He was very supportive and enthusiastic about what we were going to do. Our district-level meeting would also follow suit in its Red and White theme as part of Golkar's second-round campaign. At the meeting we would not put up or use the Golkar emblem. It would become a forum in which voters could talk to us heart to heart under the Red and White. Pak Achmadi's original plan for a campaign agenda that started small like a *tumpeng* from the district level and up was finally in the making, though not in the format he had envisioned. We were busy ordering bamboo poles and the national flag to be widely distributed everywhere. Red and White stickers were also ordered in various sizes.

Just as our second round of the campaign was about to kick off, Bambang Warih Kusuma (BWK) turned up. He was my old friend at ITB who had got himself elected to the Student Consultative Council through an innovative campaign. His personal appeal was considerable; he was friendly, good-looking and he had a way with words, so much so that his friends called him ITB's own JFK.

He came bearing a stack of 15×9 cm Red and White stickers that he said he happened to have. We decided to use his stickers for the campaign, handing them out to motorists around Senayan as they were leaving town for home. Sudarko Prawirojudo, who had just come back from his campaign in Merauke, had also prepared several banners that we might put up if the situation allowed while monitoring the sticker hand-outs. Our plan was to hand them out without saying a word, though we would behave friendlily. We informed the press of our plan.

The Red and White Action was a tremendous success. Motorists accepted our stickers with absolute delight. While the event was unfolding, some young people approached us and wanted to volunteer. One of them introduced himself to me and asked if he could help out, producing his student card from the University of Indonesia. There were three of them, and naturally BWK and I were only too happy to oblige.

The media reported the event and it was called by some newspapers as "Golkar's sympathetic action". We rejected this characterization because whether something was sympathetic or not could not be determined by those who carried it out. Our small action was conducted by just five people, but it was covered by both TVRI and the print media, and it had a considerable impact. In today's parlance, it went viral. Both the DPD and DPP Golkar offices were inundated with activists and ordinary citizens.

My colleagues and I—the *cleret gombel*, or flying lizard politicos, like Djoko Sudyatmiko, Rahmat Witoelar and Sudarko—had taken the initiative of putting together the Red and White Action without being told to do so by anyone. The activity was in fact characterized by the strength of our networking, which was based on mutual trust, leading to the participation of grass-roots Golkar sympathizers. The action happened because of the common perception among us, and not as a result of hierarchical authority.

"Occupy" DPP Golkar

Inadvertently, the DPP Golkar headquarters was transformed overnight into the headquarters for the Red and White Action. My colleagues from the FKP and I utilized the space there without permission or a mandate. Our presence was de facto. We made Pak Sugiharto a kind of patron to legitimize our "occupation" of the Golkar office.

We then discovered that Pak Sugiharto refused to be an idle patron and he used his own network to further the action. Almost by default, liaison between DPP and DPD for the action was carried out by Heru Suparto and Yudha Irlang—without an official mandate, of course. Later on, another action centre was set up at the DPP AMPI office in Jalan Pejambon. AMPI was recovering from being tarnished in the Banteng Square incident and was doing its best at consolidation. In the lead-up to the final round of the campaign, AMPI members in full uniform conducted parades in riskier areas and handed out Red and White stickers.

The volunteers that showed up at the Golkar office in Slipi were truly the best representation of Golkar's extended family. Individuals from various grass-roots groups and Kosgoro, MKGR, SOKSI, Satkar Ulama, AMPI, Majelis Dakwah Islamiyah and other civil society groups were represented there. Members of the Mahajaya Regiment, or the student regiment, also volunteered. A contingent of thirty members of Baladhika Karya arrived and took the initiative to guard the office complex. We all gathered in the auditorium to discuss the next phase of action and to listen to reports from the field, which seemed to suggest that an interesting experiment was in order. From the discussion, most agreed that we would go around the city carrying Red and White stickers and Golkar banners using three pick-up trucks.

"But it's not our turn yet [to campaign]", one of the volunteers quipped.

"If an official questions you, just say you are on your way to headquarters", I said.

We then had a specific discussion to finalize the plan to have three pick-ups going around the city. My instructions to those who would be on the pick-ups were that they were to just make the round, with no shouting throughout. They were to act in a friendly and natural manner with anyone they encountered. They should avoid any conflict with others and refrain from songs likely to provoke a response.

In the afternoon, at around 3 p.m., our participants for the city-rounds came back on their open-top pick-ups, having finished their circuits. They were in a jubilant mood. They had received warm welcomes from the public, many of whom had greeted them with Golkar's two-finger gesture while shouting "Long live Golkar!" There had been no backlash, even from government officials.

In the meantime, our stickers, bamboo poles and the Red and White flags kept arriving at our headquarters. We started to plan for the next round. The basic outline was simple: our last round of the campaign, just before the pre-election silence, would take the form of a great parade, one that was usually referred to as an allegorical parade. It would still take the theme of Red and White, but with pronounced Golkar attributes. Whatever we did next was geared towards preparing for the parade, including our next campaign schedules in five different locations.

Outside the campaign round, the Red and White Action was concentrated on handing out stickers at major roads, offices and traditional markets. No Golkar emblems were to be displayed or uniforms worn during this. It was strictly a hit-and-run activity, with an emphasis on mobility and the range of coverage. Our goal was to give the impression that the Red and White Action was taking place everywhere, but we did not want the timings or locations to be predictable. We split the team into small groups that would plan their own actions.

The hit-and-run concept came from Bambang Warih Kusuma (BWK), who trained volunteers how to use the stickers and banners to achieve maximum effect with the minimum of personnel. One of the groups taking part in one such training session consisted of young women activists from diverse backgrounds who did not necessarily know each other. A small group of these women sitting in a corner were visibly smitten by BWK. They then started to flirt with him using coded signs, whispering and laughing among themselves. BWK was annoyed with them and asked them to stop interrupting the briefing. Other activists also thought they were out of line. An angry BWK, however, seemed even more attractive to these young women, and things soon became noisy and out of control.

Faced with pandemonium, I immediately called off the training session and tried to find out who these fans of BWK were. It turned out they hailed from a particularly old profession in which the service given was of a physical nature. Old as it was, this trade had never been officially recognized as a "functional group" in society by any of Golkar's guidelines. As such, they were not qualified to take part in our action. In terms of income, they were probably on par with most small or medium enterprises, though their preferred place of trade tended to be inconspicuous and quiet. In terms of locality, their habitat was centred around Taman Impian Jaya Ancol. We kept BWK out of sight and I asked the women to leave. With the distraction gone, the session resumed and was completed satisfactorily.

Free Buses

A brilliant idea based on the desire to be of service to the community was conceived by Uncu Natsir and Johnny Baginda, both of whom were activists of Generasi Muda Kosgoro (Kosgoro Youth). The idea occurred to them since many Jakartans at the time were having difficulties with public transport because of the vandalism and arson attacks on several public buses. Our two young friends from Kosgoro suggested we run two free bus routes: one linking Cawang, Kampung Melayu and the Banteng Square, and another running between Cawang, the

Pancoran roundabout, Slipi and Tomang. I asked them where they expected to get the money to rent the buses?

"We will come up with the money. Don't worry about it", Uncu Natsir assured me.

Thus, Golkar's free bus services came into existence. They were an immediate success. The standard etiquette was enacted: broad friendliness, and only bringing up Golkar if the situation was conducive—not to mention handing out Red and White stickers.

Arresting Sectarian Sentiments with a Covert Operation

With the Red and White Action in full swing, supporters of sectarianism became more vocal, especially at night, when they came out to put up huge posters about the Iranian Revolution at strategic places all around Jakarta. I heard from friends and colleagues who stayed in touch with the PPP leadership that the latter was dismayed at what was happening and they were doing their best to diffuse the tensions within their ranks.

Golkar had come up with its own initiatives to deal with the problem through the activists of Golkar-affiliated organizations such as Satkar Ulama, Majelis Dakwah Islamiyah and Al Hidayah, which was based at the DPD Golkar office in Jakarta. Our public Red and White Action was in need of complementary action that would be out of the box.

I brainstormed what alternative approach we could take with Mazuki Darusman. Like Bambang Warih Kusuma, Marzuki was good-looking and very refined in manners. But there was another side to him; he was a master at organizing covert operations, leaving no trace whatsoever. Very few people knew about this hidden talent of his.

Both of us discussed a strategy to get rid of the provocative posters and billboards. We agreed we could not report their existence to the Electoral Commission because they did not originate from any entity that was a participant in the election. If we waited for the police to act, there might have been complications. I left the matter in Marzuki's hands without going into too much detail because I knew he understood what I meant.

Two days later, I heard news that the posters and billboards in question had disappeared. It was reported to us that the clean-up act had been carried out by a group of well-built men clothed in black with their faces covered. They worked fast and neatly. People called them ninjas. Speculation was rife as to who had conducted the covert operation. Some boasted about having done the deed. Overall, it achieved what it set out to do, as incidences of provocative agitation became less frequent.

Red and White a Success, Golkar Gets Most Votes in Jakarta

Days ahead of its last round of the campaign, Golkar had rows and rows of its flag planted along major thoroughfares, such as Tomang-Cawang and Sudirman-Thamrin, with Semanggi as a focal point. The current tradition of planting organizational flags originated with Golkar's 1982 campaign.

The distribution of Red and White stickers continued. Small stickers were meant for office workers, both in government and the private sector, with a suggestion that people should put them on their car windshields. Larger stickers were handed out on public transport and at terminals and markets.

Two days before our last round in Jakarta, the roads were full of cars with Red and White stickers. I never found out who started it, but several drivers sounded their horns twice and others followed suit. They also wound down their windows to share the two-finger greeting. Preparations for our allegorical parade were being carried out day and night, with attention to detail being the priority. Participating floats were recorded and given their respective numbers. A beautiful surprise presented itself when colossal paintings worked around the theme of development by Samsul Hadi, an artist from Yogyakarta, arrived. At the suggestion of Sugiharto and Moerdopo, the paintings were installed above the trucks used for the parade, all of which were parked at the East Senayan Lot according to their respective numbers.

On the morning of our last round of the campaign, the Red and White allegorical parade was all ready to go. At the head of our convoy was a jeep driven by a member of the Mahajaya Regiment, with five youngsters standing alert, all of whom were in white, wearing *peci* on their heads, and holding poles bearing the national flag.

Behind this jeep was another one with AMPI members holding Golkar flags. In their wake were the numerically arranged trucks carrying mostly young people in various costumes of red and white, including headbands, sashes and flags. Golkar's identity was visible, though not overwhelmingly dominant.

The orderliness of the parade did not last long, as independent floats came to join us, and many of them ended up going different routes to ours. Still, the parade was a joyful occasion, and visually it created a sea of red and white. In effect, it was a sort of productive disorderliness. In the afternoon, the parade came to an end in an orderly fashion.

After PDI's last round, we all entered the election silence week, which we spent by cleaning up our campaign props. Accordingly, the DPP Golkar headquarters reverted to its original state, as a sign of the cessation of our "occupation". We used the week off the campaign trail to visit and thank those at the grass roots who had helped us during the campaign, and this was the first time I became truly acquainted with them.

When the results of the 1982 elections were announced, Golkar managed to come first in Jakarta, with 45 per cent share of the vote— up 6 per cent from the result of the 1977 election. I became an MP representing Jakarta.

Back to Normal

I then asked for Pak Sugiharto's permission to go on holiday with my family. Nini, my children I went to the United States for ten days, visiting Los Angeles, Nevada, the Yosemite National Park and San Francisco.

Our holiday in the United States meant a lot to us as a family, considering I had mostly been busy in politics, with all its tensions, while Nini worked as a lowly civil servant. So the family needed a bit of consolidation as well. Our family consolidation was achieved during the trip, with Nini becoming pregnant. In February 1983, our fourth child was born, a girl whom we called Kendisan, better known to us as Keke.

Another act of consolidation was for Mimi to relocate to Jakarta, the process of which was arranged by Mochtar. The Bandung house was turned into both an office for the Wawasan Nusantara Foundation and a guesthouse for our relatives.

Mas Isman Passes Away

At the end of 1982, I heard that Mas Isman, founder and Executive Chairman of Kosgoro, had passed away. He had previously had problems with his heart, but his will to live was very strong. He was hospitalized for a while, but then he pulled out all the tubes they had put into him and left for home. After this, he became active again at the meetings in Jalan Cik Di Tiro. Not long after, though, his heart began to give him trouble again, and he was flown to the United States for treatment, where he succumbed to his struggle and passed away.

As I have mentioned, Mas Iman was an interesting individual, open-minded and egalitarian. We often kept him company as he lay in his bed and held discussions. People who came to see him in the house—later christened as Wisma Mas Isman—came from diverse backgrounds, professions, political persuasions and age.

I was then reminded of the 10th November Study Group from my university days in Bandung. I suggested that PPK Kosgoro set up the Kosgoro National Discussion Group as a forum in which priority issues could be dissected. I shared my thoughts on how important it was to nurture the organization in a more methodical way. The vision of Kosgoro needed to be disseminated systematically, with a focus on three spheres: education, grass-roots economics and the cultivation of political potential. A communication channel was then formed under the name the Face-to-face Forum (Forta).

My opinion was that future organizational development could not be expected to happen organically, because the next generations of Kosgoro would be pluralistic with various backgrounds and roots, unlike the founding generation, most of whom shared the experience of being in the Indonesian Student Soldiers Regiment (TRIP).

Subsequently, I was appointed Chairman of the Kosgoro National Discussion Group (GDN), while Mas Isman was still around. In its development, GDN became a forum for orderly and thematic brain-storming. Topics that were discussed in GDN were then submitted to Forta to be further developed. Forta eventually had its own regional branches. The systematic fashion in which issues were discussed and developed within GDN and Forta was a departure from the discussion groups of the previous generation. Although they were very invigorating, the issues discussed back then rarely made their way out of the groups.

Benny Moerdani's Surprise

In early 1983, ahead of the MPR General Assembly, CSIS invited several Golkar activists to attend a meeting with Lieutenant General Benny Moerdani, the Intelligence Assistant of the ABRI Commander. When we entered the meeting room, we saw that senior Golkar figures of the likes of Ir Haditirto and Moerdopo were in attendance.

Benny Moerdani elaborated on the projection of the ABRI-Golkar relationship for the future. He pointed out that, in the long term, ABRI could not be expected to be Golkar's lifeline, because the military needed to focus on its main function of the defence of the country.

"If you in Golkar expect to rely on the military indefinitely, you will not get the best people from us. Those in ABRI who don't get postings in our main function in defence get categorized as personnel with specific interests, including politics. Golkar can't rely on the civil service indefinitely either because eventually civil servants will have to prioritize their main job, which is to administer government policies."

"So Golkar must undergo extensive transformation into a civilian political force. The key here lies in the post of Secretary General", he continued. "And we have just the right man to do it. There's Sarwono who is sitting in the corner over there", Benny Moerdani said, pointing a finger at me. "As for the post of the Executive Chairman, we will leave it to the Chairman of the Board of Patrons [President Soeharto]." I could not help reacting through a bit of banter, which elicited laughter from those present at the meeting.

"You seem to have the habit of speaking in an unguarded manner, just like Mochtar", Benny Moerdani said somewhat accusingly. There was no trace of humour in his voice or on his face.

Then one of those present asked a question, "Is this the institutional view or your personal view, Pak Benny?"

"I'm the Intelligence Assistant to the ABRI Commander. I don't need to answer your question", Pak Benny replied. Then he asked, "Any other suggestion for the post of Secretary General?" The room was still. No one made an answer. And then he concluded the meeting.

From that moment onwards, the characterization that "Sarwono is Benny's man" stuck. The candidacy of Pak Sudharmono at this point had not surfaced.

MPR General Assembly, 1983

The MPR General Assembly of 1983 went ahead as planned. In my opinion—shared by many of my colleagues—the session produced a most strategic product in the MRP Act No. IV/1983 on Referendum, which regulated the prerequisites for amending the 1945 Constitution. Any motion to amend the Constitution would need to be done in consultation with the people through a referendum, the conditions for which alone were hard to meet.

With the new mechanism in place, the government had less need to rely on the military to guard against political tinkering with the Constitution. Both ABRI and the civil service could also expect greater professionalism since they would not be burdened with functions beyond their job descriptions. The people would decide whether the 1945 Constitution needed to be changed or not, should the occasion arise. Judging by the state of things in society at the time—although political upheavals did occur from time to time—there were signs of a growing understanding among the people of how constitutional law worked for Indonesia, partly because of the success of the P4 programme by BP7.

While the Referendum Act was important strategically, it was barely noticed by the majority. It was probably too strategic to be a daily topic of conversation by the public, whose concerns tended to be about practical things. So the Referendum Act became a dormant legal product.

During the MPR session, I was a member of the MPR Task Force as well as Fractional Secretary on behalf of Golkar. It was all plain sailing, as far as I was concerned.

Golkar's National Congress, 1983

Another major political event that year was Golkar's National Congress. In the lead-up to the event, Pak Sudharmono—who had just been reappointed as Minister of the State Secretariat—was discussed as a contender for the post of Executive Chairman. There was no resistance towards Pak Sudharmono, except for the question of whether he would be suited to the job, given that he was known to be "a man of the Palace" whose existence inevitably was far removed from the average Indonesian. Very few knew that Pak Sudharmono was one of the founders of Sekber Golkar in 1964, as he was then the representative of the Indonesian Advocates' Association (Persahi).

There were also those who questioned my suitability as Secretary General. Interestingly, TVRI presenter, Tuti Adhitama, played a recording for me while we were lunching at the Hilton Executive Club, on the sidelines of the Congress. The recording was of one of the officials at the State Secretariat commenting on my candidacy. The commentator predicted that I would be unsuitable as Secretary General for Pak Sudharmono, who was, he said, a meticulous worker, a neat deliverer and polished in his manners.

"Sarwono is unruly, often speaks out of turn and likes to offend people", he surmised. I could understand the official's view of me because I probably would not meet most people's standards or expectations of what a politician should be like. Tuti did not reveal the identity of the official, and I could not guess who it was either. But his view impressed me in a profound way. I then thought that if I did indeed become Secretary General, it stood to reason that I should try to adapt and mend my ways to suit the Executive Chairman who would be my superior. But did that mean I had to act out of character? This became something for me to ponder upon.

My candidacy for Secretary General became a topic for congress participants, in the sense I was labelled as "Benny's man". There were also other candidates beside myself, both ABRI and civilian.

The congress was held in October 1983 and was officially opened by President Soeharto. The President's speech was in line with what Benny Moerdani had told us—that Golkar needed to be more independent, mature and deeply rooted in society. The President also stressed the importance for Golkar to foster democracy internally and externally through consolidation in ideology, scope of thought and organization.

I was on the Steering Committee for the Congress, tackling things that had become my "brand" in policy harmonization. I paid no attention to the rumour mill that had been directed towards me, since I did not feel I had it in me to control what post anyone could occupy, which was often up to other people.

Sudharmono Leads Golkar

Pak Sudharmono was gaining momentum fast as a chairman-to-be, and we were told he planned to make his appearance at the congress. The assistant to the Minister of the State Secretariat in Inter-departmental Relations, Sukarton Marmosudjono, was already on the premises busy preparing for the arrival of his boss. Naturally, his appearance drew a lot of attention from those present, but Pak Dhar was calm and friendly. Colleagues on the Committee for the Congress who had worked with me on the Red and White Action suggested that I introduce myself to him. I turned down their suggestion, saying, "If I do become Secretary General, I'll get to meet him often. If not, what's the point of introducing myself to him now?"

I then ran into Siswono Yudo Husodo, my old friend who started at the School of Civil Engineering at ITB in 1961. To the best of my knowledge, Siswono had been a supporter of PDI, but at Golkar's congress here he was in charge of accommodation and transport for the participants. He did his rounds and introduced himself to people at the congress and he seemed to have done a great job. I was pleased to see him, since Siswono had a reputation of being an entrepreneur who successfully built his business from scratch to become the established property giant, Bangun Cipta Sarana.

Towards the conclusion of the congress, the Chairman of the Selection Team announced the new lineup for DPP Golkar for the period 1983–88. Pak Sudharmono, better known as Pak Dhar, was Executive Chairman. My name was mentioned for the post of Secretary General. Senior Golkar figures that had played a major role in developing the organization such as Moerdopo, David Napitupulu and Jusuf Wanandi no longer occupied key positions. At the General Secretariat, Akbar

Tandjung, Oka Mahendra, Soedarmadji and David Napitupulu became my deputies. Regeneration had taken place in the formation of DPP Golkar. When the new DPP functionaries were introduced to those present, everyone looked dapper in their long-sleeved batik shirts. The only one to appear in a short-sleeved shirt was I. After the congress was officially declared closed, Pak Dhar called Akbar and me to give us instructions for a plenary session in three days' time.

Another Surprise from Benny Moerdani

Naturally, as "Benny's man", I took the first opportunity to seek a meeting with the general, who agreed to see me in the office of the ABRI Commander in West Merdeka. I will never forget the conversation I had with him. I started by thanking him for his support and efforts in making me Secretary General, a position that in the past had always been held by a high-ranking army officer. "But we never got to discuss in detail what I should do in that capacity. Please give me some guidelines", I said.

"If that's what you want, why don't you ask Pak Harto [President Soeharto], who told me to make you Secretary General of Golkar?" he replied. I was taken aback to hear this.

"Well, it was you, Pak Benny, who mentioned my name as a candidate for the job when we met early in the year at CSIS", I reminded him.

"At the said meeting, I only interpreted for everyone Pak Harto's thinking for Golkar's future, including the part where you become Secretary General", he responded. "Personally, I don't care one way or another", he continued. "I'm a soldier and my superior's view becomes my own and whatever he says, I do."

Because the news was still a surprise for me, I asked him another question, "Would you tell me more, as to how it all started, Pak Benny?"

"Well, it started in December 1979 when I was asked by the President to conduct intelligence observations on several people, you included. From our conversation, I knew the type, format and content of the report required. So I got my men to work at once", Pak Benny explained. "Did you feel you were being watched and followed?" he asked.

"No, I didn't", I replied truthfully because I had no idea whatsoever that I was being watched.

"That's why I asked to be introduced to you and why we met each other in South Korea in 1980", he added.

"Then when Pak Yusuf was Minister of Defence and Security in the last cabinet, he seemed to give me special attention. Why was that?" I asked.

"As the Intelligence Assistant to the Commander, I had the duty to report the findings of my operations, including the one on you. It's possible Pak Yusuf asked Pak Harto about it. I don't know and I don't want to know because it's none of my business."

Then Pak Benny related that at the beginning of 1983 he was ordered to bring along the reports on me and the others to the President. Three days later he was summoned again. Pak Harto said, "Based on your report, please make an effort to make Sarwono Secretary General of Golkar; Akbar Tandjung as deputy. The other posts are open to anyone."

"It was a surprise to me", Pak Benny continued, "because the post was usually reserved for the military. And now a young civilian whom I had just met was to be Secretary General. Then Pak Harto explained to me his way of thinking, which was what I related at CSIS the other day."

I was truly stunned, and perhaps Pak Benny could see it reflected on my face. But I still wanted to ask him another question, without expecting him to answer. "Pak Benny, does anyone else know about this?"

"Moerdiono does. Pak Dhar has no idea whatsoever", he replied. "So it's simple. Please ask Pak Harto what he wants from you and carry it out as best as possible. I am a soldier. Politics isn't my thing. But if you want my personal view, it's this: this nation, including Golkar, isn't ready for democracy. So I can only hope that you will succeed. Good luck and all the best."

Afterwards, we talked about other things, and it turned out both of us liked to read books. We also liked to read the same type of books. Pak Benny was fluent in English, and a great part of our conversation took place in English.

I went to the DPP Golkar office that afternoon with a sense of respect and admiration for Pak Benny. He could have refrained from telling me about my being tailed by his men. He could have let me think I was his "man". But he chose to tell the truth. What was odd was that during our exchange I was the one who had asked the questions—a rather inverse situation for a master of intelligence.

Days later, when I saw Moerdiono, I asked him about the things Benny Moerdani had told me. He said that I had been told the truth; Pak Harto had paid special attention to me. Moerdiono recounted to me what President Soeharto had told him: "Sarwono is a cadre. He understands strategy. He thinks like a soldier. And he is good at crisis management".

4

True to the Middle Course

First Step

Once, as I was working on something connected with the technical side of administrative affairs, I fell into a reverie of thoughts, tracing my own journey in politics. At this point in my life, as the Secretary General of DPP Golkar, I was responsible for many things, including important state matters that only a few were privy to.

I reflected that my journey in politics had been a long one. What had started out as a part-time activity was now a full-time career, with me finally within the main circle of the elite in the country. If anyone asked me how I had got this far, I would not find it easy to come up with an answer.

To deal with the day-to-day business at the secretariat, Pak Dhar immediately appointed Sudarsono, an echelon II civil servant at the State Secretariat. In his capacity as the Head of the DPP Golkar Secretariat, Sudarsono and the staff he brought from his previous post managed to integrate themselves well with the existing staff, and both teams were able to work in tandem with each other.

Later on I discovered that Sudarsono had done his post-graduate studies at L'Institut International d'Administration Publique, a prestigious educational institution in France. Sudarsono was a consummate admin-istrator and was excellent at communicating with others. He always came on top as well in various training workshops held by the state administration agency.

When I became State Minister for the Environment in 1993, I appointed him Secretary of the Ministry of the Environment. Pak Dhar, who was then former Vice-President, was surprised by my choice of Sudarsono. There was another side of Sudarsono that Pak Dhar had not had an opportunity to see, which was his intellectual capability. Apparently, while he was at the State Secretariat, Sudarsono managed to hide his superior intelligence from everyone else.

Soeharto's Man

My political journey for the last two decades had led me to rub shoulders with Indonesia's top politicians. If I could just create the map, it would be very interesting. I often found myself pondering on what General Benny Moerdani and Moerdiono told me. I did keep that bit of information to myself for a long time. In practical terms, based on the testimonies of both Benny Moerdani and Moerdiono, I was really not "Benny's man" but "Soeharto's man" — in addition to those others close to the President long before me.

On the other hand, Pak Dhar professed openly that he did not know me, and even hinted that he had had someone else in mind for my job. It is possible that Moerdiono might have spoken on my behalf to Pak Dhar, but of course he could not just rely on the word of one man. It all meant that my appointment as the Golkar Secretary General still left some questions unanswered.

Being inside the circle of the political elite made me even more conscious about being consistent in staying on the Middle Course. It meant that I needed to keep my distance from the elite and to prioritize performance and public communication, including maintaining good relations with Golkar's Executive Chairman, within certain boundaries. Pak Dhar was known for his hobby of playing golf; did I feel the need to start playing golf? That, in my view, would have been overkill.

It was in this frame of mind that I asked to see Pak Dhar at the State Secretariat the next afternoon, before Golkar's first plenary under the new leadership.

First Face-to-Face Meeting with Pak Dhar

Before my first one-on-one meeting with Pak Dhar, I made sure I was presentable. I went to the barber's so that my hair was neatly trimmed and did not look too disheveled. I clipped my nails. I prepared a set of neatly ironed clothes consisting of a pale blue safari shirt and a pair of navy blue trousers. I applied some coconut oil to my hair since I did not have any pomade. I brushed my shoes to a good shine. Satisfied that I was properly attired to the Chairman's sartorial standards, I set off for the State Secretariat.

Pak Dhar welcomed me to his workplace warmly and bade me to sit down. His ministerial office at the State Secretariat looked spartan compared to those of other ministers. Without further ado he shared with me the main points for Golkar's plenary in the evening. Seeing that I was jotting it down, he said, "No need to do it now. You can do that later this evening. I'd like to see if the new DPP Golkar is capable of working fast and accurately as a team."

Although Pak Dhar was friendly towards me, a far cry from his perceived image of being aloof, I still felt there was a considerable distance between the two of us, which was probably understandable since we had just met each other for the first time.

Then, unexpectedly, he asked, "It's not like you to be this dapper. Have you just had a haircut? Your clothes are spick and span. But in this environment, the colour of one's shirt must match the trousers."

It occurred to me that I needed to have a quick retort for Pak Dhar's comment. "Thank you for your attention, Pak. I took great care in my personal grooming before coming here. Naturally, it's not perfect yet, but I'd like to assure you that both of my socks are of the same colour."

I then observed an example of body language that was apparently characteristic of Pak Dhar—previously described to me by a few friends—when something unexpected happened, he would tilt his head back. That was what he did after hearing what I said. Then, as his head returned to its original position, he laughed loudly. "Have you worn socks of different colours before?" he asked.

"Once, Pak Dhar. I had to leave the house very early in the morning to catch a flight. My wife would drive me there. It was still dark and

I hurried along because I didn't want to be late, so I didn't turn on the light as I was putting my socks on. When the sun was up, I saw my socks were of different colours."

Pak Dhar then asked me to stay for lunch with him. I was delighted to see the dishes on the table because they were just like the ones I often had as a child at the Sentiong house. There were fish *pepes*, savoury tempeh, and stir-fried long beans in sweet soy sauce.

"Wow, this is what my mother would serve at home when I was growing up", I said, beaming.

"My wife made these. She cooks for me every day. If you like her cooking, I'll tell her to make sure there's enough for you. She deliberately comes here at around midday so that I can eat well", Pak Dhar explained.

"That would be wonderful, Pak. I'll make time at midday especially to taste her cooking."

We talked lightly as we ate and then I took my leave. As I was about to leave his room, I remembered to ask him, "What should we wear for tonight, Pak?"

"No particular dress code really, as long as it's neat."

"So what I wear on top doesn't need to be colour-coordinated with my trousers then?" I joked.

"Of course not. You are free to wear anything. But please wear shoes, not sandals. And, most importantly, both shoes must be the same colour", he replied, grinning widely.

Pak Dhar was to remember this conversation of ours. In our out-of-town trips together, he would sometimes joke about me to break the ice.

"Can you please check Sarwono's socks? Are they the same colour?" he would say. Everyone else would burst out laughing.

First Plenary Meeting

As evening came, the post-Congress DPP Golkar functionaries made their way to the Ministerial Housing Estate Widya Chandra for our first plenary meeting. It also served as an introduction since some of us did not yet know each other. The rest of the evening was taken up by Pak Dhar who, in his capacity as Executive Chairman, explained the duties of each functionary and our programme.

Pak Dhar steered the meeting well, with no hint of awkwardness. Broadly speaking, he spelled out the distribution of responsibility among the eight sectional chairmen in their respective fields and territories. The Secretary General and his deputies and the Treasurer and his deputies were the supporting framework, led by the Secretary General, and they were known as Team 8.

We had the following types of meetings: the Core-Team Daily Meeting for the Executive Chairman with the other sectional chairmen, the Secretary General and Treasurer; the Full-Team Daily Meeting featuring the Executive Chairman with the other sectional chairmen and Team 8; and the Plenary Meeting, with all forty-five DPP members. Expressed in numbers: seventeen for the Full-Team Daily Meeting, eight for the Team 8 Meeting and forty-five for the Plenary Meeting. The combination could be interpreted as 17-8-45, Indonesia's Independence Day.

Our new Chairman also elaborated on President Soeharto's speech at the opening of our Congress. In the speech, the President stated the importance for Golkar to nurture democracy, internally and externally, through consolidation of ideology, scope of thought, and organization. The cultivation of democracy would also be achieved through the regeneration of activists, territorially and functionally.

Our mid-term programme had the aim of Triple Successes: successfully drafting the Five-Yearly Development Programme in parliament, successfully conducting the General Election and successfully conducting the 1998 MPR General Assembly, as mandated by our recent congress. The sectional chairman overseeing Organization, Membership and Regeneration (OKK) and his department were charged—with the support of Team 8—to formulate in detail the Code of Conduct and the Programme. Throughout the meeting, Pak Dhar stressed the need to build an atmosphere of collegiality in carrying out our organizational duties.

Chatting with Soeharto

A few days after our meeting, we gathered in the evening at the residence of the Chairman of the Board of Patrons, President Soeharto. It was an informal affair and we were free to sit ourselves in the drawing room. The Executive Chairman General M. Panggabean and the other members of the Board of Patrons were also present. The impression given was that those gathered there were key figures—retired high-ranking ABRI officers—but they did not necessarily reflect the organizational make-up of the Board of Patrons.

I was there because the Golkar Executive Chairman had asked me to come along. Other DPP chairmen present were Pak R. Soekardi and Pak Manihuruk. I quickly realized that I was the only one in the room with no military background. As it happened, the chair to the right of Pak Harto was unoccupied, and I decided to sit there to start my first ever conversation with the President. He gave me pointers so that the proposed publication of *Media Karya* as Golkar's monthly magazine could go well. "As for the printing, ask Bob Hasan to help out because his printing company still hasn't reached its full capacity", Pak Harto told me.

In my first encounter with the President, I could feel his air of authority. As if by reflex, I conducted myself with care in front of him, as befitting someone much younger than him.

Afterwards, Pak Harto asked Pak Sudharmono to make his report on Golkar's activities. Pak Dhar briefly related the way the plenary meeting had gone and the outline of the programme adopted for the future. Pak Harto responded by underlining the strategic value of regeneration, especially the programme Karakterdes. A short discussion ensued in a relaxed manner among those present, after which the President asked his guests to have dinner together.

You Rotten Egg … Arsehole … Damn You!

As the new functionaries were settling into their routine, something amusing happened. One day I arrived at the DPP Golkar office in the morning to start work. As I entered my room, I saw a technician installing something. He was, as it turned out, installing a buzzer so that the Executive Chairman could summon me to his room by pressing a button. I did not think such a mode of summons was in line with the spirit of collegiality that the Executive Chairman insisted on.

"I don't want to be summoned like that", I told the technician. "If Pak Dhar wants me in his office, he can call me on the phone or send someone to tell me. I don't want to be ting-tonged. Take it off!"

Then I sat at my desk and saw four white buttons, which were my own buttons to summon my deputies.

"Do I take these off as well?" asked the technician.

"Hang on. I want to try them out first." I then pressed all four buttons one by one.

I was bemused to find my deputies turning up with a pad in their hands. I then told them my opinion on the buzzer. "How come all of you were willing to put up with something like that, to be ting-tonged? We are all colleagues, elected at the Congress. Pak Dhar also wanted us to be collegial with each other. I can send someone to get you if I need you here. I can call you on the phone or even go to you", I explained.

"You rotten egg!" said David Napitupulu.

"Damn you!" Akbar Tandjung joined in the chorus.

Hearing the swear words, Oka Mahendra kept smiling.

"Arsehole!" said Soedarmadji, who was at other times a serious man. The Javanese swear word Soedarmadji used was *dobhol*, which actually means haemorrhoids, and he would typically say this word about four times a year. In this instance, he said it to denote his annoyance at having been played like a fool by me.

The swear words did the trick. The working atmosphere at our office reverted to the cheery state it had always been.

DPP Golkar Plunged into a Hectic Schedule

The work schedule given to us by the Executive Chairman proved to be extremely challenging, given that the next plenary meeting was a month away. But, under Pak Manihuruk's leadership and with solid teamwork, everything was done to perfection, thanks to the "Manihuruk Method", which I explained earlier.

At the time, Pak Manihuruk was Head of the Administrative Agency for the Civil Service (BAKN). We sometimes had our meetings in his office. He took the opportunity to explain that BAKN was in the process of developing a staff database, of which the manual version was up and running. A computerized version was on the way. The Civil Service Information System was then known as SIMPEG. We could not fathom how complicated the system had to be to be able to record data on around two million civil servants.

"Name someone you know who works as a civil servant. Wherever that person is posted, his or her data can be accessed in just three minutes", he said. "It could also work by using the person's civil service code number", he added. Turning to me he said, "Your wife is a civil servant, isn't she? What's her name?"

I gave him Nini's full name and he told his staff to find her data. It was true. In a matter of minutes, my wife's documents were found, with data including alternative future career direction. Then someone else asked for a few other names to be located. They were all found.

Pak Manihuruk in his capacity as head of OKK, Team 8 and the Department of Organization, Membership and Regeneration became the driving force behind DPP Golkar. Other departments would often ask us to help them out with their projects. With the Secretariat Team under Sudarsono's capable leadership, Golkar's organizational machine was very well oiled indeed.

We were able to finalize the concept for the Code of Conduct and the outline for the programme on time, and the next project was started immediately, which was to formulate the membership and regeneration scheme and its direct application. All of this needed to be completed by the end of 1983, which gave us less than two months. Consequently, we had to work non-stop and intensely. Our Executive Chairman also arranged various visits to state institutions and certain government ministries, on which we accompanied him—a programme that started with a visit to President Soeharto to report on the Golkar Congress.

All of our policy initiatives were approved by the Executive Chairman, with minor adjustments. We the young ones at DPP learned a lot from our seniors by working in tandem with them. Their past experience of formulating policy was invaluable to us. Our most helpful seniors included Moerdopo, Cosmas Batubara and the undisputed master, Pak Manihuruk.

On 1 January 1984, we kicked off our Golkar membership programme, with the first two official members being President Soeharto and the first lady, *Ibu* Tien. They both received membership cards. Afterwards, membership applications were opened throughout the country.

Next on the list was the mandatory visits by the DPP heads in their capacity as regional coordinators to the respective regions allotted to them. Team 8 and the Secretariat played a pivotal role in arranging those visits. After the regional visits were satisfactorily concluded, the next wave of activities ensued, which included Functional Regeneration (Karsinal) and Village Territorial Regeneration (Karakterdes). All these policies were up and running by the first quarter of 1984.

Media Karya

Another Golkar project we worked on at this juncture was to prepare for the publication of the monthly magazine *Media Karya*. The first edition of the magazine was slated for March 1984, to coincide with the anniversary of the decree of 11 March 1966 (Supersemar). Our Department of Publication and Mass Media, its Head and Team 8 worked hard to meet the deadline, with supervision from the Executive Chairman.

In the official structure at the magazine, Pak Dhar was the Managing Director, while I was Editor-in-Chief. Almost all DPP members were involved in *Media Karya* in one way or another, supported by our own magazine staff, including the reporters from *Suara Karya*. I was lucky that among the staff was Rum Aly who had worked with me on the West Java edition of *Mahasiswa Indonesia* until its permit was revoked by the government following the Malari incident. In a later development, Rum Aly snugly fitted into the role of Managing Editor and received special attention from Pak Dhar.

Media Karya was designated as a monthly magazine featuring not only organizational news but also analyses and quality writing. We worked hard for our first issue, the cover of which featured a portrait of President Soeharto. Pak Dhar then asked me, as Editor-in-Chief, to have an article on the issuance of Supersemar, which was a difficult task given that Pak Dhar was himself in the midst of it, and we were only given very little time.

Prior to the date of publication of *Media Karya*, I went to see Pak Dhar to show him the proposed layout of the magazine and my article.

Before I went into his office, Zaenal Abidin, an administrative staffer at the Ministry of the State Secretariat, browsed through the magazine mock-up and commented, "Pak Dhar might not like this."

So I entered his office with some anxiety. Unlike our first meeting, he looked serious this time. As he went through the magazine, my main article on Supersemar obviously intrigued him. He read it very carefully with a pen at the ready in his hand. Before he could even use the pen, he looked up and with an expression of being pleasantly surprised said, "This is good." I was relieved.

He then went over the rest of the magazine and told me it could now go to the printers. I was next told by Jusuf Wanandi that Bob Hasan's printing company indeed had available printing slots. Jusuf Wanandi worked hard to help us meet the deadline for *Media Karya*.

Next we started to prepare the second issue for April 1984. After Pak Harto had graced the cover for the March issue, we naturally wanted Pak Dhar for April. We decided against using a photograph and commissioned an artist from the Ancol Art Market to paint a portrait of him instead. When we showed it to Pak Dhar, he laughed and commented, "That's not me. Too young. That's my younger brother."

As Secretary General of Golkar, I also became Editor-in-Chief of *Media Karya*, Golkar's internal magazine.

I suggested to him that, in the interests of efficiency, members of Team 8 take turns in accompanying him when he carried out his duties as Executive Chairman. All of us were incredibly busy because of Golkar's hectic schedule, and I myself was often invited to speak at a number of forums as Golkar's representative. It only made sense that I complied. Pak Dhar agreed with me.

Ironically, even with the hectic schedule at work, I in fact found myself with enough time for all the things I wanted to do. This was made possible by the full participation of all DPP members. Our

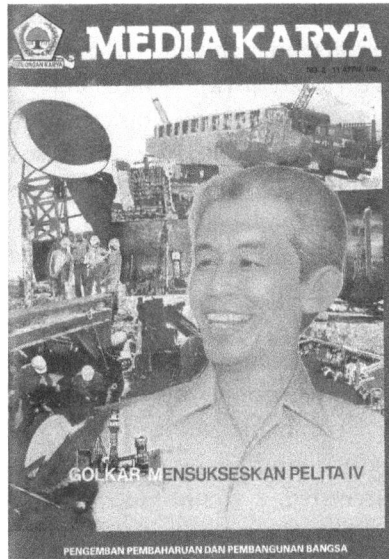

programme-management cycle was crafted with high precision. Almost nothing unexpected occurred as a result, which would have meant wasted time in damage control or improvisation, possibly leading to yet more unexpected and detrimental consequences.

Birth of Kosti Jaya

Since I had some time to spare, I remembered something I had promised Awan Karmawan Burhan (Mang Awan), the Deputy Secretary General of DPP Golkar (1978–83). Mang Awan had asked for my help in consolidation efforts at the Greater Jakarta Taxi Drivers' Cooperative (Kosti Jaya), a new body resulting from the amalgamation of two cooperatives, Koptain and KSTI. The amalgamation had been made mandatory by a new law that forbade the existence of more than one cooperative of the same kind in a single province. Even though the two had been merged by Jakarta's Regional Office of Small and Medium Enterprises, the new cooperative was dysfunctional on account of infighting.

Many people had warned me against taking on Mang Awan's request because transport cooperatives were usually bad news, perhaps even the worst. My own thinking was that since they were known to be unmanageable, I could not lose by trying. If I failed, people were bound to be understanding, since it was a difficult task. If I succeeded, it would have brought me a sense of satisfaction, apart from the obvious benefits. So I stepped up to Mang Awan's challenge and, together with M.W. Datubara from Dekopin and Mazuki Darusman, became an advisor for Kosti Jaya.

During my tenure as the Secretary of the FKP (1977–82), I had the opportunity of getting to know the administrators of the cooperative. My observations did identify the internal situation of Kosti Jaya to be problematic. Its members were mostly migrant workers from other parts of the country who were accustomed to subsisting on odd jobs, including being taxi drivers. Most were also unused to working within an organization, not to mention the general atmosphere of uncooperativeness towards one another that existed there.

In its first few years, the cooperative saw administrations come and go because of the frequent motions of no confidence from its own members. On the other hand, government policy on cooperatives at the time was unsupportive. The structure of a cooperative was set up like that of a mass organization, and not as a commercial venture. The performance of any cooperative was judged by the government based on criteria more suited to a bureaucracy.

Kosti Jaya Needs a Solution

In the lead-up to Golkar's 1983 Congress, I had a discussion with Muslimin Nasution, who was then Head of the Research and Development (R&D) Department at the Ministry of Cooperatives. We came up with a key point in any solution for cooperatives like Kosti Jaya: that drivers must become owners of their taxis, which we called the concept of owner-operator. Muslimin Nasution also promised to look into the matter at his department for me.

When I had enough spare time to devote my energy to Kosti Jaya again, I asked to meet with Muslimin Nasution to discuss the concept of owner-operator further. His department had reviewed the concept and concluded that it was in line with the principles of the cooperative because taxi drivers were essentially stakeholder-owners in the co-operative and not employees.

To make the concept work, an accountable management system was needed, as well as a change in orientation for cooperatives to see themselves as business entities. However, our idea necessitated two things: a change in government regulations on cooperatives, and making car credit loans accessible to the drivers.

An idea then occurred to me, which I shared with Muslimin. "Why not make Kosti a pilot project under the auspices of your department, as a gauge in generating information and input for possible changes to regulations? As for car credit loans, we could go to the Minister of Cooperatives for assistance."

Muslimin seemed pleased with my suggestion and we agreed to submit the idea to the Minister of Cooperatives, Bustanil Arifin. We wasted no time and immediately went to see him. He agreed at once and telephoned the Head of the Regional Office at his ministry to inform them that Kosti Jaya was now under R&D and therefore off-limits to the regional office.

There remained the question of credit loans. "I will instruct Bukopin to provide the loans", Pak Bustanil said. Subsequent development saw Bukopin and the Head of R&D in negotiation, leading to a document spelling out car credit loans and their terms and conditions in detail. Both sides soon signed a loan agreement at DPP Golkar, Slipi, Jakarta with Muslimin Nasution and myself bearing witness to the event.

After the signing ceremony, the Managing Director of Bukopin, Ismeth Abdullah, told me that he had essentially written off the loans given to Kosti Jaya as non-performing loans. "I signed the agreement because I had been ordered to do so", Ismeth said.

The taxi drivers present at the event were also sceptical. They saw the signing ceremony as play acting. One of them said—I remember his name was Daus—"If we do end up with cars, I will shave my head bald."

Even though the risks were obvious, Muslimin and I saw the milestone in a positive light. The R&D at the Ministry of Cooperatives and I now had a "laboratory" to conduct tests in order to create better regulations. For me, the effort was also another kind of laboratory on functional regeneration, with consolidation in ideology, scope of thought, and organization thrown in. I hoped that in the end the drivers might, of their own volition, apply to become members of Golkar, not only for the cars alone.

Prospective loan recipients were selected based on stringent criteria by the R&D Department of the Ministry of Cooperatives. The ministry also set up an office and a car pool area for Kosti Jaya, free of charge, in front of the Amalgamated Cooperatives of Indonesian Batik (GKBI) building, near Semanggi. Pak Suhanda was appointed pool caretaker.

Kosti Jaya in Operation

Two weeks later, a hundred new Ford Lasers were parked in rows at the car pool. There was a great commotion at Kosti Jaya in reaction to the news. After the handover ceremony, Daus drove me to DPP Golkar as his first passenger. I saw his hair had been shorn clean off. I tried to insist on paying for the ride but he refused. The first months of Kosti Jaya were chaotic. All the administrators there, who were taxi drivers themselves, were ill-prepared to run an organization.

Staff members of the Ministry of Cooperatives had to be deployed to ensure credit payments from the drivers, which was also an uphill struggle.

By coincidence this period also saw newcomers to the FKP with whom I was eager to make my acquaintance. I started interacting with them when they met me during their orientation period. A new member who was attracting a lot of attention was Mubha Kahar Muang, an economics graduate from the University of Hasanuddin in Makassar. The woman activist was unique in many ways, having experience as a member of the Student Regiment, a parachutist, a soccer player and a keen windsurfer.

On one occasion, Mubha asked me to find her something difficult to do. She basically liked challenges. I was sufficiently intrigued to find out more about her from my friends in South Sulawesi. Every one of them told me she was special. By another coincidence, the Treasurer of Kosti Jaya had died. I immediately asked Mubha to fill the vacancy.

Mubha worked fast to iron out the credit repayment system and soon became a leadership figure for the taxi drivers. In two years' time, Mubha successfully created a computer-based information system on finance for Kosti Jaya, a considerable feat at a time when information technology had only just entered its second generation. Using the system, taxi drivers were able to keep track of their finances on the computer screen. But the system had its detractors at Kosti Jaya. A group of them came to the DPP Golkar office to protest against what was displayed by the system—which was still undergoing upgrades— because it was wrong. "If the system is to be believed, we all joined Kosti for nothing", said the leader of the group.

Dealing with Recalcitrants

Almost all of the fifteen delegates took turns to voice their protests, and in a very crude manner. I was aware of the background to the problem they had come to tell me about. Previously I had heard that there were signs that data was manipulated at Kosti Jaya, which necessitated improvement in the information system on finance and the management of the car pool. In addition, I had gone undercover as a Kosti

Jaya driver for three days. I had been able to do so incognito because I was then far from being a celebrity.

From my brief stint, I knew that in four hours of active driving there was enough income for a driver to pay for his daily financial obligation as owner-driver to Bukopin and Kosti Jaya. The rest was ready cash that could be taken home or deposited in a bank account to speed up the loan repayment.

Knowing what I knew, I felt that the grievances of these drivers were just a ruse, but to what end I did not know. So, in response, pounding on the table, I raised my voice. "Be quiet!"

They appeared shocked and fell silent. I explained to them what the problem was with the data on the computer, and I told them that their conduct was grievously dishonest. This was a carry-over from the days when they were employees in a transport company with a record of treating its workers badly. This led them to cheat the company to earn extra income through the manipulation of purchases for spare parts and car tyres.

"You have forgotten that you are now owners. What you used to do before joining Kosti would only hurt yourselves if applied here", I said. I also related to them my stint as a taxi driver. I was so angry with them. "You are all liars! Leave now!"

I was vexed because, despite the stringent selection process, people such as these had managed to slip through the cracks.

Then something I did not expect came out of the group leader's mouth. "Secretary General, we only came to test you. You are truly smart. You deserve to be our advisor."

Afterwards, they took their leave. But in the courtyard they were still arguing loudly. Alas, the problem did not end here. I received word that a group of people were stirring up trouble at the car pool.

"I have tried everything I know to keep them in line but I have failed. It might be better if you came over yourself to see it", Pak Suhanda said.

I then went to the car pool late at night to see what was going on. I saw for myself that some of the people who had come to DPP Golkar were among those who gathered at the stall of the spirits hawker. They were clearly drunk.

"They refuse to go, and would sleep here", Pak Suhanda said.
I thought their presence could no longer be tolerated because some
of the other members had also complained about their behaviour.
Complaints from passengers could also be traced back to the same
few individuals. I tried to work out what I should do. It had to be
something they least expected, but that would be effective. If we dealt
with them through conventional disciplinary measures, it might lead
to more unexpected problems. An idea however presented itself.

Solution for Kosti Jaya

The following night I went back to the car pool with a group of people
with a spotlight and Betamax video recorders. I asked them to record
what the troublemakers were doing. Since the rowdy individuals were
all drunk, they behaved even more outlandishly when they realized
they were being filmed. The fifteen-minute footage we shot was edited
at my request. "Choose the most ludicrous acts. Please edit it for a
short presentation. Two minutes would suffice", I said.

After viewing the final edit, which I found satisfactory, I invited
Kosti Jaya members on Sunday night to come to the car pool for
a family viewing of comedy films. They all came with their wives
and children. The first film to be played was a silent movie starring
Charlie Chaplin. Then came an old movie starring Bud Abbot and
Lou Costello. Everyone was enjoying themselves.

"Please don't go home just yet. Here's a film that only lasts two
minutes but everyone must see this", I told them. I then asked the
operator to play the clip of drunk drivers. The whole room erupted in
pandemonium. The people seen in the film were berated and punched
by their wives. The children cried, too, seeing their fathers behave in
such a depraved manner.

"You told me it's hard to earn money and you often don't come
home because you work long hours. But in fact you are squandering
our money on getting drunk. You evil man!" admonished one of the
wives.

Not long after, Kosti Jaya members decided in a meeting that the
ten people who made up the drunken gang were to be sacked. The ten

did not even try to defend themselves. They never came to the meeting. And things got better after this. There were no more problems with credit repayments. Indeed there were indications that some members would be able to repay their loans in full sooner than the scheduled five years. Bukopin was even willing to finance a second round of loans. Mubha then came to me with news that she suspected markups in the prices of cars, and that she would resign as treasurer if the issue was not resolved. It was however successfully dealt with in the end.

Mubha was eventually elected as Chairwoman of Kosti Jaya. Under her extraordinary leadership, the cooperative came on in leaps and bounds and became the second-largest taxi company in the country after the Blue Bird Group.

Why did Kosti Jaya end up being liquidated while Kosti Solo and Kosti Semarang—both of which were founded after Kosti Jaya—still exist today? It is a long and interesting story. However, at this point, I would like to go back to writing about my job as Secretary General of Golkar.

Pak Dhar's Leadership

In spite of his tight schedule as both Golkar's Executive Chairman and the Minister of the State Secretariat, Pak Dhar was very attentive to us and would from time to time visit us at DPP Golkar or call us on the telephone. Once he rang when I was at DPP Golkar. At the time, Team 8 was occupied with preparations for various policy proposals. Pak Dhar asked me how David Napitupulu was doing. I understood straight away that the question had something to do with the psychological well-being of senior functionaries who had been superseded following the appointments of new and younger team-mates at the Congress, including the prestigious post of Secretary General.

"Oh, David is always hard at work", I told him truthfully. "He is always here and as busy as the rest of us."

"Is that so? I'm so glad to hear it", he said, clearly relieved.

After moving on to other things, we ended our conversation. But, one night, after I got home from a plenary meeting, Pak Dhar rang me. He said he was deeply concerned about the intense three-way debate between Tatto Pradjamanggala, Anang Adenansi and myself at the plenary. As chair of the meeting, Pak Dhar had asked us to stop squabbling and declared the issue over which we argued to be taken over by the chair. Then the meeting resumed. Tatto, Anang and I were sure to quickly forget about our arguments because fierce debates were common among the younger FKP members.

"In the future, please don't use such harsh language", Pak Dhar said. "We must be unified and do our best to prevent animosity among ourselves. If there are problems to be smoothed over, you come to me immediately and we'll find a solution", Pak Dhar said earnestly.

When Tatto, Anang and I met again, I knew that they had been reprimanded as well. We all laughed and shook our heads.

"We must get him used to debates and jokes. Let's fight over something again and see what happens", Tatto said.

In truth, as explained earlier, Pak Dhar did his best to adapt to our style by becoming less uptight since being appointed as Golkar Chairman. However, Tatto was correct in that he still needed a crash course in adaptation.

In the meantime, Golkar's machinery was in full operations mode. Pak Dhar and his entourage—the composition of which varied from one visit to another, for the reasons I mentioned earlier—always undertook visits to the regions every weekend to meet the grass-roots Golkar sympathizers and to see the application of Karakterdes in all its phases. The DPP functionaries were busy not only in organizational tasks but also with our duties as MPs, in addition to being figures in society. Our departments held weekly thematic forums. We used these forums to recruit potential cadres from functional groups of diverse professions and to be exposed to new ideas.

At the same time, at the provincial and municipal levels, Golkar regional conventions were held to elect new functionaries for the 1984–88 term and to formulate regional programmes. It is safe to say that Golkar was then very much alive throughout Indonesia.

P4 Classes

Amid our obviously busy schedule at Golkar, out of the blue, Pak Dhar asked to see a few DPP functionaries and myself. "All of you haven't done the P4 classes at BP7, am I right? That's unacceptable. Please

Myself (seated far right) with the Executive Chairman of Golkar Sudharmono attending a Karakterdes session.

register yourselves to do the classes. It would look bad for us to go around the country putting Golkar's programmes to work if we haven't even taken the classes ourselves", he said.

We naturally agreed and proposed that we do the P4 classes alternately in small groups. Moerdopo and I were the first to register—the P4 34th Class. When the participants gathered at the BP7 building in Pejambon, I met middle-ranking military officers from all the forces, police officers and business managers, both from state-owned enterprises and the private sector, all manner of figures from different organizations. Among the middle-ranking military officers were Colonel (Army) Zainal Basri Palaguna who would become Governor of South Sulawesi and Colonel (Navy) Dr Tarmizi Taher who went on to become Minister of Religious Affairs.

In our first meeting, I was appointed head participant because, according to state protocol, I outranked the other participants, going by precedent, whereby the Secretary General of Golkar had been a high-ranking army officer with the rank of Brigadier General. My duties as head participant included welcoming VIP guests alongside the Head of

BP7, preparing the classroom for VIP lectures and upholding discipline among participants.

I was asked if I was familiar with military ceremonies. I answered in the affirmative since I had become acquainted with the subject while I was an ITB student. Then the Head of BP7, Major General Hari Soeharto, who would one day become Attorney General, entered the room to brief us. Lieutenant General (Rtd.) Sarwo Edhie Wibowo, the former Commander of RPKAD in 1965, who would later become father-in-law to President Susilo Bambang Yudhoyono, was the coordinator of our instructors.

The classes were conducted in an interesting manner. What surprised many of our participants was the elaboration on the 1945 Constitution, be it its preamble, the main text or the roles of state institutions in constitutional governance. Many participants were obviously ignorant of these matters, so lectures on these subjects, both at the plenary session or in small group discussions, were alive with interest.

The VIP speakers we invited largely turned up without substitution. The Minister of the State Secretariat and the Commander of ABRI came to speak and appeared pleased to see me carry out preparatory work ahead of their lectures with perfect military ceremonies. Towards the end of our classes, participants were interviewed by the instructors, especially about the thirty-six points of P4. It was a shame, however, that several instructors put undue emphasis on our ability to memorize rather than on our understanding of the essence of Pancasila.

Prior to the commencement of our classes, I heard that as participants we would be continually ranked depending on our performance. Initially, I was ranked number one, but I had fallen to seventh place by the time the classes had concluded. It was easy to see why my rank had plummeted. One of the reasons was that I was too quick with my interjections, liked to ask difficult questions and came up with unusual arguments. Still, at least people found out I knew how to conduct military ceremonies properly. Ranked first was Moerdopo. Those in the top ten were entitled to further training to become instructors. Throughout our classes, Pak Sarwo Edhie liked to do his rounds and drop in on and participate in our discussions. He seemed to enjoy his role.

Instructor Training at the National Level

Sometime later, the training for prospective P4 instructors was held at the Bogor Palace, opened by President Soeharto. The number of participants from DPP Golkar and the FKP was quite high, around thirty, including Mrs Tati Dasoyo, Usman Hasan, Johnny Sukirman and Albert Hasibuan, as well as colleagues from Bandung. We were required to sleep over, with one room housing four to six people. I shared the same room with, among others, Bawadiman, a Golkar MP representing West Nusa Tenggara.

There, I was introduced to Abdurrahman Wahid, better known as Gus Dur, who had studied in Cairo, Baghdad and Leiden. He was at the time active in grass-roots empowerment efforts as well as being a prolific writer of articles on sociopolitical issues. Other new acquaintances were Slamet Effendi Yusuf, Chairman of the Ansor Youth Movement, and Iwan Jaya Azis, a renowned economist who later taught at Cornell University.

Unlike the classes at the BP7 building, the training at the Bogor Palace had a more relaxed atmosphere in which the exchange of ideas took place in an animated manner and was more substantial in responding to fundamental problems. I took part in the discussions normally, as I was relieved to be in surroundings that were conducive to speaking freely and meaningfully. Time seemed to fly by. After fourteen days, our training was over, and I was awarded with a letter stating that I was a certified National Level P4 Instructor.

During our stay at the Bogor Palace, I was particularly struck by Gus Dur, who was capable of articulating his opinions well, creatively and sometimes hilariously. I felt that we were kindred spirits. Slamet Effendi Yusuf was also interesting because of his wholesome patriotism, fine articulation and warmth, which won him many friends.

Sarwono's Man

I related my having made the acquaintances of Gus Dur and Slamet Effendi Yusuf to Pak Dhar. I suggested to him that Slamet be recruited into Golkar and be inducted into the Steering Committee for Golkar's

National Leaders' Summit (Rapimnas). The Rapimnas was an annual event conducted in October to coincide with Golkar's birthday. Pak Dhar agreed with me. Slamet Effendi Yusuf did not hesitate in accepting the offer and he soon fulfilled all the requirements in applying to become a member of Golkar.

Unlike Siswono Yudo Husodo, whose presence at the 1983 Congress and his subsequent appointment as a DPP functionary were welcomed, Slamet Effendi Yusuf was a lightning rod for controversy. His presence caused anxiety among some of Golkar's younger activists. Their antipathy towards Slamet Effendi Yusuf reached its climax when he was appointed as the only representative of the younger generation on the team of Formulators of Political Statement on the Rapimnas Steering Committee.

Immediately a rumour spread that Slamet was a "turncoat" and "Sarwono's man". I thought the latter did not sound so bad. Within Golkar, there were those labelled as "Dharmono's men" or "Benny's men". Apparently there was a new breed: "Sarwono's men", starting with Slamet Effendi Yusuf, Chairman of GP Ansor, which had hundreds of thousands of members.

After this, a number of functionaries of DPP AMPI, in full uniform, visited me in my office. They protested against Slamet Effendi Yusuf sitting on the team of Formulators of Political Statements because Slamet had been a campaigner for PPP in the 1982 General Election. The AMPI functionaries then demanded Slamet be expelled from Golkar. One of them threatened he would quit Golkar if their demand was not met.

I took full responsibility for their protest. If I had said that Slamet was there by the consent and decision of the Executive Chairman, they might have accepted it, because it was the kind of language they understood. But I took a different path. "If you want to quit Golkar, place your membership cards on my desk now. No one would shed tears if you left!" I said firmly. "If Slamet were expelled, millions in the Nahdliyin (NU) extended family would be disappointed and offended, and we would lose votes and potential support", I added.

They were shocked to hear what I had to say. They looked at each other and then decided to leave my office.

At the Rapimnas, Pak Dhar believed that I had taken an important principled measure, which was to formulate a Guideline on Golkar's Principle in Fortifying the National Unity. After the principle was discussed in the summit, it was accepted and enshrined as an organizational statute.

Coming to the Defence of H.R. Dharsono

In the aftermath of Golkar's 1984 Rapimnas, Awan Karmawan Burhan (Mang Awan) turned up at my doorstep one night. He was in profound distress at the arrest of Major General H.R. Dharsono, the former Commander of Siliwangi, on a charge of involvement in the bombings of the offices of Bank Central Asia (BCA) in Jakarta and Borobudur Temple. Several other alleged perpetrators had also been arrested. Something fishy was going on, since three of the signatories of Petition 50—H.M. Sanusi, A.M. Fatwa and H.R. Dharsono—were detained and had been charged with being present at the preparatory meetings for the bombings.

Of the three, H.R. Dharsono, whom we called Oom Ton, was close to Bandung's '66 activists. Oom Ton was even accused of being the mastermind behind the bombing of the BCA offices. We knew him well and thought the charges to be outrageous. Those of us from Bandung talked about nothing else, and Mang Awan suggested that we who knew Oom Ton personally sign a petition to request he be placed under house arrest instead. I told Mang Awan that it was not easy to arrange a petition with many signatories in such a short time. Moreover, it might lead to an unforeseeable chain of consequences.

At this particular juncture, I was in fact getting ready to leave for Japan, having been invited by the Japanese government to meet with the leadership of the Liberal Democratic Party (LDL), Japan's ruling party. Therefore, I told Mang Awan I would write the letter myself, to represent the concerns of our friends. I wrote the letter the next day, addressed to the Attorney General, carbon copied to the Commander of ABRI and the Minister of the State Secretariat. In the afternoon, I left for Japan.

A week later, after my return from Japan, I discovered that my letter had been received and had caused an uproar. I immediately went to see Pak Dhar at the State Secretariat before noon.

He received me with a serious expression on his face and asked me without further ado, "Why did you write a letter defending H.R. Dharsono? He is involved in sedition."

I replied, "With all due respect, you are a lawyer and no doubt understand that he is innocent until proved guilty. What's more, I wrote the letter in my private capacity as a citizen and did not use the DPP Golkar letterhead. Neither did I refer to my post [as Secretary General]."

Pak Dhar then asked me to tell him my reason for writing the letter. I explained why I had done so in great detail and he listened to me earnestly, his elbows resting on the table while his hands were joined before his face. His eyes looked afar. Then I said something that stunned him. "Pak Dhar, let us look at the whole thing this way. Life is like a wheel. We may now be on top, but there may come a time when you may be on the bottom and suffer the same fate as Pak Dharsono. If you ever did, I would also write a letter to ask that you be placed under house arrest rather than be detained in jail."

Then Pak Dhar said, "All right then." He said this with such finality that signalled he wanted me to leave him. He did not ask me to stay for lunch as he used to.

I also tried to see Pak Benny Moerdani but was ignored. I heard from Harry Tjan Silalahi that Pak Benny once took a piece of paper from his shirt pocket, spread it out and held it between his index and middle fingers, then dropped it on his desk, as if he had cast something disgusting away. "That was Sarwono's letter in defence of Dharsono", he apparently said with great vexation.

I then remembered having met Colonel (Navy) Dr Tarmizi Taher at the P4 classes at BP7. I felt I needed to see him because I had seen him talk intimately with General Benny Moerdani, who had come to deliver a lecture. I remembered thinking he was different from the other military officers there, who had simply saluted the general and stood at attention, without engaging the Commander in conversation.

I was able to see Tarmizi Taher, who alternated his duties in the Navy between the Health and Spiritual Divisions. Born in Padang on 7 October 1936, the Colonel would one day be appointed Minister of Religious Affairs (1993–98). On seeing me, he listened to my explanation as to why I had written my letter. "Did I do something wrong by writing the letter?" I asked him.

He answered that I had done the proper thing under the circumstances. However, he said further that Pak Benny in his capacity as ABRI Commander had the necessary reasons to feel aggrieved by my letter. Colonel Tarmizi Taher then tried to console me and promised he would speak to Pak Benny on my behalf.

In the meantime, Pak Dhar had reverted to his old self with me. In the FKP plenary, which he attended as the Executive Chairman of Golkar, one member aggressively asked how the Secretary General would be penalized for standing up for H.R. Dharsono, a suspect for seditious activities.

Pak Dhar turned to him. "The letter was written in a private capacity by Sarwono. I have studied it and understand why he did what he did. There's no need to make a big deal out of it", said Pak Dhar, smiling, and he then turned to me.

A few days later, Colonel Tarmizi Taher rang me. "Mas Sarwono, I have spoken to Pak Benny", he started, sounding quite pleased. "He has mellowed towards you. Why not ask him to see you? I hope everything goes well."

I at once requested a meeting with Benny Moerdani, and he received me in his office in Jalan Merdeka Barat. I began by apologizing for having put him on the spot.

"Oh, is this about the letter? Forget it! Let's talk about other things!" He offered me a Gudang Garam cigarette and we started talking like before.

Flashback to "Petrus"

My letter in defence of Oom Ton was the second instance I had drawn ire from Pak Benny. The first instance occurred prior to the Golkar Congress of 1983, just when it was commonly known that I was the candidate for Secretary General backed by the then Intelligence Assistant of the ABRI Commander, Lieutenant General Benny Moerdani, before he was promoted to become the ABRI Commander.

Around about this time, Oka Mahendra and I, separately and simultaneously, expressed our concern about the murders of known street criminals by unknown actors, especially in Jakarta and Yogya-karta. The string of vigilante executions was known as *penembakan misterius* (mysterious shootings), or *petrus*. General Benny Moerdani only deigned to respond in a cursory manner, dismissing it as gang fights.

Both Oka Mahendra and I released similar statements that the government could not sit by and let *petrus* continue unpunished because it had the potential to erode the rule of law and encourage further violence. We were both quoted by the media the following day. Later that day, at around 11 a.m., I received a phone call from Benny Moerdani. I was then in the office of the Secretary of the FKP. Pak Benny and I had a rather testy conversation over the phone and in the presence of the *cleret gombel* colleagues of mine.

I set off immediately for Jalan Merdeka Barat, having been summoned by Pak Benny to his office. After I arrived, we continued our fierce conversation from earlier for a brief moment before he fell silent listening to my arguments. I explained to Pak Benny that if allowed to go unchecked, *petrus* would lead to an increase in the number of murders motivated by mundane matters like political rivalry, business competition or even private issues. Such a phenomenon, I argued, had taken place in other countries. Pak Benny stayed silent listening to me. I later learned that Jusuf Wanandi had given him similar arguments to mine. Afterwards, we had lunch together and talked about other things.

At 2 p.m. I arrived back at the FKP Secretariat to retrieve a few things and found that my colleagues were still there waiting for me. "Well, just as we were going to buy you a toothbrush, toothpaste, soap and a towel in case you had been arrested on Benny's order", Djoko Sudyatmiko jokingly said.

So, even before my appointment as Golkar's Secretary General, there was the *petrus* brouhaha that made Pak Dhar think I was unsuitable for the post, although he changed his mind later. In Pak Benny's book, I was even a repeat-offender, having twice fallen in his favour—first when I was Secretary of the FKP and next as Golkar Secretary General. However, over time, all the harsh words said between us were forgotten entirely.

In all, I strayed just a little from the Middle Course three times, but did not suffer from undue consequences. Perhaps I was just lucky.

DPP Golkar in Running Order

Throughout 1985, time passed us by as the range of activities at the DPP Golkar office became more varied. Our office was always full of visitors engaged in the different forums organized by our departments. These were usually well-attended, not just by Golkar members but also by members of the public, business people, social activists and civil servants. Everyone seemed to be able to find something interesting in the wide range of ideas under development. We at the DPP were keen on monitoring these events, at which we often encountered new talent suitable to be invited to strengthen Golkar.

The Three Stream meetings also ran like clockwork. Initially, as Chairman of the DPP Golkar, Pak Sukardi acted as liaison within the Three Stream network, with me as his assistant. However, Sukardi then decided to hand over Stream A (the ABRI Headquarters), represented by middle-ranking military officers, and Stream B (the Directorate General of Sociopolitical Affairs). All parties often got together to exchange ideas and impart important information to be relayed to our respective superiors. From within these informal and off-the-record meetings came follow-up actions for various ongoing issues, particularly gubernatorial elections in the provinces.

In those days, I would often tour the provinces, either as part of the Executive Chairman's entourage or as an invited speaker at various forums and discussion groups. Each time I was in Lampung, I would be accompanied by Siti Nurbaya, Head of AMPI Lampung, who worked at Bappeda, and who is currently the Minister of the Environment and Forestry. In full AMPI uniform, she would drive me around in an open-top jeep.

Siti Nurbaya was and still is an energetic and smart woman. It so happened that she was good friends with my wife, Nini, who at the time worked at the Directorate General Cipta Karya under the Ministry of Public Works as a civil servant. When accompanying me on the visits to the regions, Nini always tried to act in a way she thought befitting her own position, and she detested the special treatment she was bound to get as the wife of Golkar's Secretary General, as well as the sister-in-law of the Minister of Foreign Affairs. When in Lampung, Nini would find a refuge from sycophants in Siti Nurbaya, with whom she had worked through their respective departments.

The DPP's relationship with the Board of Patrons, however, had reduced in intensity from the previous year, although from Golkar's own charter the latter had the prerogative to intervene in the DPP's policies. Our meetings with the Board of Patrons were usually held at President Soeharto's residence in Jalan Cendana, typically in a relaxed atmosphere. As I earlier observed, I often found myself to be the only person there with no military background.

The strategic position of the Board of Patrons within Golkar was still supreme with regard to financial matters, as it continued to be Golkar's main benefactor at all levels of the organization. As Secretary General, however, I was not directly involved in Golkar's finances, the rules of which were never set in stone. There were guidelines for the distribution of budgetary funds for the DPP and the DPD in each province, but these were not under the purview of the Secretary General. What we felt as functionaries was that there was always sufficient funds for our activities.

Should a member of the DPP have the need to travel out of town on Golkar business, we were entitled to the standard facilities prevalent for civil servants, which were far from being extravagant.

When a Golkar or society figure wanted to make a donation, the secretariat would show them a list of goods we required, and the donated goods could only be accepted after being approved. The unwritten rule was to treat money in a proportional manner, which in turn encouraged solidarity among Golkar members. At times, we would encounter budgetary difficulty and would be saved by the generosity of fellow Golkar functionaries or members.

Preparations for a visit to the regions would be conducted under the watchful eyes of Pak Dhar, as he always wanted to ensure our hosts would not be encumbered in any way. Accommodation and transport expenses for the whole entourage would be paid in advance by a task force under the DPP Secretariat, which would usually be sent ahead of us to our destination. With such stringent financial discipline within Golkar, the diversity of backgrounds among its members never became a serious problem. It was in fact quite the reverse. Our accountable financial management created a trusting environment for all the different people with their varying needs and interests, further fostering solidarity among us.

Through my interactions with Golkar members who came from different cultures and professions and with differing personal predilections—all involved in politics under the same umbrella—I came to identify two dominant types. First, there were the idealists—those who prioritized aspirations, ideas and the contribution to society above anything else. Second, there were the career politicians—those with an eye for opportunity, who, in their linear view, always had to aim for higher positions.

Friendship and Rivalry

I discussed this particular topic a lot with Sukarton Marmosudjono, the assistant to the Minister of the State Secretariat in Inter-institutional Relations, Ashub Mensesneg for short, who was also the head of Golkar's Board of Patrons' Secretariat. Both of us effectively became the two poles of influence in Golkar for those wanting something. We were highly sought after by Golkar's stakeholders who expected us to sponsor their annual conventions.

This predicament of ours in relation to the youth organizations under Golkar was unavoidable. Consequently, we decided to come up with a protocol for exercising our influence in relation to one another. The protocol revolved around two criteria when assessing those who petitioned us for funds or other forms of assistance—priority and preference. Priority was connected with the general competence of the petitioner as a Golkar cadre and his leadership potential. According to Pak Dhar, the quality of a cadre had to satisfy his formulation of PDLT: *Prestasi* (performance), *Dedikasi* (dedication), *Loyalitas* (loyalty) and *Tidak Tercela* (unblemished record). Preference was our own subjective assessment of the petitioner.

We considered the unofficial protocol to be important so that the existence of the two poles of influence could be properly managed, preventing internal competition from getting out of hand. After all, we were both Pak Dhar's men: Sukarton as Pak Dhar's underling in the Ministry of the State Secretariat, and I as Golkar's Secretary General to Pak Dhar's position as the Executive Chairman. It was interesting to note a subsequent development in which Golkar's young cadres were polarized into two camps: "Karton's men", who liked to hang out at the office of the Board of Patrons in Jalan Teuku Umar, and "Sarwono's men" at the office of DPP Golkar in Slipi. There was also the third kind known as KKO, for Kanan Kiri Oke (left or right is fine), those who alternated between the two poles.

In managing rivalries for leadership positions within Golkar's youth organizations, Sukarton and I would support our respective candidates that fulfilled the criteria of priority and preference. If Sukarton's candidate won, I would congratulate Sukarton, and vice versa.

After two years of applying our protocol, both Sukarton and I were satisfied with the results. Both sides competed fairly, sometimes fiercely, but still within acceptable parameters. Once, we compared our respective wins and found we were evenly matched. There was both friendship and rivalry in my relationship with Sukarton. When we happened to find ourselves in the same entourage during a visit to the regions, we often had to share the same bedroom, especially when there was no other to be had. We also had a protocol for that: I would go to sleep first because Sukarton snored.

Nini is Unwell

In mid-1985, Nini unexpectedly complained that the lump on her chest had seemed to have grown bigger. We talked about it and agreed that it had to be removed immediately. We were optimistic the tumour was benign, and Nini otherwise felt strong, able to work and manage the household well simultaneously.

Both of us then went to see Harry Tjan Silalahi and his wife, Trees, because Trees had undergone surgery for the same problem and she had recovered well. Trees had been treated at Academisch Ziekenhuis Maastricht in the Netherlands by a surgeon called Dr George Sie, who was related to Trees.

By coincidence, I was about to head for Houston, having been invited to attend an international forum. Nini and I agreed to fly to Maastricht first before continuing to Houston. We arranged our schedules accordingly and left Indonesia after securing permission from the Executive Chairman. I did not feel the need to notify Pak Dhar of Nini's condition because I was under the illusion that her tumour was benign and did not expect any complication.

We arrived in Maastricht and went to see Dr George Sie, who had been born in Indonesia but had made his home in the Netherlands. He was a micro surgeon with the post of *Hoofd Chirurg*, a senior surgeon. Dr Sie examined Nini, performed a mammogram and took a biopsy of her tumour. Two days later he came into Nini's room at the hospital and gave us most unexpected news.

"At first I only found one tumour growth, but I had a feeling there was another one hidden somewhere, and I was right. Nini, you have stage-four cancer. Your breasts and other infected tissues must be removed", Dr Sie said.

We were naturally dumbstruck. I then responded, "Doctor, do we have time to think it over?"

"I recommend immediate surgery. The day after tomorrow."

Nini and I looked at each other while we held hands. Then she looked at me with her round and clear eyes. There was calm acceptance on her face as she said, "Do whatever is best. I trust you."

She was composed and did not cry.

"Very well, doctor, please take the necessary steps", I said.

"Pak Sarwono, please believe me when I say that the medical costs here are far cheaper than Jakarta or Singapore. We will do our best for your wife", Dr Sie assured me.

"What about your fees, doctor?" I asked.

"The team of doctors who will be tending to your wife have had a little discussion and we agreed to do this for free", Dr Sie replied.

I was very touched and probably teary-eyed. Nini hugged me tight.

I stayed for a while in Nini's room and we spoke of the past, our journey together in life, and laughed at its funny moments. We also talked about the children and felt lucky that we had brought them up well. Nini's composure was extraordinary. I never saw any tears coming from her during her illness. After dinner, I went back to my hotel since the hospital did not allow overnight visitors. In the evening, I shared the news with my children and relatives, including my brother, Mochtar. They were all shocked. Nini's cousins in Jakarta promised to mind our children and to run our household in Nini's absence.

I then rang Pak Dhar, who was most concerned and sympathetic. He told me not to think about work for the time being and to concentrate on Nini's care. I said I would take turns with my relatives in looking after Nini during her treatment and recovery so that I could be in Jakarta part of the time. I also contacted my host in Houston and conveyed my apologies for not being able to attend the forum. I then rang Harry Tjan Silalahi and informed him of Nini's prognosis.

Two days later, Nini had her surgery and subsequently her chemotherapy. When she emerged from the operating theatre, she was between consciousness and sleep. In fact, she was asleep most of the day, only waking up intermittently. She had her chemotherapy every third day and then every five days. After spending a month at the hospital, Dr Sie informed us that she could convalesce in a home environment. His family had found us a flat that we rented for a month in Valkenburg, a small town near Maastricht.

So both of us stayed there while Nini recovered. Akbar Tandjung and Albert Hasibuan came to see us in Valkenburg. The former told me that everything at the DPP Golkar was in good order. Then, two of Nini's cousins arrived, after which I returned to Jakarta and met with Pak Dhar and my colleagues at the DPP Golkar. My children had been well looked after, and we all talked about my plan for them to see their mother in the Netherlands. Things at my house were also in good order as my mother-in-law had moved in to look after her grandchildren.

During this trying period, both Nini and I received extraordinary sympathy and attention from many people. Donations from friends came flooding in, including from Pak Dhar. I was able to go back to the Netherlands with a considerable sum to support us while Nini recovered. I immediately opened a bank account with Algemeene Bank Nederland.

While in Valkenburg, I looked after Nini and accompanied her on a daily walk, gradually increasing the distance. I cooked and washed our clothes. I then told her that I thought our third child, Adja, and our youngest, Keke, should join us there. Adja could go to an Indonesian School in the Netherlands. I told Nini that the presence of our children with us was necessary to remind us of the future life we all aspired to, instead of feeling trapped by our current unfortunate circumstances. Nini could not agree more.

After Nini's cousins came to keep her company, I immediately flew back to Jakarta to fetch Keke, who was three years old at the time. I was only in Jakarta briefly, mainly to sort out my children's passports, after which I went back to Maastricht with Keke.

Keke's presence was timely. Nini's haemoglobin had dropped dramatically to the critical level of four. She should have received an intravenous infusion but she refused. Nini had to be rushed to hospital as an emergency. At this point, Keke's presence did wonders for Nini's morale. Her haemoglobin levels improved to a safe level of ten.

The rental of our flat in Valkenburg came to an end and we moved to a hotel. Nini's condition improved swiftly. Our three other children came to us during the school holiday, accompanied by my mother-in-law. Nini made further recovery. She now had chemotherapy twice a week. She also had to wear a wig because of losing her hair as a side effect of the chemotherapy.

Adja was duly enrolled at the Indonesian Netherlands School in Wasenaar, The Hague. We rented a small house in Scheveningen. I then bought a second-hand BMW 315 and drove it in turns with Nini. By this stage, I felt sufficiently confident to return to Jakarta and stay there longer to attend to my work.

My whole family in the Netherlands during Nini's recovery period. (from R–L) Rezal, Nini, Nino, Adja and Keke.

To my delight, I found that our monthly magazine *Media Karya* had gone from strength to strength with each edition. Its content had improved considerably, encompassing a wide range of issues, well beyond the scope of directives from the Executive Chairman. It ran articles on expositions of our ideology by Moerdiono and Oka Mahendra, historical articles by H.M. Syafaat Habib, in addition to coverage on policies and Golkar activities by our departments. There was also serial fiction by Lastri Fardani Sukarton, wife of Sukarton Marmosudjono, the head of the Board of Patrons' Secretariat. *Media Karya* was now a publication with a high rate of subscriptions from Golkar sympathizers and it had a steady stream of advertisers.

Pak Dhar asked after Nini and I informed him that she had much improved and would probably be allowed to come home in three months' time.

"Pak Harto [President Soeharto] asked me how she was and I had the impression he wanted to help. He was actually disappointed you never said anything to him about your wife", Pak Dhar said.

I realized that what he meant was that the President had discretionary powers to grant medical and financial assistance in a programme known as *Bantuan Presiden*, or Banpres.

"Pak Dhar, thanks to your generosity and that of my other friends, I have enough money for my wife's treatment. If I received further help in the form of Banpres, I would be benefitting from my Nini's illness. That would be most improper", I replied.

"I understand your thinking. What's important to me is that you report your wife's condition to Pak Harto because he cares about you. No need to ask for anything; just end your letter with 'Awaiting your instructions'", Pak Dhar said.

I duly wrote a letter to President Soeharto to apprise him of my wife's latest condition and to thank him for his sympathy. I ended the letter with, "I hereby end my report and await further instructions."

Two days later, Pak Ali Affandi, an official at the State Secretariat administrating Banpres, who happened to be father-in-law to Sudarsono, Head of the DPP Golkar Secretariat, telephoned me.

"Mas Sarwono, I am on my way to Slipi with the President's instructions", he said.

Pak Ali Affandi arrived with a stack of documents and a thick envelope that probably had money in it. He told me that he had come with documents on Banpres for me. The programme, he explained, would take effect once it had been approved by the necessary officials. Ali Affandi then asked me if my wife needed an additional doctor, to which I replied no. He also asked if I needed money to transport family members, to which I also said no. He then gave me US$5,000 in cash to pay for medical bills and daily expenses, with the condition that any unused cash should be returned to the state through a special bank account.

I was touched by the President's assistance and felt a bit dazed for having that sort of cash on my person. I used the money for Nini's medical expenses and returned the unused amount to the State Secretariat.

When I look back at the time I spent with Nini and the children in the Netherlands, I cannot help but feel humbled, thankful and amazed that Indonesian embassies in three countries—the Netherlands, Belgium and France—showered us with endless attention. Initially, they may have been attentive towards us out of duty because I was the Secretary General of Golkar and brother to their boss, the Minister of Foreign Affairs, Mochtar Kusuma-Atmadja. But true friendship did come out of it, which has lasted to this day. My whole family became close friends with Harun Al Rasyid, our ambassador in The Hague, his wife Kastini, Leonard Tobing and his family in Brussels, and Jack Gaffar and his family in Paris. When Mochtar came to Maastricht to see us, Leonard Tobing managed to talk him into having a lump on his head surgically removed. Dr Sie assured Mochtar it was just a minor procedure with zero risk. After his surgery, there was no visible trace of the lump.

We were also indebted to Dr George Sie and his family, who went beyond the call of duty in looking after us. Even the nurses in Maastricht would take the time to drop in to see Nini outside their working hours. While we were there, we also had the chance to meet Nini's and my father's relatives who had made their homes in the Netherlands.

I also often ran into Dutch people who were fluent in Indonesian. Once, I was on the road, and naturally I obeyed the traffic rules as a good European would. Then I saw a blonde Caucasian driving manically, overtaking other vehicles left, right and centre. By coincidence, both of us were side by side while waiting for the green light. I sounded my horn, and when he looked over I shook my head and proceeded to point a finger at my head, indicating I thought he was insane. He lowered his window and I did the same. "Going to get into a fight with a white man", I thought.

"Please forgive me, Pak. I'm a reckless driver. Just come back from Jakarta. [The way people drive there] rubbed off on me", he replied in the Betawi dialect. Both of us burst into laughter.

Heading back to Jakarta

Having the children around her did wonders for Nini's recovery. They became the essence of her resolve and warmth in the midst of her suffering. Our youngest, Keke, stood out during this period of our life, a three-year-old who could speak fluently and was good at singing. Once she waddled her way to the middle of the town square in Maastricht and, among the pigeons, she started singing *Burung Camar* (Sea Gulls) by Vina Panduwinata. Passers-by stopped to listen to her sing. When she finished she took a bow, prompting people to applaud.

She also liked to ask people riddles. "Why does a giraffe have a long neck?" she asked. Her siblings would try to solve the riddle, but their answers would all be wrong. "It's long because its head is far from its body."

Nini was finally given the all-clear to go home by Dr Sie, but she would need a check-up six months later. Upon her return to Jakarta, she went back to work with great enthusiasm. I also went back to work, being Secretary General again. What I found on my return was amazingly encouraging. After my absence as Secretary General for almost a year tending to family matters, Golkar was still in good form.

Golkar's List of Legislative Candidates

On coming back to the DPP Golkar office, I soon became acquainted with a number of developments that had unfolded while I was away. Akbar Tandjung, for instance, was busy finishing his studies at the University of Indonesia's School of Electronics. He was in roughly the same spot I had been at ITB when I was given the ultimatum to finish my studies in 1973. Golkar, however, was in a much better position.

The DPP had just accomplished a number of important things, one of which was the public competition to create a hymn and a marching tune for Golkar. A decision had also been made for members to start paying their dues. A new guideline on the creation of both central and regional legislative lists was finally issued. The guideline detailed the main criteria to be met by Golkar's candidates for parliament, often referred to as PDLT. Another decision made while I was away was for the quota of young people on the legislative lists. The new directive stated that the number of candidates aged forty and below, as well as the number of women candidates, had to satisfy the new twenty per cent threshold.

When I returned to Golkar, the team tasked with preparing the list of candidates had already begun working, under the leadership of Pak Manihuruk. He was assisted by the Secretary General and his deputies, as well as the Head of the OKK Department. The team reported to Golkar's Governing Board, consisting of eleven people — the Executive Chairman, eight chairmen, the Secretary General and the Treasurer.

Our team was to come up with five times the actual number of seats in the DPR for every province. Candidates were made up of Golkar functionaries drawn from the DPP, the DPD, those already in parliament (FKP) and other cadres from Golkar's stakeholders. Our candidates also included representatives of the ABRI Fraction, typically comprising officers nearing retirement who were recommended to enter parliament as part of the FKP.

After the list of candidates was finalized by the team, it went up for review in the daily meeting. Suggested changes to the list went back to the team for further work. I was most interested to note our Executive Chairman's attentiveness as a deft administrator in assessing whether the proposed candidates indeed met the set criteria. For instance, he would pinpoint which provincial list failed to meet the quota for young people and women. Pak Dhar also knew precisely why A, B and C did not need to be on the list because they had already declined to be nominated.

The team set to work again by accommodating the suggested changes and other input from the daily meeting and reporting back until consensus was reached. The updated list was then submitted to the DPD in the respective province for its input and suggestions. After further back-and-forth, a working list was finalized for each province, numbering twice the actual number of seats for the said province. The working list was then submitted to the Electoral Commission (KPU) after being approved by a plenary session of the DPP. The same procedure applied for candidates for provincial and municipal councils.

Our system was open and transparent. The list of candidates was never kept under wraps, and Golkar cadres connected with the election process had access to it. Then came the candidature bourse, which was always eventful since those who really wanted to enter parliament would naturally strive to be on the fixed list or secure one of the top numbers on the ballot paper. The fixed list was determined through prediction based on the results of the 1977 election. Unlike in subsequent years, vote-getters did not receive top numbers. National figures were given bottom numbers because they were slated to become MPR members.

Maritime Discussions with Gus Dur

While we were busy with our list of candidates, our office had a frequent visitor: the interesting K.H. Abdurrahman Wahid, better known as Gus Dur. Gus Dur would often talk to Pak Dhar alone for extended periods of time. They appeared to be on very friendly terms with one another. After he said goodbye to Pak Dhar, Gus Dur would often come to see me in my office.

One of our topics of conversation was the nation's maritime history and the recognition of Indonesia by the international community as an Archipelagic State through the enactment of the United Nations Convention of the Law of the Sea (UNCLOS) in 1982. Gus Dur's knowledge of the nation's maritime history was profound and instructive in the rise and fall of the coastal kingdoms in our archipelago. By coincidence, the topic was also covered by H.M. Syafa'at Habib in an edition of *Media Karya* in which he scrutinized the history of European mercantilism that led to the colonization of the Indonesian archipelago. For my part, I knew a little about our struggle as a nation to achieve archipelagic status at the UN, which kicked off with the Djuanda Declaration of 13 December 1957.

The topic was of interest to me. As previously related, at the age of fifteen I was a witness to a UN Summit in Geneva in April 1958, which was the opening salvo of our long fight to have the waters between our islands recognized as our own. The enactment of UNCLOS in 1982 was the triumphant ending to this.

All of a sudden, Gus Dur told me, "One day I will be President. I will appoint you minister to take care of our seas." At the time, I scarcely paid any heed to this statement of his.

Pak Dhar's Transformation

According to stories by friends, during my absence from the DPP Golkar, Pak Dhar underwent a great transformation. He was often at Slipi and made himself available to all. People were free to go in and out of his office. At times, when he wanted someone, he simply went to their workspace and sat down to talk to them.

They also told me Pak Dhar had become a great improviser in the field when he conducted his face-to-face meetings with grass-roots Golkar cadres. Sudarsono, the Head of the DPP Secretariat, told me of one instance whereby Pak Dhar visited Aceh and explained Golkar's regeneration scheme to a group of people who were there to take part in the Karakterdes programme. A woman who sat in the front row listened intently to Pak Dhar and took notes throughout. Her studiousness struck Pak Dhar, who invited her to come on to the stage to have a dialogue with him. "I couldn't help but notice you were very serious in doing this programme. Congratulations", said Pak Dhar, full of praise, followed by everyone clapping their hands. "Please introduce yourself, your name and where you are from", he continued.

The woman told everyone her name and said she was from PPP and had decided to attend the Karakterdes class to learn from Golkar with a view to doing something similar at PPP. The assembled company was stunned. A few clapped their hands but the rest were mumbling unpleasant things. Pak Dhar's reaction was quick, admirable and completely unexpected.

"Well done! I wish you every success in applying our programme with PPP. My regards to our friends in PPP", Pak Dhar said, smiling. Those in the audience were even more stunned than before. Then Pak Dhar started to explain that the membership and regeneration programme in Golkar were the application of the Law on Political Parties and Golkar, and all the programmes were open books for all. Having heard his explanation, everyone felt relieved and the applause was deafening.

Sudarsono said to me, "I worked under Pak Dhar for a long time at the State Secretariat but I didn't know he could be so responsive like that."

I had an inkling of what Pak Dhar's sense of humour was like from a story he told me once. "A few days ago, the administrators of PSSI [the Indonesian Football Association] came to see me to ask for instructions", he started. "I told them that PSSI was generally very good, technically, physically and mentally. The only thing left to do is to find out how we can score as many goals as possible against the team we are up against and to prevent them from scoring any against us", he said.

Then Pak Dhar bemusedly said that the next day the PSSI administrators held a serious talk to discuss his advice with a topic printed on its invitation that said, "The Minister of the State Secretariat's Instruction: score as many goals as possible and stop the competitor from doing the same."

So that was the general atmosphere in Golkar in the lead-up to the 1987 General Election: dynamic, united and militant. It goes without saying that Pak Dhar had become a prominent figure nationally. Yet, in the distance, dark clouds had begun to gather. A smear campaign that claimed Pak Dhar had been a member of the PKI (Indonesian Communist Party) had begun; at first just whispers, but they became louder and more persistent. A hoax was also disseminated that when he signed the founding document of Sekber Golkar in 1964, he did so as a representative of HSI (Himpunan Sarjana Indonesia), which was known to be an organization under PKI. In fact, the truth was that Colonel Sudharmono S.H. was a signatory on behalf of Persahi (Persatuan Sarjana Hukum Indonesia), an independent organization for legal practitioners.

Alertness to Potential Trouble

Friends and colleagues told me that the ABRI Commander General L.B. Moerdani had openly questioned Golkar's regeneration programme, which he saw as an excess that would yield no result whatsoever. The two things needed clarifying, but I thought it would be too sensitive to do so through the Three Stream channel. So I took the initiative to see Pak Benny at his Merdeka Barat office, with the fervent hope the meeting would go well. If for some reason he became offended, that would be the third time I would have had problems with him.

Sitting across from Pak Benny, I asked him about the pernicious rumour about Pak Dhar. "Is it true he had a PKI background?" I asked.

"Absolutely not!" he answered emphatically. "That rumour was probably started by people jealous of him."

"So why do we let it go unanswered?" I asked.

"In time, if necessary, I will put it to rest", he replied. "If we respond now, in its initial stage, we might end up pouring petrol on to the fire. Let's just wait and keep an eye on it", he added.

I thought his reasoning sensible and satisfactory. I then asked him about his scepticism of Golkar's regeneration programme, which was causing concern and surprise within Golkar. Benny Moerdani sighed deeply as he blew out cigarette smoke. He admitted that as a soldier he might have gone overboard in expressing his opinion on Golkar's politics.

A moment later he said, "We have done an assessment on you. You won't get more than 65 per cent of the votes in the 1987 election, perhaps even less than that. So what you've been doing is pointless. But, all right, I'll stop commenting on Golkar because as a soldier it's not right for me to do so. I just want to say what you are doing is just a pipe dream; no use!"

I thought to myself that it was an instructive conversation that I could use as background information with some care.

At my next opportunity to have a meeting and dinner with the Board of Patrons, I managed to speak to the President about the rumour concerning Pak Dhar.

"Oh, that hearsay is false. Dharmono is clean. But let it be. It might be a good thing for him to start having problems, he…he…he…", Pak Harto replied.

My head reeled from what he had just said.

Pak Dhar's Stoicism

To illustrate Sudharmono's stoicism in facing down malicious rumours about him, I would like to relate a funny story that captures the essence of Pak Dhar's character when under pressure.

In the midst of our preparations for the 1987 General Election, he made a point of overseeing the implementation of Golkar's membership programme and asked Team 9 and the Department of OKK to report their progress to him. He then made an unexpected comment.

"*Bu* Mochtar, the wife of the Minister of Foreign affairs, doesn't seem willing to apply for Golkar membership. Why? She told me that Si Yuk told her that she didn't have to if she didn't want to do so. Who is Si Yuk? Anyone here know something?"

I told him that Si Yuk was my nickname among family members. Mochtar's wife had once told me she did not want to be involved in politics. I understood her stance on the issue because she had experienced trauma because of politics.

"It's not something we can force people to do, Pak Dhar. Golkar's membership is voluntary", I added.

"But Jeng Nini is also yet to apply", he said of my wife. "She should have applied already by now. I ask your permission to leave the room for a moment. I will ask her myself."

When I returned to the meeting, I told him that my wife had been careless and failed to fill in her application form because of the amount of documents that needed signing on her desk. I apologized to Pak Dhar on her behalf. "But she is Golkar through and through", I assured him.

Next he emphasized the need to secure Golkar's membership programme through better screening. "There's someone I know who was just released from Pulau Buru (Detention Complex) where he was a political prisoner. How come he managed to get a Golkar membership card? What happened to our security measures that he managed to slip through?" he asked seriously.

Those present were stonily silent because what Pak Dhar had just described fitted what people were saying about him to a tee, that he was PKI since most of the prisoners on Buru Island were former PKI members. My old itch suddenly resurfaced. I just opened my mouth and what many would see as an indiscretion came out. "He was your acquaintance, Pak Dhar. That was the reason he got a membership card."

The whole room fell eerily silent and became tense. But Pak Dhar's reaction was just the opposite. He laughed aloud, tapping the table before him with his left palm while his right index finger pointed at me. "Here goes Sarwono again. That was very funny, by the way", he said, still laughing.

I could feel the whole room relax with him. Then they also laughed. But I soon felt regretful about what I had just said because jokes like this could easily be misused by irresponsible people who might seek to target Pak Dhar. "Thank you, Pak Dhar. Sorry, I may have gone too far. I ask you all not to share this joke", I said.

Another example of Pak Dhar's power of endurance took place during our fundraising for the election campaign. Alas, this one is not funny at all. As I explained before, Golkar's operational funds, whether at the national or regional level, were paid for by the Board of Patrons, with clear guidelines and accountability. Pak Dhar always made sure that our working trips to the provinces did not burden our hosts in any way. However, in order to cultivate Golkar's independence, the need to raise funds from new sources was no doubt inevitable.

As a political organization, Golkar had an array of schemes and programmes, all of which required considerable expenses to carry out. Ideally, membership fees should have been sufficient to cover most of our expenses. As mentioned before, the DPP had decided to apply a membership fee of 100 rupiah a month in the near future.

We realized that to put the decision into action required thorough preparation after our membership information system was finalized. This was to be the work of the next DPP.

In the spirit of maximizing self-funding, Pak Dhar brought us good news. He told us that the Chairman of the Board of Patrons, President Soeharto, had agreed that the DPP could conduct a fundraising event attended by business people as part of the campaign. A fundraising night was accordingly held at the Graha Krida Bhakti Hall in Jalan Veteran, Central Jakarta, attended by tycoons and big names in business, numbering around 150.

I was not involved in organizing the event because I was not tasked to do so and because of my personal dislike of being involved with anything concerning money. Pak Dhar was evidently pleased with the success of the fundraising night. He asked me and the Deputy Treasurer of the DPP, Mrs Tati Darsoyo, to accompany him to see Pak Harto at Bina Graha.

The President looked at our report on the fundraising night with a furrowed brow. A moment later, he said something that shocked us. "Why did you raise money yourselves? I have always given enough money to Golkar through my foundations", Pak Harto said with a grim face. He then added, "If you don't believe that, please have a look at the report. It's been audited by a public accountant."

Pak Dhar was visibly shaken by what had just transpired. His jugular veins protruded tensely and his face bespoke of shock and disappointment. Without further ado, the meeting came to an end. Pak Dhar looked pensive and did not say a word. Mrs Tati Darsoyo and I who witnessed the sad episode were at a loss as how to console him. But the incident apparently left no lasting mark on Pak Dhar, since he was back to himself in no time and displayed resolve and enthusiasm in leading Golkar.

Original Campaign Strategy

Golkar kicked off our campaign for the 1987 General Election with great optimism. Our own internal projection pointed to the great probability that our share of the vote would exceed that of 1982. Each Golkar member was provided guidelines on how to maximize their share of the vote in their own respective communities. The guidelines spelled out a simple strategy, with the acronym 3S—*Sedulur* (relatives and blood relations), *Sesumur* (neighbours) and *Sedapur* (members of our own nuclear family)—encouraging people to invite those closest to them to vote for Golkar.

I was a candidate for the Special Capital City Region (DKI) of Jakarta. In this I was fortunate that, having won my seat in the 1982 election, I was familiar with campaigning in the city, and my social network there was solid. I started going around the city to canvass support and enlisted the help of Kosti Jaya taxi drivers.

At that point, Kosti Jaya had an armada of three hundred taxis. If each driver spoke to ten people a day about voting for Golkar, we would have three thousand people each day hearing positive and authentic messages about Golkar. We could also be sure that the message got passed around to others as well.

The drivers were extremely keen on being part of the campaign, so I felt compelled to formulate a code of conduct in communicating with their passengers. For example, taxis drivers were forbidden from taking part in campaign parades or carrying Golkar emblems. If a driver desired to attend a Golkar campaign event, they would only be allowed to do so on the condition of not being in Kosti Jaya uniform. Their priority was to communicate with their passengers politely and effectively.

Some drivers came up with the idea of writing Golkar testimonial letters for their passengers, and asked me whether this was allowed. I told them it was as long as the letter was given to the passenger on the point of leaving the car, not as they had just entered it.

On Friday, 10 April 1987, when I was at the DPP Golkar, Wawan Gunawan, the administrator of AMPI sub-district Karet Tengsin, came to see me. I had known Wawan from our 1982 campaign. He was a militant Golkar cadre who faced a huge challenge as his area had never been won by a Golkar candidate.

Wawan was one of the AMPI administrators who had organized a parade on foot through our marginal areas distributing stickers back in 1982. On this occasion, he told me that I was expected by the youth of Karet Tengsin. "They have issued a challenge for you. Will you come to them?" Wawan said. "I already told them Pak Sarwono would definitely come. So, please, come with me now. If you don't, where will I hide my face?"

The youth of Karet Tengsin had a reputation for being delinquents and of having disturbed our campaign in rather creative ways, such as by putting sand into our truck's carburettor, pretending to attend a rally and then proceeding to wreck it from the inside, and vandalizing our banners .

When Wawan came to me, I was in the middle of a discussion with several other guests. It occurred to me it might be a good idea to invite these guests to come along to Karet Tengsin because it was my view they might make good role models for the youth there. I was lucky that one of them was the late M. Sjafe'I Hassanbasari, a reporter for *Kompas*, who could cover what I suspected would be an interesting story. So we all set out for Karet Tengsin.

Another of my guests was Untung Djumadi. He had come to tell me that he had just graduated from the School of Law at the University of Krisna Dwipayana (Unkris). The story of his life is fascinating. After finishing junior high school in Nganjuk, he fled to Jakarta, determined to make something of his life because he could no longer stand how poor his family was. He wanted to be financially independent, so he had done all manner of odd jobs as of 1976. By way of accommodation, he squatted at the Security Post at the DPR. He was eventually brought to us at the FKP Secretariat, whereby he was given a job as an office boy. He performed his duties well. Three years later, he informed us that he had graduated from high school, having attended night classes. My colleagues and I were surprised and impressed.

"I have applied to the School of Law at Unkris and have been accepted. But I can only go to university if someone is willing to help out with the expenses. I don't want to impose, though, so if no one can help, that's okay", Untung Djumadi said.

I started spontaneous fundraising among my fellow FKP leadership friends and the *cleret gombel* group. In a short time we had enough money for the enrolment fee and a year's worth of tuition fees. People were more than willing to chip in because Untung Djumadi had earned his reputation as a diligent, helpful and smart person.

My next guest was Otje Soedioto who was a law graduate from Melbourne University's postgraduate programme. He then worked as a journalist at *Berita Yudha*, based in the Ministry of Foreign Affairs, before subsequently practising law. Otje was congenitally blind but was fortunate enough to have parents who encouraged him to think positively. He never went to a special school for children with disabilities. I was first acquainted with Otje at the house of one of my relatives and found him to be impressively knowledgeable as well as a pleasant conversationalist. I only found out he was blind when he started feeling the top of the table to look for an ashtray. Otje often made jokes about his being blind. He was also capable of giving directions to any taxi driver. When he came to visit me at my office, he was already a functionary at Pertuni (the Indonesian Association of the Blind).

My third guest was Muchtar Abbas, who was Acehnese and a former boarder of Mimi's in Bandung where he studied Mathematics at ITB. Muchtar became a friend of our family. After he left Mimi's house, we lost touch until I ran into him in Magelang. While I had by then become Golkar's Secretary General, Muchtar was the Village Chief of Pabelan, Magelang, Central Java.

The story of how Muchtar Abbas became a village chief is interesting. Towards the end of his studies at ITB, Muchtar conducted his compulsory work experience in the village of Pabelan, Magelang. There he developed ideas on how to reduce poverty in the village, which he eventually shared with K.H. Hamam Dja'far the cleric, who headed the *pesantren* school of Pabelan. He was then invited by the cleric to put his ideas into practice.

Muchtar was so dedicated to his project that he stopped his studies at ITB to allow him greater focus. He empowered the farmers in the village by revamping the irrigation channels for their paddy fields. He was also instrumental in getting the village administration to reduce the levies they were in the habit of imposing on villagers. His efforts paid off and many farmers managed to emancipate themselves from poverty. Muchtar Abbas's project was part of an empowerment programme under LP3ES and P3M (the Association of Pesantren and Community Development), which subsequently won the Aga Khan Award, accepted by K.H. Hamam Dja'far. Included in the award was the *pesantren*'s BPPM (The Center for Communal Training and Development).

The success of Muchtar Abbas in Pabelan led to his election as village chief, in which he beat the other candidate who had a military background. It was quite an extraordinary event for a newcomer from Aceh, who did not speak the Javanese language, to win a village election in Central Java.

Muchtar Abbas came to me at Slipi after he collected his award for Pioneering Youth (National Level) of 1986 in Jakarta.

It was these three guests of mine that I wanted to showcase as role models to the youth of Karet Tengsin who were in the habit of complaining how hard their lives were. I started by introducing our guests: "Today we have Untung Djumadi who had to do odd jobs and was away from his parents and hometown. But he managed to graduate from the Law School. We also have Otje Soedioto, who can't see but finished his postgraduate studies in Australia. Then we have Muchtar Abbas who is a Pioneering Youth as well as an elected village chief, even though he can't speak Javanese. You, on the other hand, all live in your own hometown with your parents, with good eyesight and are all healthy. So how come all you can do is whine and complain?"

Lively discussion ensued among those present, and the youngsters seemed intrigued and wanted to know more about our guests of honour.

In its Saturday edition, 11 April 1987, *Kompas* carried a small news item on our group discussion in the densely populated area of Karet Tengsin. Commenting on the article, the communications expert Alwi Dahlan, who would later become the Minister of Information in 1998, called the event a breakthrough in political communication. The event also became a topic of conversation among the residents of the sub-district of Karet Tengsin, and I was subsequently invited to a community gathering at the house of Pak Agus Lematang, RW Chief 006, Karet Tengsin, who was also Golkar's local district commissioner.

The gathering was designed as an informal event open to all residents and was, strictly speaking, not a campaign event at all. However, it could not be helped that it had a distinct political atmosphere because the local residents who had never voted for Golkar before changed their minds about us. They became even more sympathetic towards us, especially after the gathering led to a few local schemes—paid for through crowd funding—designed to revamp the area and provide assistance and training for economically struggling residents.

As Golkar's Secretary General, I held a discussion with the youth of Karet Tengsin, Central Jakarta, in 1987. As we sat on mats talking, I introduced them to three young men who, despite their limitations and circumstances, managed to be successful. I wanted them to become role models for the local youth. Photo by *Kompas*/Oemar Samsuri.

For the first time, Golkar had managed to spread its wings in the area, at the grass-roots level, without utilizing organizational intervention. Everything happened as a communal effort, set in motion by a small discussion I attended along with the three friends whose presence was timely enough to allow them to become role models for the local youth. As a follow-up activity, the youth of Karet Tengsin formed a group called 3M (Membangun Manusia Mandiri). The group would collect fees from its members to fund their own trip to Pabelan, on the invitation of Muchtar Abbas, in order to take part in empowerment training at the BPPM at the Pabelan *pesantren.*

Overall, I think it was an extraordinary experience that a small gathering attended by 150 youngsters for one and a half hours managed to change their way of thinking. Their transformation from a bunch of disaffected youngsters who liked to complain and get involved in delinquent acts to positive-thinking individuals was remarkable.

I repeated the Karet Tengsin template of action in several locations in Jakarta, in places where I had cultivated good relations with the residents since my first Jakarta campaign in 1982. The results were the same. People changed their minds about Golkar, without it having to be there explicitly with slogans and emblems. What stood out was the sense of togetherness in improving the quality of life through communal efforts and real action. Once the residents understood the importance of togetherness and communal efforts, Golkar could then take them to the next level, which was training through Karakterdes after the 1987 election, in the DPP's next term.

The personal campaign approach, known as 3S, and the campaign guidelines I formulated for Kosti Jaya and the places where I had started to accumulate social capital were a marked departure from the typical campaign style prevalent at the time. The standard campaign style in those days was a combination of mass mobilization and entertainment. As such, a campaign event was only deemed a success if attended by thousands of people in an open field or meeting hall, where Golkar cadres paraded themselves in uniform, where charismatic figures delivered their rhetorical speeches and famous entertainers gave out wonderful performances. I tended to avoid events of this category. If attendance was unavoidable, I would only appear on the stage briefly to be introduced and would then go down to mingle with the crowds.

Triumph at the 1987 Election

The result of the 1987 General Election was a great triumph for Golkar, as our share of the total national vote stood at 73 per cent, 9 per cent higher than that of the previous election in 1982. There were a number of factors at play here: unity, militancy, and a fully functional political machine, under Pak Dhar's inspirational and collegial leadership.

Secondly, the New Order government was in the process of attaining its pinnacle of success in reversing the political and economic chaos under Soekarno's Guided Democracy. An authoritarian government was still seen as a price worth paying for the relative ease of living enjoyed by many.

Pak Dhar did not wallow in the euphoria of our electoral success, and he immediately tasked the DPP to prepare the next phase in our work agenda. First on the list was the preparatory work for the upcoming MPR General Assembly, by assigning personnel to support our agenda within the FKP and MPR. Next was to set up teams to come up with legislative drafts for the MPR. Preparation for Golkar's National Congress of 1988 was next on the list, preceded by Regional Congresses at both provincial and municipal levels.

Moreover, Pak Dhar also toured the regions to express his thanks to Golkar's cadres for their efforts and their role in our electoral victory.

Team 9

With our Golkar agenda in full motion, President Soeharto summoned nine individuals to his residence in Jalan Cendana. The nine were General Try Sutrisno, the Army Chief of Staff; Lieutenant General Edi Sudrajat, the Deputy Army Chief of Staff; Lieutenant General Soegiarto, Chief of Sociopolitical Affairs of ABRI; Cosmas Batubara, the Minister of Public Housing; Ginandjar Kartasasmita, the Junior Minister for the Optimization of Domestic Goods Usage and Head of the Investment Coordinating Agency; Moerdiono, the Junior Minister Cabinet Secretary; and lastly the three of us from Golkar: Akbar Tandjung, Siswono Yudo Husodo and myself.

The President gave us a secret task, the progress of which was to be reported only to him and the details not to be divulged to anyone else. Our task was to discuss and propose names suitable for posts within the state institutions, including the President and Vice President. "If any of you think that I'm no longer fit to continue as President, please don't hesitate to say so", he said. We all felt slightly overwhelmed by the task. We had heard that after the 1982 election, five people had been tasked with the same thing, but we never learned who they were and what they suggested.

A few days later, we started to meet each evening at Wisma Yani, Jalan Diponegoro, chaired by General Try Sutrisno, to discuss the mission given to us. As for the post of President, naturally we did not have any other candidate but Pak Harto. Certainly, no one hesitated to mention his name. On the question of the post of Vice President, the three of us from the DPP Golkar enthusiastically put forward Pak Dhar's name. The others welcomed our suggestion, on the condition that if Pak Harto indicated that another post might be more appropriate for Pak Dhar, Pak Umar Wirahadikusuma would continue as VP.

The three of us from Golkar also wholeheartedly nominated Pak Manihuruk as a candidate for Chief of the Audit Board of the Republic of Indonesia. The others obviously shared our great respect for Pak Manihuruk and our suggestion was accepted. For the post of Speaker for the MPR/DPR, we all agreed to nominate Lieutenant General M. Charis Suhud, and Lieutenant General Ali Said as Chief Justice of the Supreme Court.

We reported the results of our deliberation to the President and he welcomed them. He repeated his instruction that our recommendations had to be treated as confidential. Pak Dhar was aware of the existence of "Team 9", but he also stressed on the need for confidentiality. "I am not allowed to know anything about this. Perhaps someday I will, but that will be up to the President to tell me", he said.

1988 MPR General Assembly

As the MPR General Assembly drew nearer, the public eagerly awaited the news of who was to be our next Vice President. Who was being nominated as President was not an issue at all. Pak Harto had by this stage become the accepted permanent candidate for every foreseeable MPR General Assembly. As with previous periods before the assembly, various pressure groups voiced their unanimous resolve to nominate

Pak Harto for another term. However, there was no manoeuvring to nominate anyone for the post of Vice President, which distinguished it from the circumstances surrounding the previous assembly. Consequently, towards the end of February, Akbat Tandjung and I went to see Pak Dhar and informed him of the lack of a vice presidential candidate.

"Pak Harto has already asked me to become Vice President. I replied that he should not think on it. I haven't even told my wife about this", Pak Dhar said.

Both Akbar and I were left wondering what Pak Dhar was trying to say, so I asked, "What is the matter, Pak Dhar? Surely it's very natural that you should be the vice presidential candidate?"

"I will only believe it when the Speaker of the MPR has declared me as Vice President", Pak Dhar replied. "I have been in this environment for too long [to be gullible]. Anything can change at the eleventh hour. Pak Harto doesn't have to feel he ought to offer the position to me. I am content with how things are."

Sudharmono's Candidacy

Bearing in mind that Team 9 had already approved of Pak Dhar's candidacy as Vice President and that Pak Harto had already learned of our recommendations, I believed it was time to declare his candidacy. "Pak Dhar, we in Golkar would be delighted if you were to be our candidate. I propose that we proceed with your candidacy through our organization's mechanism", I said.

"Please, not like that", he told me. "If you want to know, please go and see Pak Harto in your capacity as leaders of the FKP-MPR and the DPP Golkar and talk to him directly. Because this is about me, you should go there with Pak Sugandhi, Chairman of the FKP-MPR."

That was what we did. Akbar Tandjung and I told Sugandhi about our conversation with Pak Dhar. I also had a further suggestion for Sugandhi. "It would be better if F-ABRI in the MPR and the MPR's Regional Representatives were also present. But they must be invited by Pak Harto because we have no authority to ask for their presence", I said.

Sugandhi was of the same mind and sent a message to Colonel Suyono, aide de camp to the President, and Sugandhi's son-in-law.

On 26 February 1988, a meeting was convened at Soeharto's residence in Jalan Cendana. Representing the FKP-MPR were Sugandhi, Chairman of the FKP-MPR; Akbar Tandjung, Secretary of the FKP-MPR; and myself as the Deputy Chairman of the FKP-MPR. The ABRI Fraction had sent Major General Harsudiono Hartas, the Asospol of ABRI, and Colonel Dr Suhadi. From the MPR Regional Representatives there were Professor Ibrahim Hasan, the Governor of Aceh H.M. Said, the Governor of South Kalimantan and the Governor of Bali Professor I.B. Mantra.

Sugandhi started the conversation by saying that we were there to see the President to ask if he had made up his mind on the identity of the vice presidential candidate to be put forward in the upcoming MPR General Assembly, now that Pak Harto himself was the presidential candidate.

"I can work with anyone", Pak Harto replied. He then elaborated on a few normative criteria for the post of Vice President. "But in line with the changing times, I don't think you should ask me who should be my Vice President. It is time that a Vice Presidential candidate should be someone put forward and supported by sociopolitical forces because our future leaders will be those supported by these forces", Pak Harto explained.

After a brief discussion still on the same theme, Sugandhi asked, "My conclusion, based on your criteria, Mr President, is that you approve of Pak Sudharmono as the Vice Presidential candidate?"

Major General Harsudiono Hartas immediately reacted, "I agree with Pak Sugandhi."

"I know Pak Sudharmono well and he ticks all the boxes as far as the previously mentioned criteria go. He had a role in founding Sekber Golkar and is successful as the Executive Chairman of Golkar, as well as being widely supported", Pak Harto responded.

I wanted to make sure that Pak Harto had truly made up his mind because in a Team 9 meeting someone had suggested that Pak Umar Wirahadikusuma be nominated as an alternative. So I blatantly asked, "What about Pak Umar?"

"I have so far worked well with Pak Umar", Soeharto replied. "But unfortunately he has no experience in leading a sociopolitical force."

The Regional Representatives were silent spectators and listeners throughout, but it was customary for them to go along with whatever the President decided on. We all breathed a sigh of relief. It was definitive. Sudharmono had been given the blessing to run for Vice President. We left the President's house and decided to give a press conference, and then went to see Pak Dhar at his residence.

In speaking to the press, naturally we did not refer to the presence of either F-ABRI or F-Regional Representatives, to honour the prevalent tradition that our meetings with other fractions were informal and off the record.

In our press conference, Sugandhi explained that a meeting had taken place between the President in his capacity as Golkar's Chairman of the Board of Patrons and the leadership of FKP-MPR. He continued to say that Pak Harto had imparted a set of criteria for a Vice Presidential candidate, with special emphasis on support from the "sociopolitical force" with a majority in the MPR. The necessity for this sociopolitical support in turn led to a political process in which the FKP-MPR was in preparation to nominate a candidate. This was a marked departure from past instances in which the Vice Presidential candidate was nominated by the Presidential candidate and would subsequently be supported by sociopolitical forces.

After the conclusion of our press conference, Akbar Tandjung and I visited Pak Dhar at his residence. We brought him the good news that Pak Harto had given his blessing for him to become Vice President and the need to press ahead with the nomination process through the FKP-MPR. We also reported that both F-ABRI through its head Major General Harsudiono Hartas and F-Regional Representatives welcomed his nomination.

"Thank you both for the good news", Pak Dhar said. "I did receive information that F-ABRI supported my nomination. But I'm still doubtful as to whether support for me within Golkar is truly solid."

Pak Dhar's remark came as a shock because the matter had long been settled through a survey within the DPP and the FKP-MPR, the members of which all supported Pak Dhar. Both Akbar and I vouched for the rest of our colleagues that we were all behind him.

On the following day, the leaderships of the FKP-MPR, the DPP and the FKP parliamentary personnel conducted a joint meeting to hear the report by Sugandhi concerning our meeting with the Chairman of the Board of Patrons, the President. The meeting quickly produced a resolution to nominate Pak Dhar as Vice President, and formal action would follow soon.

Since the meeting discussed the nomination of our vice presidential candidate who happened to be Pak Dhar, Sugandhi acted as chair. I sat next to Pak Dhar who then turned to me, raised his eyebrows and asked, "Are you sure everyone in this room supports me?"

I replied, "Absolutely, Pak Dhar. There's no problem here. We will fully support you. You'll see."

I had formed a different impression to Pak Dhar's. I thought, if there was ambivalence, it would be in the support from F-ABRI. At the top level—the leadership of F-ABRI and the new Commander General Try Sutrisno—the support for Pak Dhar seemed genuine enough. However, it might have been wobbly at other levels where political manoeuvres and uncertainty of stance were afoot. With such mixed signals, it did occur to me that parts of the military were preparing an alternative scenario.

Informing Benny Moerdani

My suspicion led me to request a meeting with Pak Benny Moerdani, who received me in his office in Tebet. What he said stunned me. "Pak Harto wants Pak Umar as his Vice President", he said.

I then related the chronology of Pak Dhar's nomination, including the stance taken by Head of F-ABRI, Major General Harsudiono Hartas, as well as discussions through the Three Stream channel. Pak Benny listened to me intently and then asked, "Whom did you meet outside?"

I told him I had run into Air Marshall Teddy Rusdi.

"Did you speak to him about this?" Pak Benny asked.

"No", I replied.

Pak Benny then asked me to repeat my story. It then occurred to me that I had a piece of information that may have been of use to him. "Pak Benny, the papers on the candidacy of Pak Harto and Pak Dhar on the same ticket are now being prepared at the State Secretariat. Though not at the Palace, but at the Secretariat of the Supreme Court."

He seemed taken aback and asked, "How did you know that?"

I told him I was used to checking small details in all things. "You can verify this piece of information yourself, Pak Benny", I said.

He froze for a moment and then said, "Sar, I consider myself close to Pak Harto. He should have told me honestly that he wanted Pak Dhar as Vice President. It would have been fine with me. I would have gone along. The fact is he never said that to me. How could he not have? This won't be easy for ABRI to change course in the final hours like this. It would be like turning around a carrier ship."

Dynamics of Vice Presidential Nomination

I heard from the grapevine that following my meeting with Pak Benny, a fierce debate within the ABRI leadership erupted over Pak Dhar's nomination. When the time came for all the fractions of the MPR to put forth their candidates for both the President and Vice President, all nominated Pak Harto for President. But the United Development Party Fraction (F-PPP) put forward Hj Naro, its own Executive Chairman as its Vice Presidential candidate. The other fractions nominated Pak Dhar.

The candidacy of Hj Naro came as a surprise. Given Golkar's majority in parliament, even if Hj Naro made it through to the voting stage, Pak Dhar would still have won. Hence, Hj Naro's candidacy had to be seen as an attempt to create a precedent, possibly inspired by the President's own criteria that the Vice President had to have sociopolitical support. As it represented a change to the New Order's tradition in electing the President and Vice President, the move by the F-PPP attracted a lot of media attention. From their perspective, the possibility that there would be two Vice Presidential candidates competing in the MPR General Assembly was newsworthy because of its novelty value. Consequently, the nomination of Hj Naro became a trending topic as well as a catalyst for a range of lobbying activities, manoeuvres and ruses that do not need to be elaborated here.

The FKP-MPR chose to respond by suggesting that Hj Naro pull himself out of the race, and I was given the task of delivering this statement to the press.

"Between F-PPP and FKP, there have always been differences in opinions on the substantive issues concerning the Broad Outlines of State Policy (GBHN). Thus it is impossible for our presidential candidate to be expected to work with a candidate from F-PPP. The differences between them rule out any effective cooperation, which is a prerequisite as stated by the law for the nomination of the President and Vice President. As a result, we urge Pak Hj Naro to withdraw his nomination", I said.

Pak Naro was angered by my statement. When we ran into each other in the MPR building, he said, "If the person delivering the statement had been a senior figure, I would have been able to accept it. But because it was some rookie like you, I was offended."

Hj Naro decided to go through the whole process of nomination because he wanted to be on the record of having been a Vice Presidential candidate. "What happens after that, it's up to my party. If they withdraw my nomination, that will be fine with me", Naro said. And that was exactly what happened. Afterwards, he reverted to his old self, good-humoured and friendly towards me. His anger towards me earlier had therefore been part of his status as a Vice Presidential candidate.

Sudharmono Elected as VP

The MPR General Assembly moved to elect Pak Harto and Pak Dhar as President and Vice President respectively by acclamation, but not before an MPR member from F-ABRI, Brigadier General Ibrahim Saleh, suddenly made for the podium to speak against Pak Dhar's candidacy, without having secured permission to do so from the Speaker. Ibrahim Saleh was duly hemmed in by Pak Benny Moerdani and Pak Try Sutrisno and escorted from the podium.

When the situation was back under control, Pak Dhar was declared Vice President. While the declaration of Pak Harto's re-election as President drew applause from everyone, Pak Dhar's declaration was greeted with silence from members of F-ABRI.

Dual Office Holding

When I was appointed the Minister of State for Administrative Reform after the 1988 MPR General Assembly, I continued to hold my position as the Secretary General of Golkar until the end of Golkar's National Congress in October. As such, I was still involved alongside my colleagues at the DPP in supervising the Regional Congresses at both provincial and municipal levels, composing the DPP's accountability report for our term of 1983–88 and formulating draft resolutions for the National Congress.

In the past, Regional Congresses had been held after the National Congress. However, it was decided that our 1987 National Leadership Summit would reverse the sequence, intent as we were on starting a new tradition whereby leadership germinated from the regions. Golkar would see to it that our best regional cadres elected in their respective congresses would then compete at the National Congress.

However, in practice, Regional Congresses saw the exertion of will by Stream A to position military personnel in leadership posts. ABRI, as the more senior Stream A, had been taken aback by the speed and militancy with which the junior Stream G had grown.

As previously described, in his prediction about Golkar's result for the 1987 election, Benny Moerdani had said that 65 per cent was the highest we should expect to see, with or without our campaign strategy, which he called useless. But we proved him wrong on that score. So, reactively, Stream A launched an offensive to strengthen its control of the junior Stream G by occupying regional leaderships; if necessary, by granting officers early retirement.

As the outgoing Executive Chairman of the DPP, Pak Dhar tried his best to win support for Stream A personnel who satisfied the new criteria enacted by Golkar towards a membership system that was voluntary, volitional and individual. At the provincial level, this was successful to a certain degree. But, undeniably, the process of re-militarization of Golkar had begun in many aspects. For example, from the wide array of choices available, it was Lieutenant General (Rtd.) Wahono who was eventually elected as the new Executive Chairman, after Pak Dhar made it clear he did not want the job again. Nevertheless, the rest of the DPP functionaries still came from the G group, something that had been pioneered by the previous administration. It was, for example, reflected in the election of Rahmat Witoelar as the Secretary General of the DPP Golkar.

We also held the National Congress with great success. The resolution adopted by the 1987 National Leadership Summit was well received at the congress. The resolution sought to strengthen the foundation on which a more independent, mature and well-rooted Golkar could be built through ideological, intellectual and organizational consolidation. Our accountability report was also accepted.

Having fulfilled all my obligations as Golkar's Secretary General, I felt I needed to prepare myself for the new chapter in my life as the Minister of State for Administrative Reform.

Cendana Meetings

In the early days of my time as the Minister of State for Administrative Reform, I often found myself engaged in personal communication with President Soeharto. On several occasions, the two of us spoke together in private, which in itself is an interesting experience I would like to share in this memoir.

As a cabinet minister, I had both the opportunity and reason to request an audience with the President to seek his instructions. My requests were usually granted immediately. The President would receive me in the evening at 8:30 at his residence in Jalan Cendana, Menteng, Central Jakarta. We would meet after there was no one else around and the reporters' waiting room was empty. Some of our meetings were at the President's own initiative. He would also summon me in the evening.

Our conversation, however, was more of a monologue. Pak Harto would tell me in great detail his past experiences and encounters with the well-known figures of the day. In the beginning, I found his stories interesting and would ask him questions. But I gradually found our meetings to be strange because three months had gone by—during which I saw him once a week—but there was still no instructions of what was expected of me as minister.

I told Pak Dhar my dilemma, who was at this point already Vice President. I asked him what the nocturnal meetings with Pak Harto could mean.

"Oh, that means he is trying to suss you out first before deciding if you could be recruited into the inner circle. I think Pak Harto is trying to see if you can work with him, not merely as a minister but also as part of his inner circle", Pak Dhar concluded.

Then I asked him how I should respond.

"Well, it's up to you. It has to be your own choice. I was part of the inner circle when I was the Minister of the State Secretariat. It was a huge burden. There was a lot that we knew as an insider but at the same time we had to keep our mouths shut about. There were times when the President would order us to do something while our conscience made us question the order. He would sometimes lay down guidelines that needed to be interpreted accurately, which wasn't easy at all", Pak Dhar explained.

"Do what you think best. I merely want to remind you that it's not easy being in the inner circle. The psychological burden is considerable. People have been known to not be able to withstand the pressure and end up disoriented or acting strangely", Pak Dhar added.

I also went to see General Benny Moerdani to tell him my experience with Pak Harto. His answer was similar to Pak Dhar's and he told me it was my decision alone as to how to proceed.

After considering the matter carefully, I was resolved to remain on the Middle Course. True to it, I would always be able to maintain my distance from the top political elite in the country. Following it, I would be able to work within the mandate given to me, of course with my own creative touch and systematic approach. My mind made up, what I only needed to do was to tell Pak Harto in an unmistakable way.

The time came during one meeting at which Pak Harto started to tell me things of a personal nature. I thought it was time to send a clear signal that I had no interest in being in his inner circle, or what many called the Cendana group.

"Pak Harto, I feel I have gained a lot through our discussions", I started. "However, with all due respect, I'm not used to speaking about things that are too private. Moreover, Mr President, you haven't given me pointers as to what's expected of me as minister, despite my having submitted several reports", I said.

For a fleeting moment, I saw Pak Harto's face harden. Then he said, "Please have a drink."

After a few pleasantries, I took my leave. I felt as if a great burden had been lifted from my shoulders!

When I requested to see him next, he instructed me to come to Bina Graha at 10 a.m., not to Cendana. It was a different atmosphere altogether. He used our meeting to give me guidelines for the implementation of *Pengawasan Melekat*. I thought it fortunate that I had submitted my report on the programme to the President and that I had actively taken part in its composition, drawing on input by the Head of the State Administration Agency, Professor Bintoro Tjokroamidjodjo, and the staff at my own ministry.

I saw that the President had indeed read my report since some of the pages had been marked. On a few pages, sentences had been underlined and his comments written in the margins.

Our discussion was animated and enjoyable, and lasted for more than an hour. President Soeharto had clearly mastered the content of my report. Such was his reputation then. He started to read all the ministerial reports sent to him between 10 p.m and 1 a.m.

President Soeharto in his official position as the Head of State and Government was coherent, effective and masterful of the intricacies of public policy. However, within his inner circle, he could be someone who was both unpredictable and unfathomable in his wishes. As I related before, around the time of the 1983 MPR General Assembly, both Pak Dhar and Pak Benny—both loyal members of his inner circle—were unsure of what the President really wanted.

All these factors led to my conviction that I was right to stay on the Middle Course, where the winds and waves were strong but still navigable, whereas being an insider would only lead to troubled waters and fickle gales.

Epilogue

This book is a record of my experiences and personal observations between 1948—when as a toddler I first had limited awareness of my surroundings—and 1988, when I ended my tenure as the Secretary General of Golkar. During this period in my life, there were a great many lessons that I gained but which I could only fully discern through observation and contemplation.

I started writing this book in 2005 and continued the effort sporadically and then intensely in the first half of 2018. It was an interesting and instructive experience. I discovered that the more I wrote, the more I remembered. I also needed to rely on considerable self-discipline so that the various conclusions I made from the process of writing were commensurate with my actual awareness at the time. I tried to resist the temptation of using hindsight. In this respect, I naturally needed a process of control, which I was able to procure not only from the available literature but also from the services and help of friends and family, as I explained in the Preface.

My advice to the younger generations: record what is taking place around you and write down your experiences day to day, whether they had a little or big impact on the world beyond yourself. For my own part, I was lucky enough that certain important moments were documented by my late wife, Nini, who even when she was terminally ill, continued to file important documents, which I found invaluable for the writing of this book. Several colleagues also sent me media clippings from their collections. In the digital age of today, also known as the Fourth Industrial Revolution—whereby digital technology is expected to develop exponentially—creating a record of our life's work and the interconnectedness of different events will be easier to do. The past, the present and the future can be more easily mapped out in terms of relevance and mutual relationships. By turning it into an instrument for charting one's life experiences, information technology will not be reduced to a facilitating tool for momentary uses but will instead contribute to more meaningful choices for the future.

Here are a few of life's lessons that have accrued to me.

First, I was fortunate to be born into a family that adhered to good and sound values. My parents had different characters to each other, but they chose to put into practice what was good, rejected what was bad and they both cared about their surroundings and their fellow human beings, in the spirit of inclusive nationhood. Nevertheless, all this would have meant less had I not had an innate sense of curiosity since childhood. I always asked questions to seek to understand what I saw, what I experienced and heard. This curiosity has become an institutionalized habit of mine.

Second, often unbeknown to me, I was quietly observed by those who later made me life-changing offers. Mimi and I happily accepted Oom Son's offer for us to accompany his family to go abroad because he and his family were very close to us. I was delighted to be offered such an opportunity because, among other reasons, I acquired a brother in the process, Juwono, who was only slightly older than me. My own brother, Mochtar, whom I admired and tried to emulate, was far older than me, and therefore our relationship was not as close as it might have been had we been closer in age.

I did not take all the offers that came my way. I turned down the offer made by the Headmaster of King's School, Mr James H. Mosey, for me to continue my studies in the UK because I missed my family and homeland. If I had accepted his offer, my life might have turned out differently. I could have lived in a foreign land for a long time, even settled there with an English woman and ended up opening an Asian restaurant. Anything is possible.

Pak Harto's instruction for Lieutenant General Benny Moerdani to make me Golkar's Secretary General—which I related at the end of Chapter 3—was an implicit offer for me to step into the President's political inner circle. At the end of Chapter 4, I wrote about my conversation with the president. He gave out a signal that I should join his inner circle. By instinct, I chose to stay true to the Middle Course instead, to maintain a healthy distance from the political elite, to prioritize wholesome political life through public discourse and to take an active role in building up the system.

Third, as a family we chose to live decent but simple lives. As a politician, I had every opportunity to live affluently. We as a family did not choose to go down that path because we were used to the simple life. Besides, there were so many others who were in need that we felt thankful to be able to have all our needs fulfilled, which was consistent with the values our parents had taught us. Those values were in turn passed on to our own children during conversations at our dining table. Both Nini and I were so busy with our work that we designated quality time, one example of which was conducting a meaningful dialogue with our children at the dining table. Our children were profoundly impacted by our discourses. They told me never to sell the round marble-top table because they felt they had been brought up during the conversations at that very table.

Fourth, looking back and contemplating the multitude of events and life experiences, I can safely say I regret nothing. Of course, there were things I might have done differently, for instance my obsession with rectifying my weaknesses and with perfection could have been more balanced if I had paid more attention to my innate abilities. When I was little, for example, I had a knack for drawing pictures. But I chose not to develop this ability because I was too fixated with overcoming my weaknesses. As a result, this ability vanished and would be difficult to reawaken.

I managed to moderate my obsession with achieving perfection in work by incorporating teamwork. The role of each team member was determined by their individual strengths, so in the end it was the collective strength that stood out, with weaknesses being corrected in the process.

Between 1948 and 1988, great changes took place in Indonesia. I did not discuss all the events in the period. I managed to put forth my own impression of Indonesia's role in the Non-Aligned Movement in Chapter 2. At the time, I was in Europe and liked to visit Yugoslavia for every school holiday between 1956 and 1959. So I was intimately aware of the struggles of newly independent nations and the friendship between Indonesia and Yugoslavia within the Non-Aligned Movement. Consequently, the awareness was present in me as a high school student, not with the benefit of hindsight.

The transformation from the era of Guided Democracy to that of the New Order was characterized by the shift from Soekarno's emphasis on nation and character building—as it was called then—towards national development under the New Order. The new paradigm was carried out using both security and an economic approach, subsequently formulated in the slogan of the Trilogy of Development: dynamic national stability, high economic growth and even distribution of development and its fruits.

The awareness of continued commitment to nationhood is the reason why the Unitary State of the Republic of Indonesia is still standing today, despite the drastic political changes and conflicts throughout its history. Alas, this memoir, which contains my personal experiences, lacks the scope to describe all of our nation's growing pains, even in the period it tries to cover.

It is my hope that in the next memoir I will be able to remedy this defect to a certain degree by sharing my experiences and observations of the period when I was the Minister of State for Administrative Reform, the Minister of the Environment and the Minister of Maritime Affairs and Fisheries, and a sitting member of the DPD, as well as what my life is like after a lifetime in politics, government and society.

Glossary

A

Anak-anak Soekarno was the term used to describe university student activists who were admirers of President Soekarno but who chose to be critical of him.

Apotek de Gedeh was a pharmacy set up in the Dutch colonial era, which subsequently changed its name to Apotek Kimia Farma

B

Barisan Soekarno was a pressure group that surfaced amid the political chaos of the 1960s. The public was divided between those who were for and against groups that supported President Soekarno.

Belgrade was the capital city of Yugoslavia. After Yugoslavia broke up into a number of independent states in the 1990s, Belgrade became the capital city of Serbia.

Boat people is a term that refers to the thousands of Vietnamese refugees who fled their country on makeshift boats during the Vietnamese civil war in the early 1970s. The war raged between the Communist North, backed by China, and the nationalist South, backed by the United States and its allies. Thousands of the boat people entered Indonesian waters, and they were temporarily housed on the island of Galang.

BP7 – Badan Pembina Pendidikan Pelaksanaan Pedoman Penghayatan dan Pengamalan Pancasila (Supervisory Agency for Education in the Directive for the Realization and Implementation of Pancasila) was a government agency mandated to disseminate Pancasila across Indonesian society through P4 "classes", which were mandatory for most Indonesians. The agency was disbanded during the era of Reformasi.

BPI – Badan Pusat Intelijen (literally, Central Intelligence Agency) was Indonesia's intelligence body formed by President Soekarno on 5 December 1958 under the name Badan Koordinasi Intelijen (BKI), headed by Colonel (Navy) Pirngadi. On 10 November 1959, BKI became BPI, headquartered in Jalan Madiun, under Dr Soebandrio.

C

Centre for Strategic and International Studies (CSIS). This was founded in 1971 as a forum for policy research by Ali Moertopo, Soedjono Hoemardani, Harry Tjan Silalahi and Daoed Joesoef.

Cleret gombel (Javanese), literally flying lizards, a reptile belonging to the Agamidae family. The term was popularized by Sudarko Prawiroyudo, a member of the DPR representing Irian Jaya (West Papua). He first used it to describe politicians who felt they could shake the government's tree, while in reality a bigger force was at work in creating political upheaval. He often used the animal's name to refer to our own group in a bid at self-irony.

Corpus Studiosorum Bandungense (CSB) was founded on 2 September 1920 at Technische Hoogeschool (TH), now ITB, under the name Bandungsche Studenten Corps (BSC). Its membership is open to all, regardless of political ideology, race, religion or ethnic group.

D

Dasasila Bandung was a ten-point declaration that resulted from the Asia-Africa Conference held between 18 and 25 April 1955 in Bandung, Indonesia. One of the resolutions was "a statement regarding support for peace and global cooperation". Dasasila Bandung incorporated principles contained within the UB Charter and those of Jawaharlal Nehru.

Deklarasi Cirebon (Cirebon Declaration). After Japan's Emperor Hirohito issued his country's surrender to the Allies in World War II, Dr Soedarsono and members of PSI immediately declared Indonesia's independence in Cirebon on 15 August 1945. The declaration was later deemed a prelude to the Proclamation of Independence on 17 August 1945 by Soekarno-Hatta.

De-Soekarnoisasi (De-Soekarnoization) was a directive issued by the New Order regime under General Soeharto to belittle the role and presence of Soekarno in the nation's official history and memory and to eradicate his cult of personality.

Diplomatska Kolonija (Serbian), meaning "the Diplomatic Colony", which was an elite housing complex in the centre of Belgrade reserved for ambassadors, attaches and foreign diplomats.

Dwikora – Dwi Komando Rakyat (Two Commands by the People). President Soekarno was of the view that the Malaysian Federation sponsored by Britain represented a threat to Indonesian sovereignty. Dwikora was declared in 1964, marking the start of "Confrontation" with Malaysia. The two commands were (1) Fortify the resilience of the Indonesian Revolution, and (2) Assist the revolutionary struggle of the peoples of Malaya, Singapore, Sabah, Sarawak and Brunei

F

Floating mass. A political concept that roughly defines belonging to any sociopolitical force based on voluntariness, volition and individual choice. According to the floating mass theory, an individual could not be claimed to belong to any group unilaterally.

G

Gang of Four. A term used to refer to a political faction comprising four leaders of the Chinese Communist Party during the Cultural Revolution (1966–76). The four members were Mao Zedong's wife

Qiang Jing, Zhang Chunqiao, Yao Wenyuan and Wang Hongwen. They were in charge of decision-making in the party. In Bandung, the term was used to refer to four student activists who worked in tandem: Rahmat Witoelar, Wimar Witoelar, Zulkarnaen Yusuf and Sarwono Kusumaatmadja.

General Certificate of Education (GCE). Measuring the academic level of competence that is a prerequisite for entrance into tertiary education for students in Britain and other countries following the British education system.

H

Hollandsch Indische Kweekschool (HIK). A teacher-training school for natives set up by the Dutch colonial government in 1848 to train teachers to provide elementary education for the local population.

Hollandsch-Inlandsche School (HIS). A school intended for the upper classes of the native population in the Dutch East Indies. It was set up in 1914 as a result of the reorganization of Year 1.

Hoogere Kweekschool (HKS). A teacher-training school one level up from HIK. This category of school only existed in a number of large cities like Medan, Jakarta, Bandung and Semarang.

Hundred-Minister Cabinet. This was the last cabinet headed by President Soekarno. It was sworn-in on 11 March 1966 and was intended as an improvement to the Dwikora Cabinet. It was the cabinet with the most number of ministers in Indonesian history.

I

Institut International d'Administration Publique (IIAP). An education institution based in Paris, originally founded to educate and train officials of the former French colonies in Africa on matters of good governance and government administration. The school was established by the order of President General de Gaulle in 1966. IIAP eventually admitted students from other developing nations, including Indonesia.

J

John Birch Society. A lobby group in the United States advocating anti-communism, limited government intervention, a constitutional republic and individual freedom.

K

Karakterdes – Kader Penggerak Teritorial Desa (Catalytic Village Cadre) was a Golkar regeneration programme at the village level.

Kelompok Bangbayang (Bangbayang Group) was a group of university students in Bandung in the 1960s who met at a boarding house in Jalan Bangbayang. Several of its members came from educated and wealthy families, such as Arifin Panigoro and Aburizal Bakrie.

Kelompok Cipayung (Cipayung Group). In early 1972, leaders of off-campus student organizations (HMI, PMKRI, GMNI and GMKI) met in Cipayung, Bogor and duly issued a resolution critical of the government. The group, and other student organizations, continued to be critical of the government.

Kelompok Petisi 50 (Petition 50 Group). This group had its origins in a petition signed by fifty national figures expressing their concern about and their criticism of the way President Soeharto was using Pancasila to silence his political opponents. Among the signatories were Ali Sadikin, Hoegeng Imam Santoso, A.H. Nasution, Baharudin Harahap and Mohammad Natsir. It later became a pressure group critical of the government. Before signing the petition, the signatories held a forum called Yayasan Lembaga Kesadaran Berkonstitusi.

KL – Koninklijk Leger (Royal Dutch Army).

Klein ambtenaar (Dutch) referred to a lowly civil servant from the native population during the Dutch colonial era. Most such officers worked as clerks.

KMKBDR – Komando Militer Kota Besar Djakarta Raja (Military Command for Greater Jakarta). Established on 24 December 1949, this command was in charge of security for Jakarta. Its name was later changed to Komando Daerah Militer V/Jayakarta (Kodam Jaya).

KNIL – Koningklijk Nederlands Indisch Leger (Royal Netherlands East Indies Army). A special division in the Dutch Armed Forces intended for operation in the Dutch East Indies (Indonesia). The personnel of the force were drawn from diverse nationalities—Dutch, German, Swiss, French—as well as from the native population: Javanese, Ambonese, Sundanese and others. The name KNIL was officially adopted in 1933, but the division had existed since 1830, after the end of the Diponegoro War (1826–27).

Komando Operasi Mandala (Operation Mandala Command) was the name of the task force formed by President Soekarno on 2 January 1962 with the mission of taking back West Papua from the Dutch. The task force was commanded by Major General Soeharto later President Soeharto.

Konsultasi Tiga Jalur (The Three Stream Consultation). A Golkar-specific term used to describe the communication mechanism between the three forces in society that were behind the functioning of the New Order: the military (ABRI), specifically represented by the army, called Stream A; the civil service (bureaucracy), called Stream B; and Golkar itself, called Stream G.

Koridor Tengah (literally, "the middle corridor"; translated in this book as "The Middle Course"). A term used by Sarwono Kusumaatmadja to describe the boundaries for political freedom under the New Order. The boundaries could be elastic. The red lines not to be crossed were Pancasila, the 1945 Constitution and presidential succession. Anyone crossing these lines would be dealt with.

Kursus Reguler Lemhanas (Lemhanas Regular Course). A form of leadership training for people occupying important posts in the military, civil service, business, press, etc. The organizer of the training was Lembaga Ketahanan Nasional, or the National Resilience Agency (Lemhanas). The material used in the training sessions dealt with strategic reviews of national resilience and the consolidation of nationhood values.

M

Mahasiswa Indonesia. A weekly print magazine run by Bandung students between 1966 and 1974. Because of its frequent criticism of the government, the magazine was shut down by the government in 1975, following the Malari incident on 15 January. In addition to a Jakarta edition, the magazine also had a West Java edition, which was distributed across the country.

Mang. A mode of address for young Sundanese males.

Mas. A mode of address, originally Javanese, for young males. It is applied before someone's first name; e.g.: "Mas Sarwono".

Masyumi (Majelis Syuro Muslimin Indonesia). An Islamic political party founded in 1943. Disbanded by President Soekarno on 13 September 1960.

Meer Uitgebreid Lager Onderwijs (MULO). A type of school during the Dutch colonial era, equivalent to a junior high school.

Membat mentul (Javanese). An expression describing springing and reverberating motions. The term was used by Moerdino to describe an approach to communication that sought to minimize tension in a discussion.

Menteri Beras **(The Rice Minister).** A sobriquet given to the Minister of Social Affairs, Dr Soedarsono, who was given the task of helping India face famine by sending its population rice shipments.

Moerdiono Connection. A term used to describe politicians close to Moerdiono. The connection bestowed access to the president, which very few politicians under the New Order had.

N

Nasakom. The acronym for Nasionalisme (Nationalism), Agama (Religion) and Komunis (Communism), a concept of President Soekarno's for keeping the country's political forces in balance. It represented the middle path in the face of contestations and confrontations threatening unity of the nation.

Non-Aligned Movement. A grouping of newly independent nations that came together after World War II. The countries in the movement chose to neither side with the United States nor the Soviet Union during the Cold War period.

O

Operasi Khusus (Opsus), or Special Operation, was an intelligence unit formed to carry out clandestine operations.

Orsinalmas – Organisasi Fungsional Kemasyarakatan (Functional Community Organization) refers to organizations with functional themes founded by Golkar members and those that declare themselves as affiliated with Golkar periodically.

Orsosmasinal – Organisasi Sosial Kemasyarakatan Fungsional (Functional Civil Society Organization) refers to the founding organizations of Golkar from when its membership paradigm was organizational rather than individual. After the individual membership paradigm was adopted, these organizations became to be seen as entities with historic links to Golkar.

P

P4, or Pedoman Penghayatan dan Pengamalan Pancasila (Directive for the Realization and Implementation of Pancasila), was a set of guidelines on the application of Pancasila during the New Order era. It drew for its legal existence on act MPR No. II/MPR/1978 on Eka Prasetya Pancakarsa, which elaborated the five principles into thirty-six practical guiding precepts.

Pak. A mode of address for adult males as a sign of respect. Originally from the Javanese word *bapak* (father). It is used before someone's first name, often in the abbreviated form, e.g.: Pak Soeharto or Pak Harto, Pak Sudharmono or Pak Dhar.

Partizan. The Yugoslavian guerrilla forces led by Josip Broz Tito against the Nazi German forces.

Peperti, or Penguasa Perang Tertinggi. Created by President Soekarno in 1962 in preparation for military action to take back West Papua. This body was empowered to mobilize civilians as auxiliary forces.

Pertemuan Seperempat kamar (Quarter Chamber Meeting). A term used to describe a meeting between the Golkar Fraction and the government, without F-ABRI. This was similar to a Half Chamber Meeting but would not touch on matters relating to defence or security.

Pertemuan Setengah Kamar (Half Chamber Meeting). A term used to describe an off-the-record meeting between the parliamentary fraction of ABRI, Golkar and the government in order to harmonize the policy approach in the DPR and when managing public communication.

Petrus, or Penembakan Misterius, was a covert operation to eradicate crime, which lasted from 1982 to 1985. On 24 July 2012, the National Commission on Human Rights stated that the operation had produced up to ten thousand casualties and that it constituted grave violations of human rights.

R

RPKAD, or Resimen Para Komando Angkatan Darat, was an elite corps within the Indonesian Army. The special force was endowed with great mobility, shooting accuracy, and abilities in surveillance of the enemy and counterterrorism. Its name changed a number of times over the years. In the early 1950s it was known as KKAD (Korps Komando Angkatan Darat), before being changed to RPKAD in 1955. In 1956 it became Pusat Pasukan Khusus TNI AD. In 1971 it was renamed Kopassanda (Komando Pasukan Sandi Yudha). At the end of 1985 it became Komando Pasukan Khusus (Kopassus).

S

Sekretariat Bersama Golongan Karya, or Sekber Golkar. Founded on 20 October 1964 by the Indonesian military, in particular by army officers, such as Lieutenant Colonel Suhardiman from SOKSI. It worked hard to bring together dozens of youth, women, university graduates, and organizations of workers, farmers and fishermen into a shared secretariat.

Sekretariat Bersama Organisasi Mahasiswa Lokal (Somal). Activism by students in the 1960s saw the formations of many local organizations. To qualify as a member of the KAMI Central Presidium, various student organizations came together to form Somal. Those organizations were Perhimpunan Mahasiswa Bandung (PMB), the Bandung Student Association; Ikatan Mahasiswa Jakarta (Imada), the Jakarta Student Association; Ikatan Mahasiswa Bandung (Imaba), the Bandung Student Association; Gerakan Mahasiswa Surabaya (GMS), the Surabaya Student Movement; Masyarakat Mahasiswa Bogor (MMB), the Bogor Student Society; Corpus Studiosorum Bandungense (CSB); and Ikatan Mahasiswa Pontianak (Imapon), the Pontianak Student Association.

Surat Perintah Sebelas Maret (the Decree of 11 March) was a presidential decree by Soekarno to Major General Soeharto to restore order and security in the country.

T

Tahir Case. A scandal that was exposed in 1976 causing ripples of outrage. Tahir, a director with the state-owned oil company Pertamina, died on 23 July 1976. His wife, Kartika, reportedly tried to cash a term deposit of her late husband's totalling USD 35.8 million at two Singapore banks. The Indonesian government duly filed an intervention with the Singapore courts to repatriate the funds on the basis that the money had been embezzled from Pertamina.

Tamblong Group. A Bandung student group based in Jalan Tamblong. Its leader was Rahman Tolleng, who was also the publisher of *Mahasiswa Indonesia* magazine.

Tjakrabirawa – the Presidential Guard, the personnel for which were drawn from the four forces: the army, navy, air force and police.

Tri Tuntutan Rakyat, or Tritura (The Three Demands of the People). A statement of three demands issued to Soekarno's government by Kesatuan Aksi Mahasiswa Indonesia (KAMI; Unified Action of Indonesian University Students), supported by Kesatuan Aksi Pelajar Indonesia (KAPI), Kesatuan Aksi Pemuda Pelajar Indonesia (KAPPI), Kesatuan Burug Indonesia (KABI), Kesatuan Aksi Sarjana Indonesia (KASI), Kesatuan Aksi Wanita Indonesia (KAWI) and Kesatuan Aksi Guru Indonesia (KAGI), as well as the army. The three demands were to disband PKI and its sub-bodies, reshuffle the cabinet and bring down food prices.

Trikarya – The three "mother groups" that founded Golkar: Kosgoro, MKGR and SOKSI.

U

UNCLOS (United Nations Convention on the Law of the Sea). The international agreement resulting from the third United Nations Conference on the Law of the Sea that took place between 1973 and 1982.

Y

Yugoslavia, meaning South Slavia, was a nation state that existed in the Balkans in the southeast of Europe from 1918 to 2003. It was a monarchy before becoming a federal republic, with Belgrade as its capital city. After the death of Josip Broz Tito in 1980—who had been declared President for life—Yugoslavia became embroiled in ethnic strife and separatism. In 2003, Yugoslavia disintegrated to form seven new countries: Slovenia, Croatia, Macedonia, Bosnia-Herzegovina, Montenegro, Serbia and Kosovo.

Bibliography

Ahmad, Rafiqul-Umam dan kawan-kawan. *Berusaha Turut Melayani: Memoar Politik Jakob Tobing*. Jakarta: Konstitusi Pers, 2008.

Basuki, Fira. *Wimar Witoelar: "Hell, Yeah!* The New Chapter*. Jakarta: PT. Gramedia Widiasarana Indonesia, 2014.

Departemen Penerangan RI. *Himpunan Pidato Presiden RI Tahun 1983 Bidang Polkam, Ekuin, Kesra*. Jakarta: Departemen Penerangan RI, 1984.

Dwidjowijoto, Riant Nugroho (Penyunting). *Manajemen Presiden Soeharto: Penuturan 17 Menteri*. Jakarta: Yayasan Bina Generasi Bangsa, 1996.

Dwipayana, G., dan Ramadhan K.H. *Soeharto: Pikiran, Ucapan, dan Tindakan Saya (Otobiografi)*. Jakarta: PT. Citra Lamtoro Gung Persada, 1989.

Effendy, Bahtiar, Hajriyanto Y. Thohari, Kholid Novianto, M. Alfan Alfian et al. *Beringin Membangun: Sejarah Politik Partai Golkar*. Jakarta: Grafindo Khazanah Ilmu, 2012.

Elson, R.E. *Suharto: A Political Biography*. Melbourne: Cambridge University Press, 2001.

Friend, Theodore. *Indonesian Destinies*. Cambridge, MA: The Belknap Press of Harvard University Press, 2004.

Golongan Karya. *Kumpulan Majalah Media Karya*. Jakarta: DPP Golkar, 1984–1985.

Hasibuan, Albert. *Memoar Albert Hasibuan: Perjalanan Penemuan Diri*. Jakarta: Kata Hasta Pustaka, 2012.

Hendrowerdojo, Soeparno, et al. *Fraksi Karya Pembangunan DPR RI: Kehadiran dan Peranannya*. Jakarta: FKP, 1987.

Husodo, Siswono Yudo. *Warga Baru*. Jakarta: Lembaga Penerbitan Yayasan Padamu Negeri, 1985.

Kusumaatmadja, Sarwono. *Sketsa Politik Orde Baru*. Bandung: PT. Citra Aditya Bakti, 1989.

Moechtar, Hasyrul. *Mereka Dari Bandung: Pergerakan Mahasiswa Bandung 1960–1967*. Bandung: PT. Alumni, 1998.

Pane, Nina. *Rekam Jejak Kebangsaan Mochtar Kusuma-Atmadja*. Jakarta: PT. Kompas Media Nusantara, 2015.

Patmono Sk. *Dinamika Senayan: Kumpulan Karangan Patmono Sk.* Jakarta: Lemuel, 1995.

Patmono Sk. et al. *Golkar Baru: Dalam Fakta dan Opini (Buku I)*. Jakarta: Lembaga Studi Demokrasi, 2001.

Patria, Nezar, and Rusdi Mathari. *Keputusan Sulit Adnan Ganto: Kisah Anak Buloh Blang Ara Tiga Dekade Menjadi Bankir di Kelas Dunia*. Yogyakarta: Circa, 2017.

Rahman, Zaini, Rofiqul Umam Ahmad, Muhammad Saefullah, Saiful Anam. *K.H. Slamet Effendy Yusuf: Konseptor di Pusaran Perubahan*. Jakarta: Yayasan Aji Yumika, 2016.

Raillon, Francois. *Politik dan Ideologi Mahasiswa Indonesia: Pembentukan dan Konsolidasi Orde Baru 1966–1974*. Jakarta: LP3ES, 1985.

Said, Salim. *Dari Gestapu ke Reformasi: Serangkaian Kesaksian*. Bandung: Mizan Pustaka, 2013.

Sudharmono, S.H. *Sudharmono, S.H.: Pengalaman dalam Masa Pengabdian (Sebuah Otobiografi)*. Jakarta: PT. Gramedia Widiasarana Indonesia, 1997.

Tandjung, Akbar. *The Golkar Way: Survival Partai Golkar di Tengah Turbulensi Era Transisi*. Jakarta: PT. Gramedia Pustaka Utama, 2007.

Wanandi, Jusuf. *Shades of Grey: A Political Memoir of Modern Indonesia 1965–1998*. Jakarta: Equinox, 2012.

Index

About the Author

SARWONO KUSUMAATMADJA was born in Jakarta on 24 July 1943. He graduated, majoring in Civil Engineering, from the Bandung Institute of Technology (ITB) in 1974, after being elected as a member of the House of Representatives (DPR) from Golkar in the General Election of 1971.

In 1983 he was appointed Secretary General of the Central Governing Board (DPP) of Golkar. He was a minister in three different cabinets. Under President Soeharto, Sarwono became the Minister of State for Administrative Reform before moving to take on the Environment portfolio. In the era of *Reformasi*, he was appointed as the Minister of Fishery and Maritime Affairs under President Abdurrahman Wahid. He was subsequently elected as a member of the Regional Representative Council (DPD) representing Jakarta.

Sarwono currently occupies a number of advisory posts to President Joko Widodo's administration, businesses and environmental organizations.

www.ingramcontent.com/pod-product-compliance
Lightning Source LLC
Chambersburg PA
CBHW060329100426
42812CB00003B/933